FEARFUL PLEASURES:
THE COMPLETE POEMS,
1959-2007

FEARFUL PLEASURES: THE COMPLETE POEMS, 1959-2007

Lewis Turco

FEARFUL PLEASURES: THE COMPLETE POEMS,
1959–2007
Lewis Turco

Copyright © 2007
by Lewis Turco

cover art by George O'Connell

jacket design by Trish Hadley

All rights reserved.
No part of this book may be used or reproduced in any manner
whatsoever without written permission from the publisher,
except in the case of brief quotations
embodied in articles and reviews.

Published by

~ STAR CLOUD PRESS® ~

6137 East Mescal Street
Scottsdale, Arizona 85254-5418

ISBN:
978-1-932842-19-7— Cloth — $ 49.95
978-1-932842-20-3— Paperback — $ 32.95

www.StarCloudPress.com

Library of Congress Control Number: 2006928731

Printed in the United States of America

OTHER BOOKS BY LEWIS TURCO

The Museum of Ordinary People and Other Stories, 2007
Fantaseers, A Book of Memories, 2005
The Collected Lyrics of Lewis Turco / Wesli Court, 2004
The Book of Dialogue, 2004
A Sheaf of Leaves, Literary Memoirs, 2004
The Green Maces of Autumn: Voices in an Old Maine House, 2002
The Book of Forms, A Handbook of Poetics, Third Edition, 2000
The Book of Literary Terms, 1999
A Book of Fears, 1998
Shaking the Family Tree, 1998
Bordello: A Portfolio of Poemprints, with George O'Connell, 1996
Emily Dickinson, Woman of Letters, 1993
The Public Poet, 1991
The Shifting Web: New and Selected Poems, 1989
The Fog: A Chamber Opera in One Act, with Walter Hekster, 1987
Visions and Revisions of American Poetry, 1986
The Compleat Melancholick, 1985
American Still Lifes, 1981
Poetry: An Introduction Through Writing, 1973
Pocoangelini: A Fantography & Other Poems, 1971
The Inhabitant, 1970
Awaken, Bells Falling: Poems 1959-1967, 1968
First Poems, 1960

ACKNOWLEDGMENTS

The Sketches of Lewis Turco and Livevil: A Mask originally appeared as an American Weave Chapbook Award volume from American Weave Press of Cleveland, Ohio, copyright © 1962 by Lewis Turco; an expanded version was included in *Pocoangelini: A Fantography and Other Poems* published by Despà Press of Northampton, Massachusetts, Copyright ©1971 by Lewis Turco. Reprinted by permission of the author.

Awaken, Bells Falling, Poems 1959-1967 was published by the University of Missouri Press, copyright © 1968 by Lewis Turco. Reprinted by permission of the author. Lines two and three of "A Dedication" are quoted from the poem "Argonauts" by Joel Sloman. "Trilogy for J. F. K.," © 2007 by Lewis Turco, appeared originally in *Words of Protest, Words of Freedom: Poetry of the American Civil Rights Movement* edited by Jeffrey Lamar Coleman for Duke University Press, 2007. The parts of this trilogy were first published as follows: "The Moment Before" in *In the Poet's Hand*, edited by John J. Zimmerman, Frostburg State College Library, 1965; "Ode on St. Cecilia's Day 1964," in *The Iowa Alumni Review*, 1965, and before its publication in *Awaken, Bells Falling,* "November 22, 1963," appeared in *Poetry* in 1964.

The Inhabitant was published by the Despà Press of Northampton, Massachusetts, copyright © 1971 by Lewis Turco. Reprinted by permission of the author.

The Weed Garden was published by the Peaceweed Press of Orangeburg, South Carolina, copyright © 1973 by Lewis Turco. Reprinted by permission of the author.

The depictions of humanoid creatures in *A Book of Beasts* were previously published in a chapbook titled *A Cage of Creatures* from The Banjo Press of Potsdam, New York, copyright © 1978 by Lewis Turco. Some of the remaining poems appeared in another chapbook, *A Maze of Monsters,* from Livingston University Press, copyright © 1986 by

Lewis Turco. "Uroboros" appeared as "The Worm" in *The Weed Garden*. All are reprinted by permission of the author.

Seasons of the Blood is based upon the Tarot deck of fortune-telling cards; it originally appeared as a chapbook from Mammoth Press of Rochester, New York, copyright ©1980 by Lewis Turco, reprinted by permission of the author. The forms in which the poems are written are from the Japanese; they are the mondo, katauta, sedoka, choka, tanka, somonka, waka, haiku and senryu. Descriptions of these forms may be found in *The Book of Forms: A Handbook of Poetics, Third Edition*, by Lewis Turco, University Press of New England, 2000.

American Still Lifes was published by the Mathom Publishing Company of Oswego, New York, copyright ©1981 by Lewis Turco. Reprinted by permission of the author and the publisher.

The Compleat Melancholick was published by The Bieler Press of Minneapolis, Minnesota, copyright ©1985 by Lewis Turco. Reprinted by permission of the author and the publisher.

The new poems from *The Shifting Web, New and Selected Poems*, published by the University of Arkansas Press, were copyright ©1989 by Lewis Turco. Reprinted by permission of the author.

"A Sampler of Hours" is reprinted by permission from *Emily Dickinson, Woman of Letters: Poems and Centos from Lines in Emily Dickinson's Letters* by Lewis Turco, the State University of New York Press, copyright ©1993 State University of New York. All rights reserved. Reprinted by permission of the publisher and the author.

Phobiamania is an expanded version of *A Book of Fears, Poems*, with Italian translations by Joseph Alessia, winner of the first annual Bordighera Bi-Lingual Poetry Prize in 1998, copyright © 1998 by Lewis Putnam Turco. Recent poems previously unacknowledged were originally published in *The Antioch Review, The Café Review, New York Quarterly* and *Ploughshares*. "Ideophobia" first appeared as part of a memoir, "The Hillsdale Epistles Revisited," in *A Sheaf of Leaves: Literary Memoirs*, Star Cloud Press, copyright © 2004 by Lewis Turco. All are here reprinted by permission of the author.

The Green Maces of Autumn, Voices in an Old Maine House, was published by The Mathom Bookshop, Dresden, Maine, copyright © 2002 by Lewis Turco and reprinted here by permission of the author and the publisher. Of the poems that appear in the series, "Albums" was first published separately as a pamphlet by The Writer's Forum of the State University of New York College at Brockport, copyright © 1979 by Lewis Turco. "Albums" and several other poems subsequently appeared as *A Family Album*, winner of the *Silverfish Review* Chapbook Competition for 1989, copyright © 1990 by *Silverfish Review*. Another selection appeared as *Murmurs in the Walls*, winner of the Cooper House Chapbook Competition for 1990, copyright © 1992 by Lewis Turco.

*For Jean,
after fifty years
and more.*

Foreword

In a recent article on the demolition of an old house ("Demolition," The New York *Times,* November 25, 2005) Verlyn Klinkenborg writes, "I wish that the house were more articulate, or that I were better at hearing what it has to say. I can hear the most recent occupants pretty clearly — they obviously hated the thought of exposed wooden beams and brickwork. But the ones who lived here before them, all the way back to the first settlers, are nearly inaudible to me."

It occurred to me, reading that and remembering the work of those authors who have most persistently haunted my imagination and shaped my view of the world, that Klinkenborg has it right: the writer is — ought to be — a living ear so finely tuned to all environments that everything becomes articulate, and the walls erected by time and circumstances become porous to the dead and the nonexistent, including those others who preceded us, those waiting in the future, and those selves we imagine being but that we never become. Writers with that kind of "hearing" enrich us by enlarging our experience, taking us through the walls they almost annihilate and out of the confinement of ourselves.

I can think of no poet working today whose hearing is better than that of Lewis Turco, whether he uses his own ear or that of some one of his alternate selves, with their distinctive quirks and obsessions. In book after book, this remarkably inventive poet, critic, prosodist, translator and teacher enables us to hear from past generations, as he does with exquisite lyricism in *The Green Maces of Autumn, Voices in an Old Maine House,* or from the dark, fearful core of joyless ordinary lives, as he does in the relentlessly ominous and yet humorous *Phobiamania,* in gorgeous language that works perfectly without attracting attention to itself.

A learned and omnivorous reader, Turco can borrow tricks from colleagues as various as gypsy balladeers, Rabelais, Swift, and Robert Burton, all conjured up by the close-to-surrealistic language of *The Compleat Melancholick*. In *A Book of Beasts* Turco draws on the Old Testament, Medieval lore from various cultures, and New World folklore in poems depicting such "monsters" as the Golem, the Zombie and the Yeti to represent the elementals of creation:

> I am the Worm Who Lives,
>   each thing and All: water of life,
>   torment's fire, wind-breath, stone and soil from which these
>   green things spring. Uruboros.
>   Look inward where I coil in blood.

Nothing escapes this poet's obsessive surveillance, as if Turco were certain that everything human had something of value to communicate to him, and through him to the poem, and through the crafty, beguiling playfulness of the poem to its reader. *Seasons of the Blood*, for instance, plays with Asian forms and Zen concepts, existential questions, the insights of physics, images drawn from the Tarot, and a Lorca-like treatment of wind, river and moon. "Do not be afraid," he writes in "Correspondence": "What disappears is not lost. The snake is eating its tail."

Like Charles Simic, Turco is fascinated by the object, the initially mundane inanimate thing that upon close observation becomes as grotesque as it is ordinary, and speaks for itself with uncanny persuasiveness. Like Kenneth Koch, Turco knows how to invest the commonplace — the physical place in particular — with iconic significance. His closets and stairways, living rooms and fields, forests, deserts and small town squares — particularly in *The Inhabitant* and *American Still Lifes* — breathe the lives of people often omitted from the poems they inhabit only as the faint phosphorescence we associate with ghosts.

Turco's imagery, like his listening — always riveting, whatever it turns to — becomes most persuasive and affecting when its focus is the individual caught in the act of changing, of moving through those finely-drawn landscapes and becoming suddenly aware of his own passage through time. Four of his books are especially relevant here. The first, *Awaken, Bells Falling: Poems 1959-1967*, contains poems dedicated to famous literary and political figures, as well as to family members, fictional characters and nameless acquaintances. The tone of these poems can best be described as restless, dissatisfied affection for something understood to be lost or in the process of being lost. A kind of hopeless longing flickers in such poems as "Burning the News," which begins with these eerily timely lines:

> The fire is eating
> the paper. The child who drowned
> is burned. Asia is in flames.
> As he signs his great
> bill, a minister of state chars
>
> at the edges and curls
> into smoke....

Although more recent poems, like the author's own words in conversation, acknowledge grave disappointment with human beings and their behavior toward each other and the planet, what this poem suggests is that disappointment is often the child of high hope and frustrated devotion. The poems that Turco devotes to the human — even those of a satirical nature — are imbued with affection, with a regretful desire to think better of what it once loved and perhaps still does. I think much of the power of these poems comes from the painful combination of enduring love, disappointment in the object of that love, uncompromising truthfulness, and the desire for hope that the hoper himself thinks is unrealistic. And, of course, a prodigious imagination, and an irrepressible urge to play with language in the process of embodying difficult thoughts.

Pocoangelini: A Fantography (which may be found in the poet's other volume, *The Collected Lyrics of Lewis Turco / Wesli Court, 1953-2004*), and *The Sketches,* perhaps the two most autobiographical of Lewis Turco's collections, consist of surreal character sketches of his father and other persons remembered from an eventful childhood. The language is wildly metaphorical, narrative, dramatic, illustrative of all the nuances of the immigrant experience and the tensions between generations. Language itself is almost another character in these stories told in poems filled with dialogue, almost cryptic revelations, sad humor and comic sorrows. Although the figures dealt with, particularly in *The Sketches*, are human oddities conveyed in language that refuses to settle down to the ordinary, these barbers and butchers, former girlfriends and old relatives remain "ours" by virtue of their compelling strangeness and intimacy. Here, from "Dorothy," is a backward look at youth:

> You were a willowy virgin
> > through youth's sad laughter —
> > and I, enthralled by age's
> > inverted telescope, stroked
> > love's fur.

Regret, and the distance that time creates, have rarely been rendered better.

Regret and distance also define the eleven poems designated as "new" in Turco's 1989 collection, *The Shifting Web: New and Selected Poems.* One of those, "The Habitation," invites the reader through an apparently empty house, noting the cobwebs, dust, yellowing sheets, ashes in the hearth, and ends with a surprising call to "Rejoice! Rejoice! The house is failing!" The poem, like others in this volume, seems eager for an end to "the house" and its history. And yet there are also poems to a son, a daughter who has moved out, a friend who has died of cancer, the poet's wife and father, and the tone of those is regret sweetened, distance bridged. This collection closes with "The Shifting Web," in which the writing of a poem becomes the process of launching a kite — a "string of hours" — up and out to "ride the air" and move "above the still neighbors in their rooms." The delicacy of that motion is a perfect figure for the poet's work, which is an indirect desire to touch.

One of Turco's most ambitious projects, "A Sampler of Hours: Poems and Centos from Lines in Emily Dickinson's Letters," consists of phrases and whole lines from Dickinson's letters and the words of Lewis Turco woven together into syllabic poems. The proportion of language by each of the two "collaborators" varies greatly from poem to poem, but the interfacing is so skillful that the whole feels coherent and satisfying. What is captured is the almost surreal sharpness of Dickinson's surprising imagery, as well as her skewed and jagged syntax; what is missing is the hymn-like regularity of her meter, often so tellingly at odds with both her syntax and her daring emotional content. The effect is at once strong, pleasing, and jarring, and constitutes a particularly moving tribute, as if an art critic had removed some crucial element from a beloved painting to show both how the whole has been altered and how its essence has endured the alteration. Clearly these poems announce themselves to "be" Emily Dickinson, even while the reader's ear suffers a recognizable absence and persistently listens for what it will not find. This series, in managing to be both poetry and subtle literary criticism, bridges genres as easily as it bridges the voices of two poets more than a century apart.

I want to end with *The Green Maces of Autumn, Voices in an Old Maine House,* a recently completed work in which I think Lewis Turco has collected all his strengths — language that is at once arresting and simple, imagery as fresh as this morning and yet timeless as Genesis, and narrative powerfully charged with genuine and deliberately unresolved feeling. This collection of poems — spoken by several generations of the dead who inhabit the walls of an old house — deserves to outlive most of what passes for notable writing today, because it embodies American history at the level of the individual, gives it "a local habitation and a name," and makes it ours as only poetry can do. It constitutes, in my opinion, a book destined to become an American classic, the product of a lifetime spent "overhearing" the words spoken by the land and its people, their disposable and somehow sacred objects, their alter egos, ancestors and imagined descendants. Here, for instance, is the voice of "Amanda Pullen (1887-1980)":

> Destitute of sound, I rely upon the room
> To resolve my silences harmonically.
> The chandelier's highlights set the tone.
> The stillness is crystalline. It has been
> A thousand separate moments since I sank
> Into this drift of time....

How sobering to contemplate the "drift of time" under that chandelier, and then remember that we're all headed for that stillness.

And how fortunate the reading public is to have this wealth of writing by one of the country's most interesting poets now in one volume, not so much a book as a library of books, composed by the many persons who inhabit this haunted and perceptive poet! It belongs on the bookshelf of every reader willing to risk the joy and anguish of hearing the world, having it speak to him as vividly, ambiguously and honestly as it speaks to Lewis Turco.

Rhina P. Espaillat
Newburyport, Massachusetts
23 January 2006

Contents

FOREWORD by Rhina P. Espaillat — i-vi

The Sketches (1962)

Gene	1
Tomaso the Baker	2
Mrs. Martino the Candy Store Lady	3
Ercole the Butcher	4
Louie the Barber	5
Guido the Ice-House Man	6
Morgan	7
May	8
John	9
Luigi	10
Dorothy	11
Cass	12
Maureen	13
Ginger	14
Miss Agatha	15
Mr. Mell	16
Jones	17
Miss Burnside	18
Deacon Smith	19
Bob	20
Ray	21
Frank	22
Jean	23
Melora	24
Granny	25
Uncle Larry	26
Granddaddy Dagger	27
Al	28
Lorrie	29
Lena	31

Morton	32
Vern	33
Miss Mary Belle	34
Lewis	36

Awaken, Bells Falling, Poems 1959-1967 (1968)

A Dedication	39
The Townsfolk	40
In a White Direction	41
Lost Girl with Dog	43
Letter to W. D. S.	45
Mice in the Sunday Walls	46
Lines for Mr. Stevenson	48
He Who Feeds Pigeons	50
Trilogy for J. F. K.	51
My Country Wife	55
My Wife of the Town	56
No Reflection on You, but…,	57
Narcissus to His Fleshly Shade	59
An Old Acquaintance	60
Playhouse	61
Millpond	62
The Well	64
School Drawing	65
An Ordinary Evening in Cleveland	66
The Old Professor and the Sphinx	70
The Well of Holy Heaven	72
Old News	73
The Forest Beyond the Glass	74
The Burning Bush	76
The Face on the Chequered Field	79
The Late, Late Show	80
The Girl from the Golden West	82

Burning the News	85
The Forest of My Seasons	86
Clambake	88
Some Pinfeather Blues	90
Scarecrow	91
Raceway	92
Pumpinode	94
Awaken, Bells Falling	96
House and Shutter	98
Season	100
The Snow Devil	101
The Stroller	103

The Inhabitant (1970)

The Door	107
The Hallway	109
The Hallseat	110
The Attic	113
The Photograph	115
The Livingroom	117
The Couch	119
The Dining Room	120
The Sideboard	121
The Kitchen	122
The Linen Calendar	123
The Playroom	124
The Portrait of a Clown	126
The Study	127
The Cat	129
The Bedroom	131
The Pillow	134
The Bathroom	135
The Mirror	136
The Basement	137
The Scythe	139

The Porch	141
The Glider	144
The Guestroom	145
The Looking-Glass	147
The Summerhouse	148
The Garden	150
The Dwelling-House	151

The Weed Garden (1973)

Home Thoughts	157
The Orchestra	158
Lovers	160
As I Read My Good Friend's Book	162
The Cell	164
The Dead Sailor	166
The Fountain	167
The Voyagers	168
The Weed Garden	169
My Lord Life	170
Father Figure	172
A Rural Jetty	173
Wake Disturbing Surfaces	175
Mary Moody Emerson, R. I. P.	176
The Face in the Stone	178
The Pilot	179
The Dream	181
Tick	183
I Am Peter	184

A Book of Beasts:
An Alphabestiary (1978 & 1986)

A -Bao-A-Qu	187
B asilisk and Cockatrice	189
C himera	190
D ybbuk	191
E nt	193
F etch	194
G olem	196
H omunculus	198
I mago	200
J uggernaut	202
K amelopard	203
L eviathan	205
M inotaur	207
N asnas	209
O dradek	210
P hoenix and Salamander	212
Q uerule	213
R oc	214
S asquatch	215
T roglodyte	216
U roboros	218
V ielfras	219
W erewind	221
X oanon	223
Y eti	225
Z ombie	227

Seasons of the Blood, Poems on the Tarot (1980)

Wheel of Fortune	231
Banjo	233
Foliage	234
Bone	235
Pentacles	236
The Devil	237
The Lovers	238
Turn	239
Foxfire	240
The Moon	241
Cups	242
Swords	243
Epistles	244
Seasons of the Blood	245
Dialogue	246
Paradigm	247
The Test	248
Facets	250
The River	251
Circles	252
The Hermit	254
Death	255
Toad	256
The Hanged Man	257
The Chariot	258
Judgment	259
Correspondence	260
The Tower	261
The Fool	262

American Still Lifes (1981)

I. Twelve Moons

Cold Moon	271
Snow Moon	272
Worm Moon	273
Seed Moon	274
Flower Moon	275
Hot Moon	276
Buck Moon	277
Sturgeon Moon	278
Maize Moon	279
Travelers' Moon	280
Beaver Moon	281
Hunting Moon	282

II. Still Lifes

Landscape	285
The Colony	286
The Maple Works	288
The Meetinghouse	290
The Tavern	291
The Trading Post	292
The Fort	294
The Pharmacy	296
The College	297
The Courthouse	298
The Ferry	299
The Tollhouse	300
The Mill	302
The Ice House	304
The Rope Walk	305
The Schooner	306
The House	307

The Silo	308
The Covered Bridge	309
The Tobacco Shed	310
The Stable	311
The Depot	312
The Trestle	313
The Homestead	314
The Stockyard	315
The Observation Tower	316
The Church	317
The Barn	318
Prothalamion	319

III. Autumn's Tales

The Neighborhood	323
The Yard	324
The Trees	325
The Automobiles	326
The Street	327
The Pond	328
The Fences	329
The Valley	330
The Vista	331

THE COMPLEAT MELANCHOLICK, BEING A SEQUENCE OF FOUND, COMPOSITE, AND COMPOSED POEMS BASED LARGELY UPON ROBERT BURTON'S *THE ANATOMY OF MELANCHOLY* (1985)

The Compleat Melancholick	335
Roots	337
The Menu of Melancholy	339

The Author of Melancholy	342
Blood Deeper than Night	344
The Moon of Melancholy	345
The Symptoms of Melancholy	347
Balsamum Apoplecticum	351
Emeralda	353
Melancholy's Herbal	355
The Desert of Melancholy	357
That Particular Air	359
Winter in Muscovy	360
Stone and Shadow	362
Failed Fathers	363
The Mandarin of Melancholy	365
A Fin for the Melancholick's Thoughts	366
The Garden of Melancholy	368
The Melancholick Art	371
A Medicine for Melancholy	373
Some Food for Melancholy	374
I Pray to a Genital God	375
The Age of Aquarius	377
Taurus Sires Aquarius	379
Melancholy Love	381
The Mistress of Melancholy	383
"A Squis'd Cat"	384
The God of Melancholy	386
A Farewell to Melancholy	388

NEW POEMS FROM THE SHIFTING WEB
(1989)

Reflections at Forty-Nine	393
The Habitation	394
Vigilance	395
The Girl You Thought You Loved	397
Attic Poem	398
A Daughter Moves Out	399
Cancer	401
The Recurring Dream	403
Corral	405
Conceit	406
The Shifting Web	408

A SAMPLER OF HOURS: POEMS AND CENTOS FROM LINES IN EMILY DICKINSON'S LETTERS
(1993)

Proem: Cloth of Dreams	413
The Harper of Stillness	414
Crimson Children	415
The Ear of Silence	416
Epithalamion	417
The Mower	418
A Memoir of Evening	419
Scarlet Expectations	420
Mansions of Mirage	421
A Dainty Sum	423
Marble Rooms	424
An Old Tale	425
Morning Music	426

Twilight Touches Amherst	427
The Gift	428
Home	429
Sampler	430
The Cage	431
Four Small Songs	432
The Deep Stranger	433
Brown Study	434
Nocturne	435
The Amherst Fire	436
A Pearl Jail	437
May, Merely	438
An Amherst Haiku	439
The Miller's Tale	440
The Naked Eye	441
A Morning Picture	442
Passing	443
Theme and Variation	444
A New Year	445
Summer's Chariot	446
Small Victory	447
Housekeeping	448
Among the Stones	449
First Snow	450
Delay	451
Company	452
An Amherst Pastoral	453
Death	454
Asea	455
Just God	456
A Dream of Roses	457
Lamps	458
Fading Things	459

An Orator of Feather	460
The Winter Garden	461
Adventure	462
Winter Bouquet	463
Flowers in Season	466
Late Summer	468
Late Fall	469
Amherst Neighbors	470
Passages	472
Epistle	475
An Amherst Christmas	476
Poetry	477
An Amherst Calendar	480
The Clock	484

PHOBIAMANIA, AN EXPANDED VERSION OF A BOOK OF FEARS (1998)

SHE — *Proem*: Eratophobia — 493
HE — Papyrophobia — 494
SHE — Monophobia — 495
HE — Zelophobia — 496
SHE — Abandophobia — 497
HE — Chorophobia — 498
SHE —Parturiphobia — 499
HE — Homophobia — 500
SHE — Claustrophobia — 501
HE — Gamophobia — 502
SHE — Nomatophobia — 503
HE — Pedophobia — 504
SHE — Amathophobia — 505

HE — Phalacrophobia — 506
SHE — Aelurophobia — 507
HE — Arachnophobia — 508
SHE — Brontophobia — 509
HE — Homilophobia — 510
SHE — Apocalyptophobia — 511
HE — Apeirophobia — 512
SHE — Acousticophobia — 513
HE — Quiescophobia — 514
SHE — Catoptrophobia — 515
HE — Ennuiophobia — 516
SHE — Sabbatiphobia — 517
HE — Melanchophobia — 518
SHE — Nebulaphobia — 519
HE — Mnemophobia — 520
SHE — Gerascophobia — 521
HE — Chronophobia — 522
SHE — Oneirophobia — 523
HE — Mundanophobia — 524
SHE — Alliumphobia — 525
HE — Arachibutyrophobia — 526
SHE — Arithmophobia — 527
HE — Ideophobia — 528
SHE — Ambiguphobia — 529
HE — Alektrophobia — 530
SHE — Meteorophobia — 531
HE — Amnesiophobia — 532
SHE — Somnophobia — 533
HE — Acrophobia — 534
SHE — Mortophobia — 535
HE — Agoraphobia — 536
SHE — Dementophobia — 537
HE — Ambivophobia — 538

SHE — Bibliophobia — 539
HE — Senilophobia — 540

The Green Maces of Autumn, Voices in an Old Maine House (2002)

Albums	543
John Bourne	544
Priscilla Bourne	545
Paul Pullen	546
Hester Pullen	547
John Bourne, Jr.	549
Henry Bourne	550
Thomas Bourne	551
Francis Pullen	552
Patience Cobb Pullen	554
Thomas Bourne, Jr.	555
Caleb Pullen	556
Timothy Bourne	557
Margaret Pullen	559
Ephraim Bourne	560
Wendell Pullen	562
Jeremy Carr	564
Michael Pullen	565
Thomas Carr	566
Patience Pullen	567
Randall Bourne	568
Julia Pullen	570
Amanda Pullen	571
Harriet Bourne	572
John Pullen Bourne	574
Bertha Bourne	576
Melinda Bourne	577

Jessie Baker	579
Raymond Carr	581
Joseph Carr	583
Ruth Carr	585
Herbert Torrey	587
Jason Pullen	589
Philip Bourne	590
Nathalie Mason	591
William Pullen	593
Betty Bourne	594
Ann Pullen	596
Lawrence Mason	597
Jean Court	599
Wesley Court	601
Gary Carr	602
John Pullen	603
William Mason	605
At Home	607
INDEXES	611–639
POEM TITLES	611-625
First lines	626-639
About the Author	640

The Sketches
1962

GENE

"Ragtail Gene, don't tag along here;
    scram on home or I'll bop your nose."
Brother, come the first of April,
    that was the word the second of May
    and all you heard when our lead pipe cannon
    swallowed a cherry bomb and belched a stone
    that boomed across the Fourth of July,
    nearly crocking you where you hid
    to spy on all the older kids.
If the world grew huger in your eyes,
    that was because they went wide
    to hear the clubhouse secrets told
    in the dark garage where gasoline
    smelled about good enough to swill.
For, the first you knew of going,
    you knew because we swore our raft
    was not a raft, but a ship to float
    a boy's body out of sight
    and a man's voice too deep for sounding.

That's the way that I am going;
    ragtail Gene, don't tag along here.

TOMASO THE BAKER

Loaf here on a cool day
    and see the bread brown,
    the stone oven stoked with coal.
Watch the loaves leave
    on the long wood spatula
    as Tomaso's arms, like
    brown loaves themselves,
    move in and out among
    the rustle of the thin white bags.
There is a measured bustle here
    and "Eh!" says Tomaso, "Hey,
    make some dough, make some more dough."
And so they make the dough —
    they mix it, they knead it,
    they cut it, they mold it,
    then into the oven to bake it.
We buy it hot for a quarter, hot,
    for they're waiting at home,
    and "Go!" says Tomaso, "Go, run!"

Bread gets cold quick
    on a cool day.

MRS. MARTINO THE CANDY STORE LADY

Listen to the hum
      of the lemon ice machine, mashing
      sugar, mushing ice, crushing
      the puckerbellies of chubby lemons.
"Twenty minutes, can you wait?
      Twenty minutes for lemon ice,"
      mumbles Mrs. Martino.
"Meanwhile, have a Milky Way;
      look, they've been in the Frigidaire;
      they're hard as bricks, they'll
      freeze your teeth —
      look, have a Milky Way."
So nibble while the engine jiggles,
      the ice goes smash, the candy bars
      go limp behind your teeth
      and twenty minutes spin around;
      twenty minutes spin around.
There are shadows in the shop;
      there are candies on the counter;
      there is ice cream in the freezer —
      but your eyes are on the accordion cups
      the lemon ice is eaten from

And twenty minutes is like sluggish ice
      as the cups grow larger with your eyes.

ERCOLE THE BUTCHER

"How many you want?" asks Ercole slowly,
      "how many chops you want?
These will go nice in a big pot of sauce.
That's prime cut pork
      you got there, Missus."
Sometimes a floorsweep will earn you a bag
      of crisp chips; or, if the sun's mean,
      the big cold room door will let you in
      to sit and chill a little.
And Ercole is a black thing
      with a white apron on his barrel front,
      with some red stain now and then,
      and there goes Ercole to saw a bone,
      there goes Ercole to chop some bone.
Slip on the sawdust; slide on the floor;
      listen to the beat of the chopping block:
      chunk, chunk,
      chunk says the cleaver.
Ercole steps to wrap the pink slabs
      we'll eat tonight, redder then
      with *salsa di pomodori* simmered
      for seeming fragrant centuries.

Ercole steps, slowly, to wrap the chops
      and *chunk, chunk* go his great feet,
      chunk, chunk

LOUIE THE BARBER

Up the block, all you kids,
    it's time for the shearing of hairs;
    it's the day the sun makes Saturday,
    church day tomorrow; it's the day
    baldy Lou, he of the lollipops,
    lowers the boom on your cowlicks and locks.
No pied piper, he; behind his chair
    he's gleeman, however, once you're inside
    with your nose a trunkful of pomade smells,
    Vitalis, Wild Root Cream Oil, Charley.
Is it baseball you're missing?
Are the bats thwacking in the back lot
    while you bend your head and want to scratch,
    and the scissors snip and the mirror
    near the chair beckons you to move just once?
"Well, the Yanks won," says Louie, "yes, the Yanks
    won and the Sox lost and what grade you in
    now, sonny?
"Steady now, steady your head, one more swipe
    of the comb (wish
    I could comb *my* hair," says Louie,
    "See?") —
The bald head lowered to pat, the chuckle,
    "*Bene, bene*, go home now, you're done,
    next man, who's next?

"Who's next?" says Louie.

GUIDO THE ICE HOUSE MAN

So what if it's hot in the sunny streets
     and the gang languishes after lunch
     and the morning games?
Down you go, boys, down you go,
     sluggish with warmth, to the ice-house shade.
When you come to the dreamy door
     that roars its silence in the sun;
     where the cubes of sawdust winter rest
     waiting for us to pick up chips
     for the salving of tongues —
When you come to that best of quiet doors,
     there Guido sits with his hat pulled down
     and his lids pulled down,
     and the shadows down, down to his knees
     like an awning's ghost —
Note no movement, not even his lips
     as Guido says, with his hat pulled down,
     "Welcome, you guys, come in, get cool.

"Get cool near the ice, boys," Guido says.

MORGAN

And so it was with Morgan,
    he of the clay nose
    and Iscariot's grin.
From first to last he was
    the hangman's child.
At eight's age, following in
    his clattering shoetracks,
        I wound my clock by the time he stole
        and tied my shoe with knots
        made for the throat.
Thus it was, and the curbstone heard
    the gurgle we made in passing.
Notwithstanding the hairbrush stripes
    engraved upon his bottom,
        Morgan made a nose of clay one day,
        and the bloody alley cat we made
        furnished dye for that lump.
Thus always was my idol Morgan.

Thank God he was lost as I turned nine.

MAY

Mother named me Lewis,
    Mother with her teapot tears
    and citrus smile,
    filing disasters under *US*
    in the cabinet beside the Singer.
And as she sewed the files shook,
    the house shuddered, the world roared
    in the knuckles of her Nebraska God.
LORD, KEEP THIS HAPPY HOME FROM HARM she stitched
    on a gore-red shirt made of heavenly hair.
When it was done I wore it out
    in the world-quake my father trod
    with peaceful soles and a pastor's hat
    made of the Devil's darkest felt.
But each day there was a new shirt
    with a new boon sewn to its breast,
    and each day there was new death
    to be filed by Gabriel, clerk of The Church,
    in the cabinet mother thought was Hell.

I wore destruction on my back
    until one day it was all worn out,
    and I tried my father's soft black hat
    to see how it felt on my own dark hair.

JOHN

John had a holy eye or two
      that pricked me where my sins
      were thinnest.
And I cracked knees before his altar,
      tapped wickedly at the temple stones
      his martyred Medusa had erected.
On Sundays he and I would toast
      the saints in grapejuice, declare
      our pew the bench of a reclining Christ.
My pious eye kept lighting
      upon his jacket's back where struggling blades
      could only indicate twin hatching wings.
At last my tongue tolled curses,
      for my psalms could coax no doves
      to roost within my belfry.

At twelve I hefted a heavy hammer
      and spiked John to crossed staves.

LUIGI

My mother called me Lewis,
    but I was Son to the old man
    who brought the sunny Host of Sicily
    ashore with him at Ellis Isle.
"Child, Christ died with a gentle smile
    and a human cry on the Fascist cross,"
    he'd say as we started off to church
    where he wept in the pulpit as he preached,
    but grinned as he shook the parish hand.
If I were the son he thought I was
    I'd sing the hymn the satyrs sang
    in the cottager's wood on Aetna's slopes
    and taste the majesty of The Word
    in the rich red juice of our common grail.

We'd drink, despite the matron frown
    that cracked like lightning in a Yankee sky
    where Calvin sat in the foreman's bench
    marking an X by a certain name.

DOROTHY

We wandered gently, Dorothy, and long
      where blue dolphins leapt grey
      upon the sun's rayfields.
Among the seashells we spilled moments
      like pearls — our moons were wine;
      we cared nothing for dreams of reality.
You were a willowy virgin
      through youth's sad laughter —
      and I, enthralled by age's
      inverted telescope, stroked
      love's fur.
Time's fell glass fails:
      dolphins turn bearded walruses
      sprouting tusks of moss....

No pearls drown in the lees
      of our vinegar sea.

CASS

Cass looked the lecher I was not
      and seemed an elderly seventeen.
Bottlefed on fifths and pints,
      he hawked and lipped those bawdy songs
      and noted leeringly the pit
      of pleasure under every skirt.
And I was glad to be his right arm,
      lascivious beneath my smile
      and lewdly harmless at his side.
At all the football games I cried
      aloud no quarter, letting gum
      trip up the slanders on my tongue.
O Cass, I loved you with the male
      and vicious pleasure of seventeen!

Where you faded and the age
      of manhood took your place I never knew.

MAUREEN

Why do I recollect Maureen? —
    no mystery:
    because of spring.
Because of grass done up
    in curlers and a brass-
    bound girdle loosed.
Blue makes for gold,
    and gold for red,
    and red for evening's color.
Hound makes for bitch,
    stud for the mare —
    I made for her.
Why do I recollect Maureen?
Stop wondering,
    it's merely spring.

Her hair was done in pincurls
    and her breasts
    fell free like two white clouds.

GINGER

Ginger loved things small and furry:
    kittens and their kind.
And she kept birth
    folded deep with her mind's
    winding sheets of pain.
She would fondle claws and fur.
She would meditate on padding things,
    pawing things, for cats were gauze,
    and pink in milk was soft
    as silk in winds.
Ginger loved them, Ginger weaned them,
    Ginger watched them purr and pass.

I sometimes thought she half suspected
    kittens and their kind were more complex.

MISS AGATHA

Miss Agatha was a spinster
    of manifold cerebral convolutions.
She had memorized, leaf by leaf,
    the masterworks of Freud
    and the Reverend Peale.
She could trace in pure regressions
    of neurons, syndromes, synapses
    man's clan memories of archetypes
    to make a Jung man dance.
She'd mapped the paths from Roman type
    to fig leaves and that coily length
    of adder-in-the-hay.
Few psychologists or modern lecturers
    were left unspitted
    above the flames of her burning insights.

I watched Miss Agatha write *finis*
    upon her own last chapter in absolute
    possession of her faculties.

MR. MELL

Mr. Mell, on Monday mornings,
    chewed his toast to plug an ulcer,
    relishing it with thoughts of labor.
Over his ledgers, above his columns,
    Mr. Mell savored work liberally
    with something gnawing at his innards.
The rubble of his mind turned out
    toward the world —
    its ashes, heaped about his eyes,
    obscured his pens.
Each red scratch was a gash of blood;
    every black line, his evil fortune
    spoken darkly and bound in dun.

I could not watch Mr. Mell die,
    the ulcer unplugged still,
    his soul slipping through the hole
    in his duodenum into a place
    no medicine man's discovered,
    where something red and something black
    gnaws away life and the hostile world.

JONES

Old man Jones unwound twine
      and stuffed it down deep and safe
      in his pants pocket-pit.
He hoarded string, rope, soap,
      and even single socks
      that lost a foot at the laundromat.
No rag or careless bottle
      was unobtrusive enough.
If you were a second-storey man,
      the block whispered there was Eldorado
      in the mattress lumps Jones dozed upon —
      that is if you could pad past
      the ears; if you skulked by the eyes:
      those eyes were quick,
      nor did the lids rest twitchless long.

I've heard folks say that old man Jones'
      old man was open-handed and well-to-do...,
      when he was well-to-do.

MISS BURNSIDE

Miss Burnside knew a ruler's job
    and felt at home
    before the blackboard's midnight.
She knew her sums and numbers well enough,
    but hated "figures"
    in her heart of hearts.
Each day Miss Burnside took her stand
    for education with fusty skirts
    taped shamelessly to her shins.
All black and gray and white she was,
    and bony where there's no excuse for cloth.
Her tongue could whip her sallow lips —
    the kids all called her "Bloodless" Burnside.

Except for we few who glimpsed her cheeks
    should she be speaking in the hall
    with some young man.

DEACON SMITH

Deacon Smith was older than the pews,
    solid as the boldest
    brass pipe in the Sunday organ.
Easter to Christmas to Easter
    round and round he passed the plate
    and frowned down wraths upon the niggards.
His windy voice was huger than the choir;
    his spine seemed surely to demand
    the crossbar of his shoulders.
God-fearing Deacon Smith
    collapsed one summer Sabbath
    during the invocation.
He gasped his swan's hymn briefly:
There is no doubt at all the Deacon feared
    his God's almighty anger.

I saw his jutting eyes, before the coins
    weighed down his sight, swear it
    like Genesis and Exodus.

BOB

Bob came down with a *rumblededum*
    with the sticks like bones
    on the head of his drum,
    and pride swooped down to perch in his eyes
    as he marched along in the Legion Band.
And I was proud as he won the prize
    — my pal Bob from across the street —
    Champ of the Snares in the whole Northeast.
(But there are snares and there are snares;
    Bob, watch out as you stare ahead
    past the gay cornet
    and the bright baton
    and the sound of the rumble within your drum
    as up go the bones
    and down they come
    on the skin drawn taut on the old drumhead.)
But you switched your uniform,
    switched your corps,
    as pride flew up to lift you high
    — higher than the sight of your level eye —
    and drop you down in an airplane's tail
    to the earth stretched taut across the night.

And the sound you made on that spinning snare
    was a *rumblededum* that no man heard
    as your bones came down with a touch of death.

RAY

I met Ray just as we first thumbed
    the last of thirteen buttons.
In salty blue we swaggered and sipped
    our way through pierside bars;
    through dresses owning white,
    brown, yellow girls.
The grunting steel beneath our shiny shoes
    sentenced us to hobo courses we
    could but approve
    with windward resignation.
Evenings, coffee sloshing in our fists,
    we caught the cosmic anthems being tossed
    via short-wave by a geisha
    slanted over microphones beyond
    shrugging waves.
But sod was winking to reclaim its own,
    and when the sea
    regurgitated those of us that it
    could not digest,
    both Ray and I stopped heaving with the boat
    and tied our hawsers to the dock.

At two-and-twenty I watched Ray roll off,
    his tongue curled half around
    a chantey I'd forgotten.

FRANK

Frank was the Maelstrom in the stream
      of boola days.
My chip swung past
      to be picked up by eddies, gulped
      by his hallooing waters.
Gray matter was a mountain to be climbed
      hanging to his sturdy rope
      and listening to his hand-pick chipping
      bits and pieces from the cliff.
He'd call, "Another foot or two to go
      and we'll be on the top!" but tops
      came hard that year; the slopes steepened.
Yet Frank slogged slowly on and up.
At last I found the dangle too hard to bear —
      the swinging above the chasm
      and the roughshod rock gouging me
      at every cranny.
I cut the rope one day — the day
      I knew the climb could never end.
And then I'd reached my peak and paused
      to breathe before I broached
      my broad plateau.

The last I saw of Frank, his heel
      was disappearing in the mountain mists.

JEAN

Jean's flesh proved sheerest silk:
      I was no rogue — potential fatherhood
      demanded the release of golden rings.
Therefore I pledged an oath
      by Book and gown;
      by my best man and organ solemnly
      proclaiming me the heir to apples.
By hook or crook I'd taken her,
      or she had been the taker.
Brought home like bacon, we devoured
      each other under quilts;
      took sampler hours, fashioned from them
      good wool days stitched through
      with certain yarn.
Years are elastic now: they give,
      spring back to wrap
      a swelling love in thicker threads.

Jean will not recognize a further cloth,
      nor do I dare.

MELORA

Weep, Melora, weep and stay;
    the world's a dim place like the sea.
Weep, Melora, strange and bare:
    the shadows of your dreamings lean
    over your waking — they prepare
    to slay the silences of night
    and set the daylight's pyre adrift
    down *Styx* where stones may weight your bones,
    but words will hurt you worse than love.
Weep, Melora, but do not read
    the future in these words I write.
These palms that carry you down to life
    are forecast by the Gypsy wind
    to make you human as hate at last.
This lullaby is not for you,
    but it is written for no one else —
    this is the first sweet silence slain,
    the first conch found on the river bank
    to be held up roaring to your ear.
Come, Melora, strange and bare,
    follow me down to the silent sea.

The world is a dim place: weep and stay
    with the shadows that hover in the air.

GRANNY

It was a grain of sand, grand
    as an alabaster dust-mote lo!
    there on the stair:
    huge, hairy, hoary, mawkish
    and dissuasive.
I could not climb by.
It stuck in the rug,
    would not roll well nor far.
That was all.
In the upstairs hall
    Granny was weeping.
She swore a swallow was lodged on the windowledge
    peeping at her nakedest wrinkles.
I could not help.
The dust wouldn't let me — it
    was downright obdurate.
Where could I go?
Out.
The hell with Granny.
Had she not grown fond of grit,
    that mote might might have been inhaled
    by a tube hooked to a bag.
Now it's too big.

She may starve up there with that sparrow
    sparing no pains to grow big as a bear
    and peck down the door.

UNCLE LARRY

Old Uncle Larry, leery of losing,
      played with aces of spades in the cellar,
      cursing when he lost.
His partner was a cat
      that mewed at the mice nicely,
      nipping their shoethong tails
      as they scooted gaily, without fear,
      among the cardboard bistros
      Uncle Larry built.
Here a curse, there a curse,
      everywhere a cursecurse
      as the aces fluttered loosely,
      like black moons arched
      and pointed in a single direction.
All Larry could do was kick the cat.

That was it: a kick and a yowl
      and old Uncle Larry on his kneecaps
      cutting at the mice with tooth and knuckle
      as they scuttled by
      scourging the cards.

GRANDDADDY DAGGER

Dear Granddaddy Dagger slyly grew berries
    in his bureau drawers.
He could never hook out a sock
    to pop on his toes
        without spearing a cran- or a blue- or a straw-
        buried among the threads.
If he honked an indiscriminate nostril, *voila!*
    a ripe raspberry brooded
    in his kerchief's curve.
No one knew (or knows)
    how big they grew.
There's no entry into his chamber:
    no doors, no window, no flue....

Just the windrows in his drawers
    and the *scritch-a-scratch*
    of Granddaddy Dagger's wry digger,
    and a *plunk-ta-plunk* as of seeds
    falling minute distances,
    maybe moments tall.

AL

Al's eyes paced the cell of his head;
    his paws padded his home's cobbles,
    and his hands, hopeful, now and then
    tested the lock of his wife's face.
But all corridors were bricked to the sky.
Whenever he pulled, he felt fleshless chains
    tug at his interior.
And he wrote wicker poems about stone and steel.
Now and then he'd will his loins
    into foreign fortresses: stockades
    of camping women,
    moors and bogs of rotten grape or grain.
At times, together, we'd watch dull dawns break
    the night's back where homes were delirium;
    where no fetters seemed long enough
    to link him to his dying room.
Yet, always the noon sun
    banished the moon with a face
    like love burning.
Always he'd looked up, been blinded, gone
    groping back to iron and ice.

Now, at my century's quarter-tide,
    I've found his bottled message on the beach,
    but don't know where to search.

LORRIE

Lorrie looked good — man,
    she was a jazz band, straight
    as a clarinet, and the tunes she played
    with her hip action wowed my crowd.
Lorrie swung like a prime ensemble,
    smiled the cool blues as we sipped our
    brews in the racetrack dive while the
    bass thrummer, a basic type, swiped
    at the strings, making us think
    of beds and things.
There we were, dancing our eyes
    among the beers while Lorrie walked
    her pert way among us, mashers all,
    and we asked, "What's up tonight,
    Lorrie-love?"
"I've no time," she smiled, "no time —
    I'm a college girl, my major's law.
"By night I slide drinks down
    to your hands, and in the daylight
    I guard lives at Ryall's beach."
Then, when the jazz bunch quit and
    the horn stopped snorting
    and the drums bumped the last bum
    out the door, we went too, man,
    we went too.

Who wants to see Lorrie meet her beau?
>	Who wants to see his old eyes, older
>	than she'll ever be, and his dark hands
>	grab her wrist hard as they leave to park
>	in the raceway woods?

LENA

I grant you your grain of sand,
    Lena, an igneous beachful in fact,
    on which to spread your pallor
    and accept Apollo: the archetype
    of a household saint who somehow lives
    to make you burn.
There let you lie, at the lace edge
    of the raving sea, your beach mat striped
    and furrowed, your forehead
    forced clear of the tidal marks
    of rage or aging, or love or lust,
    or life, even.
I have come to see how you lie on sand.
This is the manner: without passion,
    only ennui; without desire,
    only fashion; without fire,
    only baking.
Lena, do you know you lie on the buried eggs
    of turtles and crabs?
Does your flesh not feel the empty houses
    left behind by small lives, nor the long
    linkages of dried weed the wind has eaten?

    Turn red, Lena — I grant you your sand,
        and the crowded beach more quiet than stillness,
        and the translucent shell that shall never be turned.

MORTON

A gust of smiles behind his beard,
    fat as the cat he itched to pet,
    by night he'd tip the inchling Buddha on its back
    so it could sleep.
No halves for him: the whole hog
    was nearly too little.
Morton would roast the boar: bristle and tusk.
Snout and twirly tail, sowbelly and jowl
    singed in the oven between his ears
    till dinner was served on paper plates.
Life was enough for him to smoke;
    tobacco never crashed his curing house
    to hang from the rafters and color his tongue.
Nor wine — he was drunk enough on air.
Morton, your seasons bedeviled my brain
    for the sum of an autumn, a winter, a spring.

Where do you roar now my oven's timer
    has rung the ruin of twenty-six?

VERN

Beyond a doubt, there was no other dusk
    the hour I found my poem
        grinning at me from Vern's paper pit.
Despite the snaking lines of ink
    I pulled its fangs and laid them side by side
    to memorize the venom in each word
    and hate the thing that Vern had pulled
    out of my craw.
Beyond that dusk, there were no other vipers
    besides ourselves; no similar coils of scales
    could stretch the measure of our lines
    with such constricting ease.
When my hate of serpents had recoiled at last
    to stab the only finger that could feed
    a wingless dragon in the night, I turned
    and gave my fangs back to the thing
    that grew them.
Now, with a pipe and a hamper stitched of straw,
    Vern's slave must hiss and slither in solitude
    to his tune of twisting syllables.

And I, alone, must squat by dusk, another slave
    who waits for a hooded head to rise
    above its pit and grin.

MISS MARY BELLE

Mary of the Charms, Mary Belle,
    see how your flesh moves in ravels
    over the landscape where your great house
    was built upon the courtings of your suitors.
Our Lady of Clocks, Mary of Sorrows,
    whose shrine is this you inhabit
    upon the hill where Shakers shook down
    the pillars of Rome
    to come out hoeing and praying among their beanrows?
Now in your Vatican of attics
    no pilgrims come to pray your hand
    and give you pause among lilacs and yews.
The last man gave you menopause
    and wrinkles and a hard eye, see:
    the walk is bare, the porch is swept,
    leaves lie in bundles, flaring like penitence,
    as winter's benediction
    begins to crowd the air.
Look, Mary, your virgin birth
    is wound in Death
    who fills your manse with phantoms
    and snows down time upon your hair and thighs.
Mary, Queen of Love, I come
    with bell and psalter to offer
    this last communion: paper host
    and a wine of words.

Drink now and go, blessed with regret,
    amid an angelus of silence,
        Mary, Mother of Snows.

LEWIS

This is your house as well,
      Lewis be clear:
      halls peopled with figures
      out of recall, and beyond its walls
      nothing but wind waits there
      in the groves of night.
And, Lewis, be cold too,
      true as the sun falling over autumn:
      early enough for pure light, but late
      as well for high color.
See each thing clearly:
      the wife among her flowers, the nodding neighbors,
      the child at work
      with toys, the furtive cat
      lurking among the mathoms.
See them together, but say them each alone.
Speak their silence and their solitude.
Beneath these aprons and these ties
      there lies the bone, and spirit of the bone.
Lewis, be clear and cold;
      Lewis, be true.

There are thin walls between the wind and you.

AWAKEN, BELLS FALLING
1968

A DEDICATION
for John Brinnin and Don Justice, on a line by Joel Sloman

           If it is true that
"the sea worm is a decorated flute
        that pipes in the most ancient mode" —
    and if it is true, too, that
the salt content of mammalian blood
    is exactly equivalent
to the salinity of the oceans
at the time life emerged onto the land;

        and if it is true
that man is the only mammal with a
    capacity for song, well, then,
        that explains why the baroque
worm swims in our veins, piping, and why
    we dance to its measure inch by
equivocal inch. And it explains why
this song, even as it explains nothing.

THE TOWNSFOLK

There is, first, the road,
which goes nowhere out of
nowhere endlessly. And beside
it, beside the road, grass
and flowers growing, some trees,

leaves covered with dust.
A barn stands caught in a
twist of the road, paint peeling in
the insensible sun.
Somewhere a dove mourns under

eaves. A phoebe calls
out the season crisply,
and the townsfolk move out of no-
where, walking, going no-
where with birdcalls and flowers.

IN A WHITE DIRECTION
for Sal

    I have come, cousin,
      to wish you good night. The hubs
of your eyes make no worlds careen now;
    the spokes of shadow are bent

    and broken beneath
      your lashes. What a wish to
wish you: good night, with its circular
    lie. You stretch beneath your sheets,

    ridged and humped like some
      winter terrain. No person's
sight will travel you again. It is
    here we must stop now, in this

    blind alley of flesh.
      The mind cannot compass you.
My breath stops and starts in its tunnel,
    the permanent wind moving

    in sentient hollows;
      it is a vague piston in
my veins pushing red motion through curbs
    time has constructed. But you,

cousin. I wish you
good night. There shall be no maps
now, no turns. Direction comes back to
this:
Darkness on winter roads.

LOST GIRL WITH DOG
for May

    Improbably fair, picture girl, your hair
settled like a mist above the closed lids of your eyes,
    you lie in the warm snow, and the collie howls

    quietly into the night. You are tacked
four square to the wall. A pattern of slatternly vines
    and rose blossoms weaves wearily behind and

    about you. You are a gateway in the
wallpaper, and she searches you from time to time. *This
is how it might have been with me,* she thinks. *I,*

    too, might have made such a lovely painting.
She nods and turns away. You are left in suspension.
    The blizzard spills on your still form like petals.

    What if the dog should move his hushed tail and go
yelping into sharp darkness for help? Little girl lost
    in the woods of sleep, what if that lone star

    came sweeping with raging feathers, nails raking
out of the glass to scatter your drab dream and hers? She
    leans and settles, neutral and thick, in corners

of the dark house. The pattern of her dress is
dry leaves and brown blossoms. Her steps upon the carpet
   drop like flakes. She passes and repasses

   you and your collie, stopping now and then to
lodge her heavy eyes in cotton worlds of snow. She nods
   and goes pressing back into brown patterns.

LETTER TO W. D. S.

    Christ, you made me sad
      with your love tunes gone awry,
  the bitter root twining mossily
among the pages of a songsheet tossed to

    wind down the wind and
      molder in a lost cranny
  of some meadow. I'm not used to loss,
though aware of it, as one is aware of

    cancer. A woman
      I knew, wrinkled like blown snow,
  died of a wild part of herself which
ravened its own life. Her children, grown to seed

    themselves, kept locks on
      their tongues, but their hearts' faceless
  prisoner snarled at the world behind
portcullises of eyes. Like those striped lines of

    yours, that scourge of ink
      and pillory of paper.
  Why did you flay yourself there, in the
marketplace? Was it because sorrow shown is

    simpler than covert
      loneliness? All of us are
  alone. The world we blow through is cold.
Snow fetters our sorrow. Still we flute and fife.

MICE IN THE SUNDAY WALLS

The gray rain, like mice scurrying about the house,
nibbles the edges of a moldy afternoon.
    Sunday's trap is set for us to trigger.
    The doorbell. The door. The whole hall hungry,
its yellow stairs snapping at our laces; the old
    lady mewing in the parlor, arching
her aching back — O! The same old tom in the same

armchair rising, dragging his sagging tail
over the carpet to welcome us back.
    The cool cat gone, off in his Olds down the alley,
    the motor purring convertibly; seduction
sloshing contentiously in the gas tank:
    gone, man, gone. Sunday rustles in the walls. We four
sit lapping the skim of our duty call.

This is the way the old folks seem at last. Death sprawls
on the couch to doze an age. But metaphor will
    not suffice to crystallize aversion;
    nor simile, our compassion. There is
nowhere to go, nothing to see, little to do
    here in childhood's hall of mirrors. Backward
and forward, reflected in each-other's vision,

distorted images of our common
love separate, then merge, then fade and fail.
    We talk. Quietly at first, for fear of shadows.
    Days, like mice, have overgenerated. They now
outnumber the old folks' hungers. Soon we
    will leave, and no one will reflect on anyone
for very long. Nor too deeply. Nor far.

LINES FOR MR. STEVENSON

       Here, music
is martial. Wars and their rumors
echo among these cold walls. I recall
       one who kept

       the beat with
his shoe — the cadence of its heel
used a desk in a way I could not have
       dreamed. A world

       speaks in so
many tongues, it is difficult
to hear truth whispering out of Babel.
       Even so,

       one must try.
At least, I believe so, and one
will be chastised for daring to believe:
       the single

       conviction
must stand against the myrmidons
of truism and rumor — must prevail
       at last, or

       there is no
hope. But flesh tires; the mind will
wear it out if the drums don't wear it down.
       Even the

>   warrior
>   need not fight forever. Where are
> the young men? There is music I should like
>   to hear; *for*
>
>   *a while, I*
>   *would just like to sit in the shade*
> *with a glass of wine in my hands, and watch*
>   *people dance.*

HE WHO FEEDS PIGEONS

    I have not been here long.
I sit in the park and feed the pigeons.
In my pocket there are crumbs and catches,
      and an old, broken chess piece
    left over from some forgotten game.
    I no longer play with pawns and kings,

    nor do I have to do with bishops —
    they are all dead men. Instead, the world
      is an aerie filled with wings.
If you should ask me why I venerate
the grass and the birds and playing children
      above all other things,

I would not tell you. There are things no man
    can tell, and none understand unless
      he is willing to bring
in his pockets the remnants of song, crusts,
    winters of memory, and drop them
      in handfuls, thus, on the ground.

TRILOGY FOR J. F. K.

I. The Moment Before

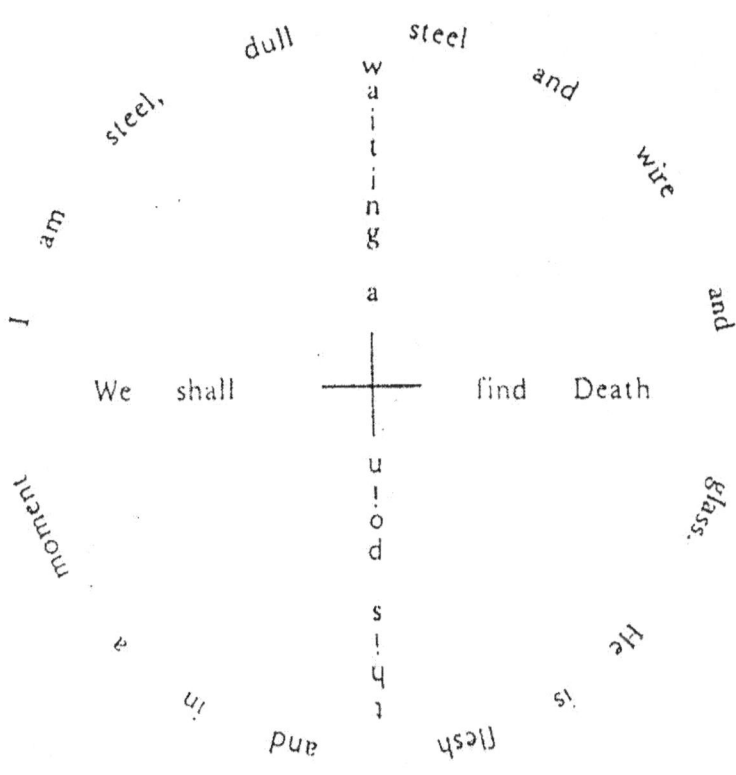

II. November 22, 1963

Weeping, I write this: You are dead. The dark
animal of the heart, the beast that bides
stilly in its web of flesh, has stolen
flight again out of the air. What is there
to say? That I wish we were gods? That the
mind of man were equal to his lusts? It
is not — not yet. You were a man, but more:
you were an idea dreamt in a sweet
hour while the spider slept. We make our
web; its habitant makes greatness of its
prey. We are ourselves victim and victor.
You were and are ourselves. In killing you
we murder an emblem of what we strive
to be: not men, but Man. In mourning you,
good Man, we grieve for what we are, not what
we may become.

               Sleep, my heart. We will try
once more. Sleep, sleep now. We will try again.

III. Ode on St. Cecilia's Day 1964

1. Of the Past

Some music, then, for this day. Let it be
Suitable to the mood of fallen snow,
The veil of a virgin saint. Quietly
Let it come now, out of the silence; now
While the birds inexplicably forsake
The elm, the oak, the seed in the lilac....
Instead, drumrolls muffled in an old year,
An echo of trumpets in the streets. Clear
But muted, there is a ragged tattoo
Of hooves, image of a sable horse, wild-
Eyed, resisting the rein, skittish among
The twin rows of witness citizens who,
Their voices frozen, give up to the cold
Air of the marble city an old song.

2. Of the Present

But it's another year, Cecilia's day
Again, another part of the land. So,
Let the phantoms of those dead days lie
Under these new burdens of snow. Allow
That chorus of stricken men to dim like
Shadows into blackening film, the dark
Merging with the riderless horse. Feature
By feature, let the scene fade into near

Distance, into perspective, then shadow.
This is music for St. Cecilia. Yield
To her the lyric due her. Let us sing
For her patronage — her martyrdom grew
Out of a summer heart: she is our shield
Against the winter. She is always young.

3. Of the Moment

Here beyond the window the campus lies.
The students pass in mufflers and coats, eyes
Almost hidden against the wind. The sound
Of radio music settles around
The furniture, into the carpeting.
Choral voices: a requiem. Distant
And urgent, the November church bells ring.
Outdoors a dog rags something. An instant
Pause in his play — he has caught a squirrel
Which tosses and tosses in the gray air.
The mongrel, in the midst of his quarrel
With life, is assaulted by three girls. There,
At the base of a tree, the limp ruff falls
From insensate jaws, starts to inch up walls
Of oak bark toward some invisible
Sanctuary. The dog begins to howl.
The girls watch the squirrel into the limbs.
Cecilia's radio is done with hymns.

MY COUNTRY WIFE

My country wife bends to rinse. Her skirt is
    unwrinkled. Its print of flowers rounds
out her womb like the rug of violets
      that mounds or dimples the chapel
burying ground. She would be grotesque where
        hydrants irrigate gutters.

Here, she is a sleight of the moon; the sound
    a mole makes. She bends and carries. She
cooks and smiles her meals down my throat. I need
      no teeth. She has done what the bee
does to clover. The sun moves around. She
        stays and stays. She sweeps and cooks.

MY WIFE OF THE TOWN

The stairs are teeth that chew her heels.
She grows shorter each day. The child
tears her with nails and with cries. I cannot hear
the night sounds that burrow
in the sheets, unwinding her like thread
onto the winter boards.

She moves in the closets mewling
among the garments as though she
were a sleeve looking for its coat. Where are they,
those sheep days, wool days, days
fleeced from green time and woven to wear?
A black rat chews her heels.

NO REFLECTION ON YOU, BUT...,

    who are you? he asked me
curiously, without conceit, yet
I could feel it, but I cannot say it
    exactly — holding something back,
      keeping it out of his eyes,

    out of his smile. He stood still, holding
out his hand, like a roadmap we were to
    travel together openly.
      His eyes were brown, warm enough,
      but with a heat that could

never fuse: the mesa of his nose was
    much too high for them to surmount,
      poor lovers. Imagine, not
      ever to cross, only
to wander side by side and worship

    from afar, as it is done in
      penny novels. His lips: one
      was thin, the other plump:
a miser bedding his jolly wife.
Under the mattress a chin was hiding.

    It was neither sturdy nor
      frail — a compromise in
a compromising situation.
But above all, a brown heath spread its hay
    over redness and ruddiness, and

yet, though he stood smiling
openly, there was that about him
which I could not fathom. No, who are you?
I asked, smiling warmly into
his face, thrusting my hand far

as it would go into the shallow glass.

NARCISSUS TO HIS FLESHLY SHADE

    I want her to be what I need
her to be, *i.e.*, a mirror for my
want. There is no man but owns his own soul.
    His lack lies in the catalyst.
Surmise it or not, what she cannot know
    is what image she replaces,

    or why the moon's in her lashes
and in mine. The moon is one mirror of
a world, but purer for perspective, for
    distance. Our man knows himself too
well for glassless love. You are too near, dear
    shade! Fall back on deeper shallows.

AN OLD ACQUAINTANCE

As we stand talking, his eye
   drops out. I am amazed.
   His socket looks funny.
   It's a nice day, I say.
His scalp is scattered on the

carpet. What's the matter with
   your nose, I ask — but it
   is too late. He laughs. His
   teeth hit something on their
way down. I must be getting

on, I suggest. But I am
   too slow to catch his ear.
   Can't you say something? I
   inquire: he opens his
mouth to show me. That's too bad,

I say, but he shakes his head
   too hard. I try looking
   into his mind, but he
   is thinking of nothing.
A spider is spinning her

web in a white cave. It is
   awkward. Well, it's getting
   late, I say. The spider
   has caught something. I smile
at him; he stands there grinning.

PLAYHOUSE

           A continuous curtain, the
mist rises and rises on no cue at all. Here
       lies the farm on bottomland. Marshmallow
             blooms blossom like cathedrals in
the mist. The stage is dark. Loam lies down with stagnant

          water to breed vapors and moss.
It is silent here, for the farmhouse wants to rot.
      By night it breathes steam from broken garrets.
         In the cellar, walls distil (drop
by drop by drop) the juices of a luminous

         cancer, and the foundations search
deeper for fundament. Rust has pilfered the plow;
       the weight of the sky has scuttled the barn;
         the willow roots in the cistern.
Bottomland lets no marker stand for long: no stone

        shows by the sycamore tree, nor
footway runs the dooryards's course. Henbane roosts in the
     parlor chair. A loveseat drowses like an
       old couple tangled in time, drugged
by blood, shedding years like hair on the flowered rug.

MILLPOND
Yaddo, Saratoga Springs, New York, 1959

    This is the place where peace grows
like a green frond set among waters aerial
      with dragonflies. Where, at noon,
  the trees section the broad falling
leaf of light, and space color upon the millpond,
    yet do not move because motion
      might be lost upon silence.

    This is the place where a stone,
given its occasional career, could disturb
      little with an arc and fall,
  for the pond would swallow all voice
and shrug circling ripples into its banks until
    moss had absorbed this small wet gift,
      showing a fancy darker.

    This is the place where one may
abet his heart's romance, deceiving his eyes by
      unconsciously confusing
  slow change with no change. But even
here, dream makes way for declensions of wind and sun.
    The alders will grow, moss will dry.
      Wings will pulsate, then plummet.

This is the place where peace rests
like ferns beyond lilies. The trick is to wear it
    as a mantle, but to know
  cloaks for cloaks, shelters for shelters.
Beneath this revery of surfaces, fish wait
  for the dragonfly's mistake. The
    trick is to lose, but to own.

THE WELL

He and his go to the spring, have gone
to the same old well, through the weeds in the yard,
   under the oak arching its limbs over
      their heads — for water have gone, to drink
   from the welling rock in the four seasons,
though good liquid has long sprung from the pipes in

      the kitchen, the clocks' hands are now turned
by sparked wire; the grandchildren's dolls no longer
   are chipped off the old block stowed in the wood
      shed, near the willow wands. Still he goes.
   Why? Time, measured by the golden rule, the
honey vine suckled in the sun inching day

      by day over his canopy of
firm timbers — those hours are over now. He knows
   no age reclaims another. But the well
      is deep and old. Its tunnel strikes through
   stone: strata which buoy up all things and all
men: himself, his — whoever thirsts in this world.

SCHOOL DRAWING

    There is a road: no
  one is walking there. Brown
paper, black paper triangles
      wrangle with the air
      to make a windmill

      striping a crayon
    sun. A black arrow points
away from the blades that turn in
        fire. It is burning,
      and there is no wind.

AN ORDINARY EVENING IN CLEVELAND

I.
          Just so it goes: the day, the night —
     what have you. There is no one on TV;
          shadows in the tube, in the street.
In the telephone there are echoes and mumblings,
          the buzz of hours falling thru wires.

          And hollow socks stumbling across
     the ceiling send plaster dust sifting down
          hourglass walls. Felix the cat has
been drawn on retinas with a pencil of light.
          I wait gray, small in my cranny,

          for the cardboard tiger on the
     kitchen table to snap me, shredded, from
          the bowl.

II.
               Over the trestle go
the steel beetles grappled tooth-and-tail — over and
          over and over there smokestacks

          lung tall hawkers into the sky's
     spittoon. The street has a black tongue: do you
          hear him, Mistress Alley, wooing
you with stones? There are phantoms in that roof's trousers;
          they kick the wind. The moon, on a

      ladder, is directing traffic
   now. You can hardly hear his whistle. The
      oculist's jeep wears horn rim wind
shields; the motor wears wires on its overhead valves —
      grow weary, weary, sad siren,

      you old whore. It's time to retire.

III.
   The wail of the child in the next room quails
      like a silverfish caught in a
thread. It is quiet now. The child's sigh rises to
      flap with a cormorant's grace through

      the limbo of one lamp and a
   slide-viewer in your fingers: I cannot
      get thin enough for light to shine
my color in your eyes; there is no frame but this for
      the gathering of the clan. Words

      will stale the air. Come, gather up
   our voices in the silent butler and
      pour them into the ashcan of
love. Look, my nostrils are dual flues; my ears are
      the city dump; my eyes are the

      very soul of trash; my bitter
   tongue tastes like gasoline in a ragged
      alley.

IV.
                    The child cries again. Sounds
rise by the riverflats like smoke or mist in time's
                bayou. We are sewn within seines

        of our own being, thrown into
     menaces floating in shadows, taken
            without volition like silver
fish in an undertow down the river, down time
               and smog of evenings.

V.

                            The child cries.

VI.
                Do you hear the voice of wire?
            Do you hear the child swallowed by carpets,
                    the alley eating the city,
rustling newsprint in the street begging moonlight with
            a tin cup and a blindman's cane?

VII.
>   The lamps are rheumy in these tar
> avenues. Can you sense the droppings of
>   flesh falling between walls falling,
> the burrowings of nerves in a cupboard of cans?
>   Can you hear the roar of the mouse?

VIII.
>   There is nothing but the doorway
>   sighing; here there is nothing but the wind
>   swinging on its hinges, a fly
> dusty with silence and the house on its back buzzing
>   with chimneys, walking on the sky

like a blind man eating fish in an empty room.

THE OLD PROFESSOR AND THE SPHINX

It is a dry word in a dry book
drying out my ear. I squat and swallow
my tongue here in this chair,
the desert of my desk, summer bare, spreading
like a brown horizon into regions grown arid
with erudition. A caravan of books treks

stolidly across my eyes while I,
the Sphinx, a phoenix nesting in my skull,
pry into inkwells and
gluepots seeking the universal solvent.
There is none. The pages as I turn them sound like sand
rattling in the sec temples of a beast gone to

earth with the sun. I lie caught in my
creaking dune, shifting with the wind of the
pharaohs, wondering if,
somewhere, I have not missed my valley. Upon
the walls of my office there are Oriental prints
hanging stiff as papyrus, whispering their brown

images into the silent air.
I know the poems on my shelves speak with
one another in an
ancient language I have somehow forgotten.
If there is rainfall, I recall, the desert blossoms —
but I have somewhere lost the natural prayer

and instinctual rites of the blood
which can conjure clouds in seasons of drought.
There is but ritual
remaining; no honey is in the lion's
hide; my temples have mumbled to ruin: they endure
disuse and despair. An archaeologist of

cabinets and drawers, I exhume
paperclip skeletons, the artifacts
of millennia: red
ball-point pens with nothing in their veins, pencils
like broken lances, and notebook citadels empty
of citizens — the crusader has squandered his

talents on bawds, grown hoary in their
service. The town is sacked: the bawds are gone
to tame younger legions.
Look into my sarcophagus: the tapes are
sunken over my hollow sockets. Slowly the waste
swallows my oasis like a froth of spittle.

THE WELL OF HOLY HEAVEN

The well of holy heaven has gone sec;
the sun begins its famous dance of wives.
Freres and handmaidens, come sip the blue from
aster's eye: pudgee and peewee liking
from free fields, milkweed stealing gold from gourd
and globe. In a word the world wags. Singing
vines take husbands from the hearth, settle them
among the clods and clouds where meadows waste.

The apple of the daisy knows it's true:
the earth is, after all, a world, though tan-
tamount to tangerines — equal in worth
to a curlew's call, a cell of bees in
amber comb, the curl of water, welter
of the summertide sunning autumn's falls.

OLD NEWS

"Six weeks gone," the doctor said,
that odd good luck look walking his lips along

the trail blazed by the tip of
his tongue. "Six weeks gone, son. She'll be fine. Lousy

in bed, though," shaking his head.
"You'll be used to the idea come daylight,"

and off he went, his eyes propped
wide with a good call's work — blasé, not quite bored

by the old wonder with which
I was left: the old bride whose acquiescence,

I now find, can swallow down
this house with its carpet silences; stillness

of pillows; the couch couching.
Outdoors, the dark lies in the hollows of trees.

Night descends like a muffled
lamp. These eyes seize on ancient things: the roadway

sleeping between its curbs, the
lurking swell of a still flat belly, and the

lidded moon risen, unwinking, on the world.

THE FOREST BEYOND THE GLASS

        Hundreds of yards of woodland
          smashed and torn.
    They had been a long while dying,
        these great beasts;
one, of a broken neck — the lucky
         one. Thirst took
the other: even on his side he'd dug
         a dozen

      holes, deep as his hooves could delve,
         trying for
  water. It had been one of those
        tremendous
agonies. There lie the two moose still,
         locked upon
love's combat, horns fused. All is as it was.
        The bulls are

      dead; so says the placard hung
         upon the
  glass; thus they were found, silent in
        the forest.
The point and object of contention
        had long since
vanished when men happened upon these hulks
        steaming in

              a spring thaw. But it was not
                    love that had
           conquered; as usual, it was
                time. Engrossed
with death's petrified grove and with the
              heart's beasts calm
in the wildwood, we stand frozen by love's
               passing glance
reflected in the forest beyond the glass.

THE BURNING BUSH

    He touched the switch
    and lit his burning bush,
    then waited for a voice
      to come chiming,
green as ever, from among

    its needles. He
    listened hard, but the spheres
    made no music of their
      colors, and the
angel sitting on top of

    everything just
    sat there holding a bulb.
    Maybe it was the wires:
      he checked them, but
could find no short anywhere —

    all the lights were
    tight in their sockets; no
    cane's cellophane was caught
      in anything
electrical. The angel

    was shedding spun
    glass hair everywhere, but
    glass is no conductor.
      He sat and he
waited. The dark windows flashed

      back the light of
        his burning bush. The house
        hummed with sleep, with couches
           stolid as cows
chewing carpet cuds. Comfort

      bleated in dim
        corners void of any
        echo. Once, the furnace
          rumbled under
him like a tame Inferno:

      for a moment
        he thought that the bush had
        started to speak. At last
          he gave up, turned
off the angel and its lights.

      In the darkness
        his bush loomed against the
        window through which cold stars
          came stabbing out
of a wind he had not heard,

      nor wished to hear.
        Snow lay trackless in his
        yard, but at his panes some
          sound, like fingers
touching for purchase or for

   entry, moved and
  scratched, scratched on the frost-etched
  glass. Open! said the wind;
   wings battered his
door. Trembling, he tried the lock

   and went to bed.

THE FACE ON THE CHEQUERED FIELD

In a drawer he found
a clock, its cord wound
among some chessmen, its crystal
broken and its digits gone dark with
dust. It needed

a spark to set it
going upon its
rounds. It would mutter some constant
monotone among queens and knights. Pawns
could listen as

they lay tumbled in
a grove of fallen
rooks: it was love's visage he saw
rising from the floor on which he stood.
She was blind to

the careful mating
moves, her blunt palms like
inexorable whispers at
his ankles, her numbers obscuring
the checkered field.

THE LATE, LATE SHOW

    It is now ten minutes after midnight,
    December 5th, 1965. In honor
        of the attack by the Japanese
            on Pearl Harbor, Hawaii, on
December 7th, 1941, all channels

    are running movies about war. On one
    channel, the come-on is newsreel footage of the
        bombing inserted into a film
            made by the Japanese. Channel
9 has topped that: also Japanese, the movie is

    science-fiction: the Third World War is just
    beginning. I'll take a gangster film — Channel 3:
        it sounds incredible, but the third
        world war is already over
over here. This one is American. Let me check

    the T. V. Guide: "'Five.' (1951).
    The only five survivors of atomic war
        revive man's ancient hostilities
            and prejudices." The whole thing
is starting again. So I have turned to writing this

    poem as I watch. I have survived one
    Armageddon; I shall build a microcosm.
        I am writing very carefully:
            the woman is pregnant, and the
Negro is building a house. I want my facts to be

        accurate, in case this is the last thing
    to be left. The sounds do not matter, only the
           sense. If you are reading this, I hope
              that it will not upset you, sir,
whoever you are. It may be that my typewriter

        was hocked, passed peacefully from dark shelf to
    dark shelf in ancient shops until it was sold for
           scrap. Grant us this: that was possible.
              But if you should find this lying
rolled in my machine, the letters of our alphabet

        scrambled in the dust, grant us this much more:
we foresaw the end too clearly for it to matter.

THE GIRL FROM THE GOLDEN WEST
for Diane, in memoriam

He was on a pale horse when he came
    riding out of the dark West,
        the manuscript of
           a novel,

beery and dog-eared, under one arm,
    and a shotgun strapped to the
        saddle. You thought you
           were supposed

to be his heroine — the girl with
    long hair, from The Golden West.
        You knew your role to
           the last dot

on the last page. And you were ready.
    The plot had to do with love
        and fidelity —
           yours, of course.

You knew he'd be true to nothing but
    art, its imitation of
        life: you were to be
           his living

imitation of love. He would write
    you down under the long wind
        out of the mountains;
           your pages

would fall like leaves into the big white
    winter of the world. It would
        be a grand book,
            a Western.

So when he came riding out of the
    West, you were prepared, even
        though he did not look
            his part: his

beard, for instance, reminded you of
    Hemingway's rather than
        Odysseus's.
            But, after

all, you were hardly Helen yourself,
    only a plump girl of woods
        and weather out of
            Cooper's verge.

So when he came you took the gun
    and wrote the last flourish. It
        was not love, though, was
            it? It was

only your revenge upon his art
    at last, and you were not his
        book, but only a
            scant chapter.

And that's why the horse bearing you out
   through the sunset is pale, not
      sable, and that's why
         we are blue,

not stricken in the wind from the West.

BURNING THE NEWS

    The fire is eating
the paper. The child who drowned
is burned. Asia is in flames.
      As he signs his great
bill, a minister of state chars

    at the edges and curls
into smoke. The page rises,
glowing, over our neighbor's
    roof. In the kitchens
clocks turn, pages turn like gray wings,

    slowly, over armchairs.
Another child drowns, a bill
is signed, and the pen blackens.
    The smoke of Asia
drifts among the neighbors like mist.

    It is a good day for burning.
The fire is eating the news.

THE FOREST OF MY SEASONS

Desire today is a cavern of snow;
  ice rimes all limbs with synonyms for wind.
    Yesternoon it was goat-time, time for horns
      rampant on a field vert under the woods
        quartered in a southern compass. Toucan
          tones rose close beneath the surface of shade,

      threatening rupture. Poet, draw your shade
today upon a mirror made of snow
      shadowed. Men may hibernate if bears can.
  Desire must sleep in a cavern of wind
    till it may be harried awake by wood-
  pecker beak and Pan's sunsharp or ramshorns —

  Too many words, like girdles built of horn,
        confined in an attic. How to say *shade*
      but make it mean more, as: tiles of the wood
  laid for light to walk on; and to have snow
    imply more than God's linoleum. Wind
        is wind, but direction matters. Who can

      help me? Where's my muse today? Shake your can,
  you errant Echo, and get home. My horns
    sprout long as the cuckoo's song while you wind
        your own clock and make love with your own shade
someplace up a cavern or down the snow
      where wild Narcissus buds among your woods.

  The forest of my seasons grows strange woods
    sometimes; this fall of words grows as it can,
not as it ought. My pen is cold as snow:
  its ink runs like chilled honey from the horns
     of silence. Lie you down, lie down in shade,
 word-warbler. Sleep sound with your mistress wind.

  And while you sleep, dream. Dream of the south wind
    needling you awake with slivers of woods:
     birch and pine, maple that sweetens in shade;
    oak on the white hillside. Dream, if you can,
of gray moles, brown mice, winter's hunting horns
blown to silence. Dream no longer of snow,

for time and flesh shall do more than wind can
to blend your words with woodwinds and woodshorns.
There will be tonics. It's time for shades now.

CLAMBAKE

        Nor was it the moon,
appointed, pure in outline,
    huge among stars, painted;
        nor was it the wind.

        Chinese firecrackers,
Chinese lanterns; O the flare
    and the pop! Acres of
        summer went well with

        the fields of light made
by the moon tugging at tides.
    And the gale mewled offshore.
        You could hear the hiss

        of rockets. The hiss of
the flames on the beach. The
    surf's hiss too, the kiss of
        sand. It was not the

        moon. Nor was it the
old wind offshore, moaning.
    It was partly these, partly
        their white permanence

        and cold. But it was
the pop too, the flare, the
    flash of flame. Short. Slight. Red and
        unappointed. The

>   scrim of those quick, quaint
> with life. The scream of bright
>   rockets; night's backdrop; summer's
>   curtain. Clams in a
>
>   bucket. Fire them, shell
> them in the summer dark.
>   A heap of shells on the shore
>   looks like the moon's shards.

SOME PINFEATHER BLUES

As you stand there, Melora, winking at
my world (doubly obscured by the
curtain's mist) your eye is
a sparrow flung searching among the morning
trees. Your gaze floats, windreft, inquiring
for its sulking mate. But it

is all to no effect, for she will not
rise from her nest for sheer pique at
weathervanes which would spin
my wet kind of world today, not your sunny
one. So the braver eye flies homeward.
Not until you turn toward

hallways and cupboard do you unwink. Those
two brown birds address their ire at
me. Yes, I'm to blame. My
wings are only knuckles now; my mind is prey
to weasels and martens, and winds are
merely the rustlers of nests.

SCARECROW
for 'Dolph

We pumpkins worship you. We orange globes,
harrowed in youth, hollow in our old age,
aspire to your straw. In the darkness
of our swelling and decay, in our days
of rook pestilence and the owl's blight
which scampers among the vines we spin in
furrows and the furbelows of weed, we
do you homage. All honor, Scarecrow! You
there, sun-struck, eminent among us, rag
lord of moonlight, crucified among stars,
sighted as none of us may be. The world
in which we root unrolls unendingly
beneath your gaze, furlongs your province.
We pumpkins worship you, we orange globes.

*I cannot see. Buttons for eyes, what would
I see? If I could hear, the crows' whispers
could tell me only of some simple fields,
potato-eyed and corn-eared, extending
to limits that would only barb my sleeve
and rend my cloth, if I could walk to them.
You worship me? a pole for a spine, a
timber for my extended bone, fingers
of hay stolen by wrens? I bleach and shake,
I shudder in the moon's dark. Pumpkins, crowd
of orange globes, I whistle in the wind.*

Scarecrow, we too would whistle in the wind.

RACEWAY

I.
        My raceway of sheets last night became
a cool trotter, unwinding with grace. Today,
    autumn peeps imponderably out of
        the soggy drought July had posted
            on the foothills. It is August

        here in Saratoga; the races
open tomorrow. Yesterday a filly
    worked out her own odds, snapping two of her
        ankles while we watched. She was done in
            by a green syringe. She lounged on

        the turf, staring from one farthest eye,
both her fore-hooves angled like ballerina
    slippers. With her, summer has staggered: it,
        too, soon will drop and the jockey sun
            grow gray above the world's brown hide.

II.
>	When a thoroughbred loses its
> pins, there's no more running. Snort if you
will, but reason, too, exhausts itself when
cause falters. Men have run down when barred from the
> race. Summer is a fragile courser

> here in the North; our racers are
> all imports from the southland. Summer
will not slow for falling leaves, nor haul our
sleighs: it will linger, pawing its reluctance
> to leave, but its strength is of only

> short will, meant for one swift effort.
> Watch the summer run its oval, it's
a winner now — nothing can stop it! The
stands urge their encouragement upon open
> air; shouts fall and rise like the fall wind

> that moves out of the foothills now, sure,
> pervasive, wild.
>> Blooded summer shies.

PUMPINODE

    I have always wanted to write
        a poem about a
      pumpkin. It is one of those
    impossible subjects. You know
the feeling, left over from childhood's

    fantasies of what childhood is
        like. Come the Indian
      summer of any year, 'mums
    and trees burning their clean colors
into the air, one thinks of

    all seasons, past and future, but
        particularly of
      the pumpkin, Ceres' good Jack,
    grinning his candlepower in-
to the scarecrow's menace. Northern spies

    engage in autumnal intrigue;
        winesaps hit the local
      cider mills, and there's a witch
    in every stook. Cozy, but the
real spice lies with that vandal made of

    air, the empty ghost our scarecrows
        cannot frighten. August:
      the field is a tangle of
    sunlight wound in vines, covered with
pillows of foliage. Blossoms flare

  briefly, then fall. Green nodes take their
    place, begin to swell. Then,
  the infant pumpkins seem to
 disappear. The patch is a great
green whirligig of tendril and vine.

  One night, only the moon watching,
    magic occurs. The dawn
  finds the bright globes lying in
 windrows, clinging to tangles of
brown twine. Next, even the vines crumble

  into film. We take October's
    flesh and make it grin. We
  set it in our window to
 frighten shadows with a hollow shell,
but wind seeps in, and the flame wavers.

AWAKEN, BELLS FALLING

    It is a dawn quick as swallows
        peeling to shear through peals belled
    from the one town steeple. Autumn
    falls from green heat like a chestnut felled
out of its prickly jacket. A single

    jay walks in the pines. A cone of
        cold sweeps chill's needles soughing
    through the day's screen doors. There can be
    no cushioning today: to wake
shall be a sharp thing. The person on his

    private ticking will be palsied
        from his sheets, his numeral
    be rung, the coils of consciousness
    spring him into good woolen light,
without armament, to meet himself in

    mirrors and still halls. Meet himself —
        find his blood walking a thin
    line, alarums unsleeping him.
    Brazen as flame leaving ash for
the elm's sere leaf, autumn will have settled

into summer's pallet — patchwork
    and quilting: that poor thread of
dreams curling at the doorsill. It
is done, the keen tone spoken, wrung
out of the bronze tongue of silence. Winter;

    allcolor; whiteness. Who will braid
        our years now into what skein
of circles? Bells fail in the streets;
the hall empties us into ice,
sheeted, sheer as mirrors, unreflecting.

HOUSE AND SHUTTER

I.
        Like a fleet thief, this sparrow has
      stolen stillness. He keeps it in a
   purse of bones. The aperture in which he
quit quickening is thin: an airy dimness
      between our house and its false shutter.

      Here's a sparrow that couldn't fall.
    I cannot even pry him loose. The
shutter has been stunned with bolts; the wall won't
drop its trophy. For certain, bird, you did not
     fly diving into quiet. It is

      your tail that caught you up and will
    not let you down. How in heaven did
you back to your demise? This December
sky seems somewhat grimmer for your defection.
     The overcast will not be cast off.

II.
       So this small absence is noted and
duly recorded. His mate impatiently
    waits near the crack into which he crept for
        warmth. It will be a cold day elsewhere,
           my lady, before the midwest

        wind hovers about his flight again.
One feather works loose. It falls. The overcast
    is cued: a flake has launched an avalanche.
        My sympathy is for both your songs,
           but less for the live, for at least

        (for all and any hurt a sparrow
feels) when winter learns to thaw there's always spring.
    Death will shrink to due proportion: a bird's
        eye view of a worm, perhaps. But right
           now, be vigilant with your grief,

           wife. Snow is vital too. It sucks what
           warmth was left today when wings hung fire.

SEASON

    In this season light
is equivocal. The moon
      rises too early.
She is the eye of the ghost

of the shadow of a world.
     She is gravid bone.
Her dust settles the season
    beneath her lumen.
We will take frostlight if we

must in lieu of blind wicking.
    The moon is an urn
burning ice and umbra. Stars
    have seeded her. Now
in season her time has come.

It will be soon our bones say.

THE SNOW DEVIL

The wind is telling rumors
to the snow; the snow listens
and takes common counsel. Drift

and drift, they bury silence
at the root of a pine which
stands forth from the forest. The

woods brandish green spears and will
not turn a cone to listen
to sophistry. The single

pine stands for all, roots sunken
in the proper element.
Snow and wind will challenge, raise

a cold champion to stand
against the pine. The wind gives
breath to frost: crystals rise in

spirals and plumes: it is a
snow devil glittering in
armored currents. The pine is

engaged, but briefly. A small
storm glistens through its boughs. At
its base silence is buried

further in a thin white rain of
mail. Nothing is finished.
The green woods wait in the wind.

The greenwood waits in the wind.

THE STROLLER

A stick strolling with an old man. Trees
messy with spring: woodland a squander
of roots. The road had nowhere to go,
so it stayed flat and listened closely
to the tap, tap of the runaway
stick. It was spring roundabout, and it
was springtime straightway. "Come, sing me songs
of death," said the old man to the sun
nearly black in his eyes. But the most
his sun would do was roust out a flock
of sparrows to swivel in the air.

"Drop in my ears sounds of worms turning
the sheets of my bed — " but the earthworms
lengthened quietly underneath moist
shadows, and quietly contracted.

"Let me hear nails driven in hard oak,"
the old man whispered to his stick. But
the cane stuttered on stones just then, made
no word out of the good green light. "Just
as I feared," the old man muttered, "there
is noplace to go when winter is
over."
      And the road stopped when he stopped.

The Inhabitant
1970

THE DOOR
On a sculpture by Ivan Albright

    There is a door
           made of faces
faces snakes and green moss

    which to enter is
           death or perhaps
life which to touch is

    to sense beyond the
           figures carved in
shades of flesh and emerald

    the Inhabitant at home
           in his dark
rooms his hours shadowed or

    lamp-touched and that door
           must not be
attempted the moss disturbed nor

    the coiling lichen approached
           because once opened
the visitor must remain in

    that place among the
           Inhabitant's couches and
violets must be that man

    in his house cohabiting
        with the dark
wife her daughter or both.

THE HALLWAY

The Inhabitant stands in his hallway. A long way from the door, still the gentleman has a distance to go before he can leave, or enter, or simply resume.

Here there is small illumination. The only window is of squares of stained glass, in the door behind him which is closed.

Things wait in the narrow aisle. Objects beguile him — each has its significance, in and beyond itself; each is an obstacle in a way to be touched and passed:

Touched and repassed, and with each touching to become more than the original substance. The Inhabitant stands in his hallway, curiosities looming ahead and behind.

It is as though, almost, this furniture had become organs, extensions of his body. If he listens, the gentleman may find his pulse booming in the hallseat, under the lid, gently, among artifacts and mathoms.

Let him proceed; let his footfall say *clum*, silence, *clum*. Let the stained light lie amber on a black umbrella in its stand, fall scarlet on the carpet, make a blue haze of a gray hatbrim rising in shadow to the level of his eye to rest on an iron antler in the hall.

The Inhabitant is home. Let him go down the hallway, choosing to pass the stair and banister this time, pass these things of his, levelly, moving from light to light, shadow to shadow.

THE HALLSEAT

This is the place where
   no one ever sits
      in half-light

the golden oak fading the
   paper fading behind a
      spotted mirror

like an entrance into flowers
   and trellises an entrance
      for eyes

only the gate guarded by
   two stags on either
      side of

the mirror where only one
   hat ever hangs but
      the true

entrance is there beneath the
   mirror and the mirror's
      stags where

no one ever rests for
   it is a trap
      opening upward

  only in the seat itself
     where certain moments repose
         forgotten now

  a rose turned to rosedust
     sheet music the dim
         notes rising

  off the page songs and
     fragrances diminishing and returning
         sometimes in

  the darkness here in this
     passageway always at some
         edge of

  recall but there is a
     volume too in the
         hallseat in

  which the rose is written
     down where music blooms
         in silence

  waiting for someone to spring
     the trap and fall
         and stay

> to listen to smell the rose
> and be written down
> like everyone.

THE ATTIC

Things, the work of dust and summer flies, upstairs over the other rooms, lying where they were created under the covers of trunks. The mathoms, original art of shadows drowsing in boxes: dresses and shirts worn by the seasons at their balls and weddings; the toys mice play with; mirrors reflecting upon solitude; cords and scissors.

Downstairs the Inhabitant moves slow among orderly rooms; his wife is a comfort, his child little trouble, and the cat is kindly for the most part.

In the attic it is quiet; rain touches the roof and falls from the eaves.

If the Inhabitant intrudes at odd times he does not notice the machine amid the clutter. It stands in a corner behind a rack of clothes in shades of brown and yellow, a red flower printing itself now and again on some fabric fading into the slanted beams.

He is mildly surprised by the numbers of mathoms. At times it is hard to remember: a photo in a gilt frame, a ribbon, someone's scroll.

They are worth an hour's musing in semi-darkness, the hum of a wasp on the ceiling, street sounds muffled. The machine is never discovered: the only mechanism to intrude — lightly, nearly beneath any threshold — is a mower in the hands of a distant neighbor.

When the door of the mathom shop is closed and the Inhabitant leaves the print of his footsteps for a moment on the wooden stair, things pause. There is no movement, not even of time. The mathoms listen until, downstairs, carpets and rugs swallow the noises of living, until the furniture absorbs motion.

Then the machine clicks on: the clock dial begins to turn; dust feeds the cogs. It is making things, making them slowly, out of the debris of afternoons and the streetlamp suicides of evening moths.

It takes forever, but the mathoms accumulate, sift into the corners like drifts, send up an aroma as of the slowest burning — the scent of must. Under the mathom shop the Inhabitant senses — at most, perhaps — a vague weightlessness overhead and, now and then, the cat acts strangely.

THE PHOTOGRAPH

    It is unwise
to trap a moment such as this
   in a frame gilt or
      otherwise for such moments

    change at any
rate no trap is strong enough look
   she lay ensnared in her
      layers of clothing among

    utter shades here
in this trunk where nothing has influenced
   her but clear glass yet
      she has grown older

    than old her
youth in its fanciful bows shocks the
   memory of grays and wrinkles
      this creature is absurd

    can never have
existed not in any light of any
   day under the sun no
      one ever lived in

    any time so
antique so suffused with ivory and lavender
    the odor of bayberry no
        camera was ever as

    clearly misty no
lens so oval she inhabits an egg
    under glass clearly she is
        unborn her maturity a

    trap for her
discoverer who falls in love with neverness
    from which there is no
        escape now that she

    has been thus
exhumed he will live with her sharing
    guilt now and despair forever
        in odd moments peering

    through crystal into
laces and shadow the long age of
    attics hearing only the hornet's
        drone and impossible songs.

THE LIVINGROOM

The chairs of his livingroom lounge thinking in groups. Couches remember what it was like here yesterday and the day before.

Lamps dimly recall old shadows in the various corners. The carpet ruminates, sometimes darkly, but again less so, running out perhaps from under a table.

Two candles counterpoint an African violet, broadleafed in a large pot; their sentinel lances prefigure a gray print in a gray frame behind them on the wall.

The gentleman's chair — gaily in complement beside the grace of a lady's rocker, yet separated from her moods by the sewing cabinet — stands in the far corner, a boy's skull growing out of the cut plush of the fabric of the seat.

The boy's ivory jaw falls and closes. The child is singing.

He listens, the Inhabitant of this room, as his furniture is listening, but the boy is not singing to him, obviously, for he can hear nothing. Yet the chairs are enthralled — even the candles seem to lean in the direction of the skull making silence vocal.

The skull is yellow, and there is yellow thread in a needle that lies on the wood of the sewing cabinet, but the dominant tone of the furniture is brown, as brown as the study into which the Inhabitant has sunken. Why can't he hear what the boy is singing, bone against the upholstery and the ornate arms, the frame of bent dark wood like the oval of an egg?

He watches the skull grow upward on its stem of spine; he waits till it is tall as a lily, and the chairs wait, the couches roar quietly.

If the boy begins to stare at him, what will he do? His hair is thinning, it is true, and he has a slight stomach — yet he is a lover of song; it is not his fault.

Perhaps it would be as well to applaud in the thin lamplight, among the uneasy things, the unsettling mood of the livingroom. Perhaps he ought, really, to pretend he has heard, for the skull is now as tall as he himself sitting in the gentleman's chair beside the grace of his lady the rocker, her spine curved now against the stair-corner, not straight as it had been when her bride's body would not bend to the will of a stripling.

Perhaps it would be as well not to listen to the song the couches recall; to forget to applaud might be wiser than to listen to the skull's yellow music which, strangely, now that he has decided, comes moving quietly across his teeth like a shadow to stir the leaves of the violet.

THE COUCH

    It waits against
the wall like some
old lion couching in gloom

    it is harmless
one can be seated
on its hide and it

    will not move
even to take its
repast look one may be

    seated here and
one will not disappear
into the plush flowers that

    camouflage hunger it
is harmless though famished
in the room on the

    carpet which rolls
into the underbrush of
an evening murmurous with crickets.

THE DINING ROOM

It is dark in the dining room. A candle studs the shadows.

Beneath the table there is an animal that eats light. The Inhabitant does not know its shape, nor does he know the color of its breath, but its ears listen to wax melting.

There will come a time when the candle shall be small enough to swallow. The Inhabitant waits wondering; the beast bides in darkness.

The Inhabitant remembers the mountains like the teeth of wolves tearing at the sky. The windows of his house are the eyes of kine.

In the mountains there are stars to be eaten, for they are fit prey and are seldom caught. In the umbra of the dining room the Inhabitant fears the animal which is his brother waiting till the feast is over.

He hoards his candle, but may not stop its burning; he fears darkness, but it is his own shadow.

Hungering, he waits in his appetite. Beasts bide at the edges of the room.

THE SIDEBOARD

    The monster in
the corner the tame gargoyle kisses
    the daily china guards

    the stainless service
serves as retainer swallows towels and
    sustains this daily bread

    till it is
served sets the tone complacent against
    the wall which like

    the lining of
a belly envelops the hours envelops
    the food of hours

    heartbeats watchticks pulses
and upon the top shelf of
    the corner familiar there

    is enshrined an
old heart a windup clock its
    pendulum counting meals stainless

    service linen and
conversation ruminant browsing continent the familiar
    monsters in the corners.

THE KITCHEN

In the kitchen the dishwasher is eating the dishes. The Inhabitant listens to the current of digestion — porcelain being ground, silver wearing thin, the hum and bite of the machine.

His wife does not hear it — she is humming, not listening. But the Inhabitant is aware of movement in the cupboards, of the veriest motion — the cast-iron skillet undergoing metamorphosis, perhaps, becoming its name: the wives' spider spinning beneath the counter, weaving and managing, waiting for the doors to open.

Each cup has its voice, each saucer its ear, and the thin chant planes between the shelves, touching the timbres of glass and crystal as it passes. The gentleman listens, is touched to the bone by this plainsong — he feels his response in the marrow's keening.

But the women do not — neither the elder nor the child — sense the music their things make. Their lips move, a column of air rises like steam, and there is something in a minor key sliding along the wall, touching the face of a plastic clock, disturbing the linen calendar beside the condiments.

It is as though, the Inhabitant reflects, the women are spinning. It is as though, while he waits, they weave bindings among the rooms; as though the strands of tune were elements of a sisterhood of dishes, the ladies, the spider in the cabinet, even of the dishwasher, done now with its grinding, which contributes a new sound — a continuo of satiety — to the gray motet the kitchen is singing.

THE LINEN CALENDAR

The background hours are
    woven among
the months which hang

upon the wall where
    meals are
taken where the months

trace one another their
    rigid files
and ranks printed upon

brown linen the smell
    of dark
coffee eggs sunnyside sound

of skillets and spiders
    weaving sustenance
as August eats July

September bites October groping
    toward winter
and the new year's

new linen against time's
    green wall
its webs and weavings.

THE PLAYROOM

Stories are done for the evening. The Inhabitant can tell that she is remembering that summer's day.

The face of the painted clown muses out of its frame, neither smiling nor frowning. The furniture, painted in imitation of noonlight, belies the sunset and reminds her of their outing — the museum, the exhibits under glass:

There lay the two moose, locked upon love's combat. Everything was as it had been: the great bulls were dead — so said the placard upon the glass — thus they were found, silent in the wood, horns fused.

The object of their contention had vanished by the time men happened upon the bodies steaming in a spring thaw. The placard related the fantastic sight: hundreds of yards of woodland smashed and torn — they had been a long while dying, these great beasts, one of a broken neck — the lucky one.

Thirst had taken the other bull at length. Yet, even on his side he'd dug a dozen holes, deep as his hooves could delve, trying for water.

Despite the bedtime tales, the child remembers. The gentleman damns that Jack, old Time, the giant killer, damns his eye: the one that — when the just-so book is closed, winks as he strangles the three bears beneath the darkled covers.

The Inhabitant says goodnight, sweet dreams of bunnies in a greening copse — forget the moose: they'd had a lovely life, free and roaming the free mountains, waters falling in the great gorge, wind in their horns, their loins and lungs bursting with love — forget the dying moose. Don't you wish that you were a happy bunny lying in a sea of daisies blooming ever?

And she has answered him in his own words. The Inhabitant had wondered how long he had been hearing those syllables couching in umbra, the stars winking in at the windows, lying about where they were by light years and by dark:

"I wish I was nothing." The fool in him asked why — "Because then nothing could hurt me."

The Inhabitant tells his daughter he would never let the giant killer hurt her. The gentleman would lie awake at night and stare the great wink down, would make his pallet on the book of hurts, and if Jack tried to slither out from among his pages and between her sheets, he'd be taken by the eye, blinded for good and all.

If these be lies, they are but slight distortion. The gentleman will do the things he can: chop down the stalk or lay the golden egg, be the harp that sings. Or he will wink and blind her with his love.

THE PORTRAIT OF A CLOWN
On a painting by Tomie DePaola

    Which way will he go
        for his lips
are at the edge of something

    shades of blue rose-flushed
        it is a
pavilion on the green wall silk

    and canvas and the wall
        is on the
edge of something the room is

    hanging on the lip of
        evening neither starward
nor sunward how will the clown

    maintain his equipoise as a
        world as a
room tips the frame tilts shades

    of aquamarine the bold lines
        of a face
ride over the sleeping child.

THE STUDY
for Donald Justice

The lamp is standing in the corner of the study: a tree with a crown
 of light rises out of the braided rug.

The Inhabitant's books form two walls which rise, like the voices of
 a thousand men, two-thirds of the way toward the tall ceiling.

He is not thinking of poems under cover, of periodicals with pages
 curling like leaves under fall trees. The Inhabitant is watching
 the lamp, for it is a tree which puts forth beams instead of
 limbs.

The tree leans away from its source. Its eccentricity is that of bias.

This is the Inhabitant's room; he shares it, for the moment, with
 Corelli and the lamp, but the study falls away from the bole, as
 the Inhabitant has fallen away from his pages and his youth.
 The lamp keeps the chairs and shelves from flying too far from
 an axis.

Behind the shading fabric there are filaments which flame at a
 touch. The tree in its foliage burns at the center of things.

This is where the Inhabitant lives. These things are his — these
 books, this music upon which the lamplight falls, upon which
 he too, once, threw a radiance now eaten by wires tapping the
 sources of silence and desuetude.

The lamp, rising out of the study's braided rug, keeps the Inhabitant from flying too far beyond peripheries. Light, he muses, uses oddly the things we use.

THE CAT
In memory of Pookah

Long-haired and black as shadow
the cat comes to drive
a pad of yellow foolscap
and a ballpoint pen out

of the Inhabitant's hands for
it is time again to
handle the palpable dark not
to compose to write about

the loom and shuttle of
shadow moving mechanically across clock
faces but to pass hands
lightly down the pelt of

smooth moments look you no
harm is meant by this
passage it is just that
things were meant to be

this way the waiting the
soft animal with sharp teeth
and claws sheathed lurking in
corners will come out to

be stroked and enjoyed for
it is lethal but sensual
as well and it means
no particular ill the hour

for striking has not arrived
it is not the enemy
but a familiar of houses
a domestic that keeps accounts.

THE BEDROOM
An adaptation from the French of Yves Bonnefoy's "A Shadow Breathing"

The mirror on the morning wall listens as swelling waters speak darkly across the room. Two beacons converge and blend among drifting lamps and tables.

The Inhabitant is an island of somnolence adrift, melding with another along stone borders where the placid seas of dream are lost — forever shaped, forever shattered. A current stirs in the vague depth of dream, and, distantly, upon the darker water of a table, the red dress, burning, sleeps.

It was midnight long ago; a static star ordered the spirals of other suns. Night's original hour bore noons in its lumen, and words were whispered into the foliage of darkness:

An indifferent star, a ship's mast — the clear trail of one or the other in still waters and firmament: whatever is stirred like a vessel which turns, which glides, which does not know its own heart in the night.

They have this sleep to traverse, like an immense, immobile sea, the Inhabitant's lone consciousness becoming eyes, mouth, and heart of the vessel's mast, loving the dark currents, drinking her eyes without memories. He was without that dream of absences which grasp and do not grasp, wishless to keep her midnight hues: blue and stone, magnificent, where nothing ever ends.

Waters of the sleeper, tree of absence, hours without beaches; in that boundlessness a night begins to end. How shall the Inhabitant name the new day — this muted mixture of crimson and sable?

In the sleepers' eyes beacons dim. Words are minted which begin to disperse the night's sparks, obscuring stars in the spindrift of meaning — it is nearly the moment of waking, already remembrance.

The Inhabitant does not know how to sleep without her; he does not dare risk without her this motionless progression. Too late he has found it to be one more dream — this region of compasses tumbling toward death.

He has wished her, on his fever's pillow, not to be — or to be dark as the clock's shadow. Yet when he spoke aloud in the empty planet, she was there on sleep's vast seaways.

Dreams urged him on — dreams illuminated with vagrant lamps. Night after night her reflection kept him from edges — darknesses beyond darkness...dawn and morning love.

The Inhabitant bent to that vale of numberless stones, listened to its grave repose. He perceived, covert among gigantic shades, the grotto where sleep's spindrift bleaches.

He listened to dream — monotonous, hollow, now and then shattered by blind rock. Her voice faded, overwhelmed by darkness; yet a freshet of narrow hope murmured in the desert.

Elsewhere, in lustrous gardens, the Inhabitant knows it is true: a pagan peacock flaunts its mortal raiment. But his single beacon suffices for her! She clothes the night with a curved phrase.

Who is she? He knows her only as alarums, as a voice urging haste in an unfinished rite. She apportions darkness to a tabletop — her eyes like suns, the only lights.

THE PILLOW

    It is stuffed with
        dreams children swim
unborn among feathers their eyes

    hooded spools rolling threads
        unwinding among the
wrinkled hands here and now

    there raveling the moon
        falling through the
window white light the hardness

    of bone needling fabric
        stitching no time
into a patchwork darkness it

    is the stuff of
        sleep and wish
turning ghosts into children children

    to phantoms touching out
        of soft darkness
for moonlight and unreachable time.

THE BATHROOM

He will wash away the dross of sleep in the thin room made of porcelain and tile. The Inhabitant will emerge another man — the old one will diminish in steam and water hissing or bubbling in taps and bowls.

The effluvia of dream will become the vapors of waking. Blades scrape away the night's stubble — those excrescences blood pushes through flesh when no one is watching.

Liquid needles spurt at his shoulder-blades, turn to spume under brisk hands. The drain sucks and gargles, swallowing sleep.

The nap and pile of toweling, with ten thousand small tongues, lick the body dry. In the mirror, under the comb's teeth, an effulgence emerges to gleam back at gaze.

Bristles and wax. Now the instar appears, palpitant in the steamy light of another morning breaking through the frosted glass.

THE MIRROR

   In the mirror this
other the heart of glass
      brave beyond
    his agate eyes

   in them currents forever
at their gaze look away
     catch him
    at a glance

   this creature of mercury
make him stop staring out
     of himself
    into crystal so

   clear so foretelling that
he can surely see floating
     in shallows
    the shoddy heart.

THE BASEMENT

The Inhabitant descends to find the child's lost doll. The door, the narrow stair, the snaky mop on sentry at the stairhead — these have been managed.

The light here is yellow; the walls drink its treacle, turn it to cobwebbing and dust, a faint odor of coal left over from another year.

The walls drink sound as well — the Inhabitant's thin whistle, the squeal of the furnace flywheel turning, saying small things, informing the spider's fretwork of minuscule agonies. The voice of a mouse is strapped to silence spinning.

Beside the set-tubs the toys lie in their boxes. In the sinks, stagnant water ebbs and tides; the curved hose of the washer arches downward, but never touches the surface — never quite touches the gray surface rising and falling in the clogged pipes, the storm drains under the cellar leading outward and downward.

The Inhabitant will find her, must find her for the yearning child. She will be in the boxes, clothed in rags, wearing her painted smile and a scraped eye, its metal beginning to corrode.

His fingers brush through the castoff things: some blocks, a partial deck of minicards — King of Spades and Queen of Hearts, Pinocchio without his rubber nose. The toys drift in the dusk like the buoys of time, shadowmarks on darkness.

Upstairs the child is waiting, having remembered, wanting the past as palpable as chain. But this is carrying water in a sieve: a toy boat rides with a ragged sail, adrift, its anchor dragging through the dust like stars.

Here she lies at last, the lost toy in her apron, smiling like yarn out of the yawning box. Take her and carry her to the stair as the wheel stands still, the tides lie quiet in the soapy tubs; do not glance back nor at the ragged doll or she shall be left at the stairhead beneath the writhing mop, and the wheel will begin to spin, its voice to whine the webs will net dust in the billowing corners when the light goes out.

THE SCYTHE

The crescent blade with its snake
    snath hangs on the cellar
      wall waiting for another
        day like last
          summer's milkweed
        day

when the bees in the great patch
    of blossoms out back made
      an electric sound as
        the Inhabitant came
          out to
            whittle

the congregation of stalks into
    a large circle then slowly
      a smaller one scything
        in spirals the
          bees moving
            always

toward the center as the ring
    of petal and stamen contracted
      the stalks falling bleeding
        milk as the
          crescent edge
            stroked

in passing and the buzzing thickened
at heart until only a
last fist of milkweed
stood crowned with
bees drinking
one

nightcap of nectar before dusk cut
into the still green air
and the Inhabitant leaned
on the snath
against his
blade.

THE PORCH

It was a quiet June evening; therefore, the noise of the collision reached across the green yards and caught the Inhabitant listening to the tickings a porch makes.

It was this evening, and he was filing cards in a mailing list; he could not sleep — it was yesterday, and the names on their white rectangles sifted through his fingers.

He ran, and the neighbors ran, collecting at the corner; therefore, six-score eyes peered into the road at the spectacle.

Before the sound there had been another sound. A siren, on this street of sirens, coming close, wiring the afternoon — stitching it with steel to the approaching darkness.

In the road — the automobile, the woman fainting at the wheel, the left fender smashed. The windshield of the car cast a spiderweb against the sun.

An ambulance, spun into the curb opposite, nosed against the grass as though it were a steel beast grazing; therefore, the doors at its rear gaped open before the crowd who could see the dying man:

Like cardboard, he lay on the floor where he had fallen. His stiff frame littered the collision.

The attendants wrestled with time; therefore, his bones gave to their ministrations, swelling the shrunken flesh, lying at last upon the stretcher in the center of the street.

It was a dead man, the hair grown long upon his parchment scalp. Or perhaps it was a woman, barely breathing, her accident compounded, her body diminished by a thousand thousand accidents of moment.

They stared at the creature; a child cried, "See his bones!" Therefore its mother said, "Hush," and the spectators listened to each other babbling, but heard nothing more than their silent periphrasis.

They helped the first woman, weeping, from her car. She had been forgotten, but now she walked with help toward the hospital nearby, past the prime cause who never had awakened, who never knew he or she had been thrown down, who lay like a sack of winter in the center of a summer street.

The body must be moved; therefore, a passing mail truck stopped, came backing down the street; its gate gaped open to receive the late delivery.

Now it is gone; the neighbors stand and talk, their voices sharp with fright, but tongues blunted with relief. The Inhabitant speaks with Mr. Smith until, at last, the failing light disperses the folk as though by accident, diminishes their number interminably.

Some of the crowd will dream; therefore, the Inhabitant shall stay awake upon the porch to work by lamplight upon his cards — ordering his neighbors' names, memorizing the streets of towns, listening to June bloom again and to a cat greeting another dawn.

THE GLIDER

Under Orion nothing
except the glider supported
by the night creaking like
chains and crickets in the yard

remnants of daylight
lie glittering or is
it dew or stars fallen
or warnings of dawn no matter

for now the
glider vessel of summer
first starship insubstantial as
its voyages enters the wind even

as the evening
is mild scented with
lilac enters winter wheels in
starlight which rimes the glider chains

crickets the night
and suddenly the silence
which settles darkly among the
lawn's glitterings for this briefest moment.

THE GUESTROOM

The Inhabitant must go around thinking of Death. Have at him, call him fool and scofflaw — he will think of Death.

There is a room where an old man lies dreaming of worms. In the moments of his eyes all the world is buried: its fables and laces are spread like tablecloths for his sons to walk on.

The feast is laid; he is watched.

He cannot stir without moving earth and water, he cannot sing without upsetting cities, he cannot tap his headboard with a hard white nail without bringing the heavens down, he cannot wink, for there would be avalanches. The Inhabitant dreams of Death, an old man who has many sons.

His daughters are the harvesters of worms. With their quick eyes they watch that there shall be no movement — no grain shall shift unless shifted by river or wind.

There will be life, they say, but life must have its color and shape, and the color we choose is brown, the shape vulgar and thin, a needle of flesh burrowing in flesh. There will be life, they say, but Death must have no mate.

Come with the Inhabitant to see the old man's stone. On it there are graven these words: *Le visage de mon Dieu est calme.*

His daughters have made his epitaph in their language, with their soft hands. They stand and watch in dark garments — no one may change their rune, for their god would tremble in Her fury.

The Inhabitant speaks of a guest who has many sons. His daughters stand on his mouth, weeping and weighting the earth.

THE LOOKING-GLASS

Once in a while
    the eye

circles like a hawk
    comes down

in a place never
    inhabited by

anything animate anything sharp
    or whole

and there lying in
    its circle

of smooth things the
    eye preens

in its own vision
    before it

rakes the wind again
    and rises

into the sun the
    fierce air.

THE SUMMERHOUSE

The gazebo looks at summer with the Inhabitant's eyes. The iris blossoms have fallen with spring, and the stalks stand naked now in the night which has gathered-in the house, the summerhouse, the lawn with its banks and peatbeds, the man standing in the darker shadows of his walls.

The Inhabitant's hands take the rough logs of the rail, and he leans to look toward the lighted windows. He grasps the round wood to see into lamplight shining through clear glass.

Inside, the woman moves across the curtains, holding her child drowsy with bedtime. They are netted, kept in gauze, their movements luminous and aquatic.

The air indoors is still and warm. The plants stand at the screens, incline toward the cool darkness where a light breeze, filled with dew, moves over the grass toward the round building in the garden.

They are real, the Inhabitant is thinking, if only for the moment. The grain and knots of the rail hurt his flesh, but he will not shift his stance, for the small pain is good under the indelible wheeling of stars beyond the room, too far to dream of touching, too near to ignore.

This is what there is. It is enough: the nightwind, the windows
    alight in the livingroom, the flowers of the garden touching
    toward the summerhouse, the neighbors on their porches, the
    road rolling outward into the darkness under streetlamps
    moth-haloed and the nighthawk's wing and call.

THE GARDEN

    Take two
  words then three
touch four words make

    earrings for
  the hearing a
necklace of the snake

    in Eve's
  garden the apple
of Adam's eye take

    two words
  touch them join
the leaf and the

    twig again
  stand naked in
the sun and the

    shading branch
  in that garden
again wearing only these

    the tongue's
  jewels the ear's
riches eyes like amethyst.

THE DWELLING HOUSE

I. On the morning of the first day the Inhabitant awoke and went out; he uncoiled the sheets of his dream and walked through the door into a blue sky hung with flowers.

In the streets of his city there moved good people. Men in love with women went quietly among children, and birds settled out of the air to light the parks with their wings.

He looked about him and saw that things were in their places — the trees made figures of light and shadow, their roots matching in the earth the patterns of limbs against the sun.

II. On the second day it was harder to lose the dream; it had shackles, it seemed, but at last the Inhabitant fought free and woke.

Outdoors the same blue sky, but edged with gray. The color of the air had not changed, but its tone was strange.

The eyes of the men regarded their women as before, gazes placid and assured, brows smooth and cheeks unlined.

Children, among the park paths, fed the winged creatures. The heads of the birds jerked and pecked at crumbs held steadily in small hands.

There was a light wind among the trees, whose leaves sometimes showed white undersides to the breathing air.

III. The dream stayed with him on the third day. The Inhabitant had trouble unwinding the night, and there were strange images attending him to the door.

A tree grew out of his doorstep, gray ribbons tangled in its branches. A trunk of steel sprang upward, and an explosion of metal limbs groped at the sky.

The men on the streets stood rigidly with the women, and the children watched. The fathers were staring, only their eyes alive, at the mothers standing among their offspring.

Wings were spread unmoving in the wind; in the parks the pigeons were frozen in the air among the vines that grew upward toward them.

But at last he blinked, and the dream was gone. The city hidden behind the veil emerged and moved upon him.

IV. His eyes were the door itself when the fourth day broke. The Inhabitant's lids opened and the black sun shone into his dream.

From the steel tree that pierced his pupils hung the world's fruit: staring out of the husks of their flesh — the eyes of neuter things, men, women and children.

Birds fed upon them. The heads of the plated fowls hunched and nodded, the sharp beaks piercing the people's eyes.

But the fruit was not diminished. Upon the limbs of the tree of steel the limbs of flesh multiplied and pressed upon each other!

The parks were merged in a garden of vines. The earth twisted upward like hair, each filament coiling toward the suspended folk, touching and holding.

V. On the fifth day the Inhabitant awoke and saw that God was dead. Silence invested the garden and the star-infested sky.

VI. On the sixth day he knew he had slept without dreaming. Behind him the night lay empty, like the cold sheets that smoothened about him, above and below.

But the Inhabitant lay with his eyes closed for as long as he could bear, until he sank into the darkness of his mind. No time seeped between his lids, but his vigil was eternal until sleep took him down once again.

VII. On the morning of the seventh day he woke and arose. In at the window the dawn blew as he stood and looked.

On his legs each hair stood in its chill; he felt the morning moving on his flesh.

In the mirror he saw a man. Upon the surface of the glass there shimmered the image of someone strange and real, bearded, the bone hung with blood's fabric.

He went to the door, naked; opened it; moved into the daylight where the world walked. With his eyes he met other eyes beyond the portal — men, women and children who knew his nakedness as he knew theirs.

It was a true flesh the Inhabitant made to walk through the city: in each eye he saw the image folk saw in his.

THE WEED GARDEN
1973

HOME THOUGHTS

    Time buzzes in the ear. Somewhere
nearby, beyond my peripheral
vision, an insect throbs its heartsong
to the couch. A twilleter fuzzes
    against a burning lamp. Outdoors,

    a common goatsucker strings twelve
yellow streetlamps on its bill. Between
its hoarse shrieks, the town sky drops pieces
of clum among my snoring neighbors.
    If I close my eyes, a crack along

    the wall comes sliving my lids to
split the mind's dry sight. Look inward: a
plaster skull sifts dust down upon old
webs that hang, buzzing, as darkness moves
    ruthlessly to feast on something

small and hollow with blind, jeweled eyes.

THE ORCHESTRA

      The ugly table is
          old music. My books
are mute symphonies lying
      among their covers. I stare
over my broken wand, over
      my pencil, my baton,

      glaring at the woodwinds
          where they quiver there
on page 13 of the first
      book, left rear corner. "Come to
your senses," I shout, "or at least
      mine!" They cannot hear me

      with their heads stuck up those
          brasses like that, words
wadded in their ears — all those
      mash notes I have sent them. "You
are vile," I say to the strings. They
      nod meekly, unstrung by

      my anger. "Useless," I
          say, "utterly use-
less." There is no answer. In
      a moment I shall raise my
arms and try again, but I know
      that silence will play

        its harpsichord; winter's
          glass harmonica
   shall be rubbed by the winds
moving against panes while night
           watches with a hard thousand eyes
           outside my brown study

beyond these curtains I have drawn.

LOVERS

      The bed frames them. Their eyes
tell little of the story. Some old passion
has been eroded. Rivulets of time have
    eaten their cheeks until their faces

      lie flat against linen
landscapes — or against each other in a dark
room, on a night empty even of owlcries.
    Their flesh is a sophistry of shadow:

nothing is hidden. They
must therefore film their eyes in order not to
notice there is nothing there to see. They sang
    songs once, to each other, in moon light.

      Now, not even night hawks
call out to the lovers in their still stead. Not
even sleep lifts the veils from their sight, returns
    each other's image for an hour's dream.

      And if the world wheel, what then?
    The grim creature of the mind stunned
by the spaces of stars hung silently
    among the dumb regions where death dwells
in an old house, watching from twin windows,

    snuttering among pebbles
  like a hag made of pimples and
sacks. She will stow her hours in odd chinks,
    fondle each old thing on her ticking
as night whines beneath the bed and her roof

    trembles with light. Then, at last,
when least she needs his flesh — when least
    they know each other in their age, the stars
will smash their windows, their roof vanish,
    and the world come burning while they make love.

AS I READ MY GOOD FRIEND'S BOOK
for Vern

his words make choochoo trains that
    derail themselves on
each other. My eyes vaguely

go searching for corpses in
    the wreckage: same old
cadavers: you can hardly

tell them from the wooden ties.
    I must gather my
thoughts — I look at them sticking

to my fingers lying in
    a puddle of brain
damage. I wish my friend well

and close his book. It will not
    lie flat; it shudders
under my touch. The Red Cross

hands out stale crackers to the
    survivors. In a
caboose on page 48

a palsied conductor plies
    the wireless: the
S.O.S. blitters out from

between stanzas, strophes. I
    pretend not to hear.
On the shelf my friend's thin book

staggers the row, throws covers
    into upheavals.
I pretend not to notice.

I think of him at home, his
    thoughts oozing out his
ear, my words steaming on the

tracks before him. I think of
    shaking his scars as
he shakes mine next time we meet,

our clasp sticky, our glances
    sliding in and out
of each-other's kindly eyes.

THE CELL

      There is the room
   of a celibate, somewhere
back of the mind. In it, a golden cage
        swings. In the cage
   a bird of paradise sings
like wind moving among the boughs of a

      ridge of ever-
   greens. The Doge is expected
at any moment. He will judge between
        the friar vowed
   to silence, who tends song with
seed, and the song itself. Reed is scattered

      on the tiles. The
   sky strikes an oblong flood of
blue light through gray stone. Magisterial
        robes, black and red,
   settle in the pool of light.
The Doge watches as the cassock tells, by

      example, of
   what may not be said. Then, judge
and friar listen without motion as
        cloth of gold is
   woven by the aureate beak
of the sky's creature. A withe of light binds

   them against speech
  in that cell where wind turns song
moving along a ridge of evergreens.

THE DEAD SAILOR

As he drowned he saw
the ship following him like
the shark of the world.

THE FOUNTAIN

      The ashen birds light
    out of the air. The sun fires
an ultimate fusillade into the fountain
     where the seagulls gather to wish
    the world goodnight: they are furnished with rainbows

      for a moment. An
    aubade shall issue from them
tomorrow, burnished sparks of matinsong banked now
     for the evening in shadows and
    dust. The square fills with strollers. In the near distance

      night flings a star skyward.
    An eruption of silence faults
for a moment this murmurous village of strangers.
     In the cafés, lights now — and in
    the fountain perpetual rain whose mist withers

      among footfall and
    laughter. But the girl who leans
against the curving basin, among the gulls, seems
     not to hear the curious voices
    of the square. No footfall disturbs her musing:

she holds the water's fire. She is beautiful.

THE VOYAGERS

        Past the worm reef and the coral,
the archipelago inhabited by dragons,
      their sail bellied silken in a wind
   sec as the sigh of a sphinx, the voyagers
           move across mirrors, their eyes

       touched with color — aquamarine
and amber — searching the curve of the world where islands
      are transformed, become porpoises and
   gulls. It is said that gold coin and amphorae
         filled with remedies lie worn

      by sand and shadow only, in
a cache the elders knew. It must be found. And the keel
     moves through glass, etching mercury where
  coral builds and anemones bloom among
        transparencies of flesh and

      quick scales metallic in shoals in
schools in light shaped by weed and eddies.
     This is where all islands have gone. Worms
build upon bullion, conchs measure amhorae.
      The voyagers look to where

      a world curves into dolphins,
     the wing and the cry of terns.

THE WEED GARDEN

I am the ghost of the weed garden.
      Stalk among stones — you will find me
remembering husks and pods, how crisp burdock
    couches in the moon for every passer.
        I am the dry seed of your mind.

      The hour will strike when you dream me, your
        hand at the sheet like five thin hooks.
I will wait for you in the old vines rattling on
    the wind, in the ground-pine. I will show you
        where rue has blossomed and eyebright,

    mother-thyme. You must name me Yarrow.
        Bitter vetch shall catch your step as
you follow, hearing the stars turning to crystal,
    sweet lovage turning sere, adder's tongue and
        Jew's-ear at their whisper. Nightshade

    will consume the beautiful lady.
        Dwarf elder, dodder-of-thyme, I
am the thing you fear in the simple of your blood:
    toothwort in the dust, feverfew, mouse-ear,
        sundew and cup-moss, tormentils.

MY LORD LIFE

     I call you Death, you mouse.
    Don't try hiding in the nest
of my flesh. Come out and let's see whether
       your pelt is smooth or coarse.

     Do you think I'm your rind?
    How's this for a trap, then? — I won't
deny you your nibble if you will come
       out from behind my eyes

     and let me stroke you in
    verse. Ah, but I hear you scurry
off to your subcutaneous revels.
       Whom do you fear? Is it

     my Lord Life? He's never
    stocked a larder you have not sacked
and scuttled. Is it indifference you
       distrust? Be merry, Mouse,

     I cannot look away
    while your teeth are at my tallow.
Or do I miscall you? Is shrew your true
       designation: pinpoints

    of fate, your vision of
  darkness; lidless eyes hidden in
entangling velvet; hairless length of flesh
      trailing behind you down

    no end of constricting
tunnel? Perhaps we are twins, my
mouse, in similar traps. Where shall we come
  out when the world opens?

FATHER FIGURE

    "I am drowning in the wind,"
    the blind man said, opening
his sack of prayers. Out flew a silver thorn
    to prick the day he could not see.
"Time past is a pool of silt and sighs,"

    the blind man said as he trod mire.
    "The wind is mud I cannot breathe.
Now is a vortex: in its eye,
    filled with omens, a vacuum
sucks and forges at the sky.

    I shall be drowning then as now,"
    the blind man said, "deaf to the daylight,
numb to thorns. Wings shall fail me and the wind
    blow from darkness into dark.
Faith to sustain me, bag and bone,

    as I lie drowning in the wind,"
    the blind man said.
The moon blew dimly on the night.
    Owls flew hugely in and out
where the fabric was rent and losing light.

A RURAL JETTY

      They converge here,
    at this rural jetty
where the houseboat stands at the dock.
    The house is made of shakes,

      unpainted and
    weathered, its barge algaed,
well-seasoned. It rocks on the swell,
    waiting for passengers

      who will appear
    out of nowhere, outward
bound. They will walk through summer dust,
    their footsteps — quick or slow —

      turning hollow
    as they touch the dock. They
will come aboard. And when they are
    settled the captain, if

      there is one, will
    cast loose the lines. The boat,
with its cottage of weather, will
    move past the stone jetty

>   into the sea
>   where waves in temblors rise
> under hulls infinitely, and
>   crews read their varied maps
>
> against the single horizon.

WAKE DISTURBING SURFACES

If we come by water,
hull down in dream,
our wake disturbing surfaces, but not
the dim currents where images swim and waver,
we will find the common island

and the serpents we
have set to guard
the hoards we have hidden in the deepest
caves. Then, with bone flute and the nerve-strung harp, we will
charm our serpents with scales other

than their own, and we
will plunder and
be plundered. Our ship will ride gunwale-low
over that sea whose tide rises and falls like old
music in the throat of the world.

MARY MOODY EMERSON, R. I. P.
for Hyatt H. Waggoner

    Ralph Waldo's Aunt Mary,
moody as all get-out, got herself
       rigged out in a shroud and rode
       through Concord on a donkey
"to get herself in the habit of the

       tomb." Ralph Waldo, though she
wore her cerements daily ever
       after, reckoned her beast of
       burden was more symbolic
than her garb. If he could transcend Calvin,

       concordantly, why not
she? Ceremonies of Innocence
       and Hope lay everywhere be-
       fore her grave step, were she but
to look: "There grow the Leaves of Grass." But what

       makes them so green? "On the
village square a concourse of elms praises
       the good Lord." In their shadow
       the moss grows. "All are Elect!"
Then why so few who can see? Ralph Waldo

    shrugged and put down to whim this
relative moodiness. When they put
    her down at last in her life-
    long weeds, Ralph Waldo blessed her
blind eyes as, no doubt, Aunt Mary blessed his.

THE FACE IN THE STONE

It was there, lying in the grain,
    only waiting to be seen.
        It is the sculptor's twin
who emerges now out of the ages,
    the rock itself groping toward

sight, its inchoate will forcing
    the hammerstroke, vision of steel
        striking fire from the heart
of matter. Halfway out of stone,
    the figure blazes like stars, arms

tearing away from the atom's flesh:
    it will touch itself, it will become
        its brother who must enter
the rock, must be the rock,
    as it was in the beginning.

Then the mountain can move. This leg,
    thrust out of the cliff, can drive
        the twin from the cave. He will stand
in the starred dark, say to himself,
    "I am, and I am the Artist."

THE PILOT

Calais, France, May 18, 1968 (AP) — Low tide yesterday uncovered a plane, presumably of World War II, with the remains of the pilot still at the controls. Its origin could not be determined immediately.

    It has been
a long flight. Like flak,
the seagrass exploded
beneath me as I fell
    out of light into
an older and a heavier air.

    My planing
continued in the tide.
When the scavengers had
done with my flesh, I found
    that still the stick would
answer, though more slowly than before.

    So I flew,
and am flying still, back
to the beginning. In
my marrow direction
    lay. Now the sea has
released me, and I have been constant.

  But I was
wrong. You see me at death's
controls, in the primal
mud where our flight began,
  but it has not been
a fleeing, as we have long supposed.

  I see that
now, with these sockets where
fish have swum. You, rising
from the shore, have shown me
  what the snail tried to
tell: the journey is the other way.

Turn me around. I am with you still.

THE DREAM

        This is the story of a dream:
the gas-station in a poor location,
        shadowed, even in daylight. The cars
                on their great tires — the 'twenties
or early 'thirties. But not many

        on the road. Perhaps evening is
coming on, darkness moving in, an air
        of something waiting in the gas pumps,
                behind the cooler. It is
summer. I am in attendance. If

        the lights were on perhaps someone
might turn off the road, drive up the old tar,
        ride over the sparse grass in the cracks,
                stop there, outside the dusty
window where I stand watching. Then, with

        the thought, they are there — four of them
getting out of the square sedan. As they
        come filing toward the door, heads turned,
                looking at me through the hard
glass with their hard eyes, I know there is

        no way out. They'll find no money,
though — something in me grins at the thought, and
        the thought worries it. They are staring
                at me: the first is nearly
at the door. As our eyes lock I am

        shocked by the pistol in his hand,
by the flame in the muzzle, the shattered
    glass, by my blindness as the bullet
            enters the brain where I know
I am lost and reeling, blood pouring

        between my fingers, bathing my
eyes, and no sensation of pain, only —

        a vague regret that I will
now accomplish no more; certainty

        that this is death; amazement that
I can think with a shattered brain; knowledge
    that if I wake again they will
            have saved me; rejection of
the possibility. But beyond

            these and above them: immense joy.
It is over. It is nothing — nothing
    I could have imagined. Mere joy, great
        relief, release and silence.
And I awake, but cannot believe

        in waking. It has not happened,
yet nothing more real has ever happened.
    Stumbling out of my blood into this
            walking dream, nothing is left
except these words, images of weed,

dust, flame in a dark cylinder, and joy.

TICK

    I am a cat with a tick
buried in my head. If I could speak,
    I would tell you I can feel
the insect head nestling within my

    brain, not just against the white
bone. I can sense its mechanical
    currents buzzing in the blood,
showing the mandibles how to clench,

    the belly how to bloat, how
to make two lives one. It is not a
    matter of will for either:
It feels my claws sliding in their sheaths;

    I feel it growing stronger
on my substance.
                    My master?
As he looks at us, I see our two

    minds sink into his eyes. We three
meet at the center of his thoughts. My
    claws unsheath there. The insect
bloats in dark vessels. Here is where we

    shall live together — a nest
of boxes, three separate designs,
    three steps in Becoming, a
skull within a skull within a skull.

I AM PETER

            I am Peter,
      the original rock. On me
          all churches are founded.
I gave my substance to be joined with water

          that all this world's
     things might have their being, even
         flesh and dust. I am no
man, but am half of All. Out of the night

         that moves through time
    like a spider without a face;
       out of suns like needles
that are the spider's eyes, I move with my fluid

        wife. Our motion
    is a begetting of motion.
      I do not think; water
does not feel. Yet I will sire thought out of

        waves, under night,
and light shall be woven into
       the fabric of being.
The penultimate son will understand that

        I am Peter;
his child will understand I Am.
        He will be the thinking
Rock, the feeling Wave — flesh, dust, heart, mind, Maker.

A BOOK OF BEASTS,
AN ALPHABESTIARY
1978 & 1986

A-BAO-A-QU

   Like a great eye it lies
invisible at the bottom
  of the spiral stair. It sleeps
until a seeker shall appear
  and prepare to climb to where

  all horizons circle
the tower, and one will cast no
  shadow by his acts. It wakes,
begins to trail the climber. Deep
  in its core a spark is fired,

  and as we mount, a glow
begins to make it visible.
  It hugs the outer wall where
the stairs have been worn by those who
  have failed. Half up the tower's

  throat one begins to see
its tentacles. As we rise, weight
  and gravity press against
us — the higher, the heavier.
  The blue light of the dim beast

    begins to coalesce:
shape is perfectible. And when
    we, too, fall — having risen
as high as we can, as we dare;
    when we turn, our hearts bursting,

    descend again to the
ordinary air, the tower's
    beast, wailing blue silences,
shall unform and fall in pain down
    to the first hard step again,

    to sleep in the flowers
and dust, vines lying along its
    shriveled heart, once more to wait
out the ages and the echo
    of a foot that would try stone.

Basilisk and Cockatrice

Out of a single shell these twins emerged:
the feathered serpent and the scaly fowl,
venomous brothers, each with its deadly
jewel searing above the eyes — crown of
ruby and emerald diadem. Neither
dared grace birth with a glance backward toward
its twin: May not looks kill, as the desert
sun's rays strike at the nest and the new flesh
risen therefrom? Therefore, to the ends of
earth they flew and slid, scales rattling the wind,
feathers sliving in sand, to find themselves
met in a circle and to flee again,
electrical poles attracted, repelled,
half of the the whole, a whole of halves: Copper
claws, fangs of stone, red coil and green comb.

CHIMERA

    Glistering on the horizon,
        the changeable shape
  swelling and dwining. For those certain
of vision, of footfall, it is a palm
    rising along a river, its fronds

      grything on the wind, an image
          engraved on water.
  Others have faltered to see silver scales
in the sand, light turning to dwale, a goat's
    foot stab, felt the air dirl in a roar.

    This may have been enough for some —
        this glimpse of wandream
  at dusk — to be confirmed, in mazle
and wistness, till an end of days, until
    tree and river have windled and run.

Dybbuk

    It is in her eyes — the odd light,
and behind it a shadow, as though
        someone were masked and helpless,
    held captive and speechless. She moves

    tautly. It is as if her flesh
were not her own: The muscles lag so
        briefly one is hardly sure
    they lag at all. The lips are hard

    as agate; the cheeks are pallid;
the eyes hollow and blue. When she laughs,
        the sound comes from far away,
    sharp as an echo from a ledge.

    The people in the room raise their
glasses and drink, uneasy at her
        approach. They cannot hold her
    gaze — the men shuffle, catch themselves;

    the women smile like wire, for
there is no way to help. One must save
        oneself first, furtively. One
    must skime her from under lowered

lids, judge her intentions, and then,
without being obvious, when she
    turns her head, move away. We
know of her possession by that

dead thing. What is one to do? Too
late, it is too late. Bad enough when
    we are at home undressing
afterward, to chance to glimpse in

the glass the unfamiliar form
of someone we nearly recognize —
    to startle; to stare until
shape and features come clear at last

and we can swallow the pulse that
has leapt into the throat, raise a hand
    awkwardly to smooth the hair,
brittle as wire, along the bone.

ENT

    Waken one clear morning and look to where,
    somehow, sunlight fills a gap in the vista.
There is a subtle emptiness that disturbs vision.
      One was used to shade in that spot, just there,
        between the blue spruce and the maple.

    The grass glitters. The birds make their morning
    music. All seems as though it ought to be well. Then,
another awakening: One's eyes widen inward
      upon recall — what happened to the elm
        you called "Graybeard," whose limbs spread along

    the pane for inches upon the far hill?
    It is gone...and then you see it, closer to
the crown, altered toward the horizon, its trunk turned
      at an odder angle. You gaze. There is
        no wind, yet the leaves swale as you watch.

    And in the dark, under the moon, your eyes
    great as moons themselves, you watch the ent walk
beyond the valley, over the crest. You can look through
      earth and rock, and its leaves are green upon
        the left, but on the right they are fire.

FETCH

    To step out of a bedroom
   into a forest of darkness;
  to find oneself naked among brambles
and shagbark, a low wind making the flesh rise.
    To turn and discover there is no door,
     only bellbloom and shadow.

    And this is waking, the path
   beaten hard beneath heaven, stars
  among limbs bare of season. And between
trees, glass — dark sheets parsing silence without
     image. In the wood only the mutter
     and crool of water wending.

    Pause and touch: Merely surface
   smooth and cold among the boles. Search:
  Only the ghost of reflection paling
under gaze. Walk, cover the ground. Know there is
     neither graith nor tackle to take the wood.
     Move as through one more tunnel.

Stop when you feel him near. Strain
to see who stands in the way, who
holds out his hand, loof and hardel: It is
another mirror of the wood — no: Likeness
of quicksilver. Behind him, a bedroom
lies rumpled in a gilt frame.

It is dark, but he is known.
He is the beast of whom they have
spoken so often in living rooms and
dreams. It is a familiar forest. This is
one's own path. It is the Fetch beckoning
welcome to the crystal glade.

GOLEM

Having dumbled through the two-hundred-twenty-one gates
    trailing alphabets; having been conjured
out of the runes of the ineffable names of Jehovah,
    the permutations of these sacred letters;
        having been branded on the forehead
            with the word "EMET" — *Truth*;

    having been summoned to sweep the synagogue, ring bells,
        this mome cumbers the table waiting for
the magic tablet to be placed beneath his tongue. With this act
    he will rise, hurkle his shoulders. He will flinch
        at the clear brass note of the shalm, ask,
            maffling, what is to do?

    The Kabbalist will hand him the broom, point to the aisles.
        He will rise, the reflection of shadow
in his eyes, walk into the daylit passages, work until
    dimpse among the scholars who flurn him, turning
        with distaste away, to the holy
            pages. Then, as darkness

    begins to deepen in the windows, panic will fall
        into the blank eyes, begin to flicker
until the old man comes to lead this oye of his lore toward a
    closet where the tablet must be removed.
        Calm will prevail. The gome will stand still
            among the cleaning tools

    until the morrow. But if the rabbi should forget —
        if the tongue should keep its amulet — then
with the moon golem shall fling down his stick
    of bristles, run spittling and moaning among
        the streets, the folk gecking and cringing.
            And if the rabbi come

    to corner him, to remove the cosmic tablet from
        beneath his tongue, he will fall like a clod
into the roadway. He will be carried, shapeless, back to where
    wisdom is studied. He will be placed upon
        the table, E removed from "EMET"
            to make "MET" — the word *Death*.

HOMUNCULUS

"Thank you," it said when she uncovered it,
having drawn the curtains, made sure the door was locked.
"I was beginning to think you had forgotten me."
It smiled, blinking in the electric light.

She sighed, began to fix a meal.
It watched as she worked slowly, gathering the few
utensils, heating the food. When she sat down it said,
"This smells good." It sniffed. It was awkward

for her to bend over the plate.
Through the door she could see the photographs upon
the wall of the other room: The dead man and the child
become an adult she rarely saw.

When she was through she washed the things.
"Please don't splash," it said. Afterward she could relax
and watch her evening show. She caught herself glancing to
the phone sometimes. "I don't think it will

"ring," it said; it was right, of course.
Outdoors the traffic faded; the lamps came on in
windows, on the streets. "It's time for bed," it told her when
the city lay stupored in its mist.

   She rose, turned out the light so that
     she would not have to see the body with its veins,
the sagging breasts, the gut — and sprouting out of it, the
     little man, perfect as a child, grown

   nearly out of her by now, as
   the other one had done so long ago.

I MAGO

Among the lianas there lies a pool
  still as a mirror, where the beasts come
    to slake their thirst, where men came once
    and some stayed, their mail rusting
     within the sun-blue depths.

      Beyond the pool lies the city of
        gold, tower
         of the
          sun.

         And
        it was
      on the path,
     in the forest's
    labyrinth of paths

   beyond, in the starlight,
    that the creature was not seen,
   only the gliming of the deep
  glass on its brow, the mirror of sleep,
where the city of gold goes shimmering.

At the edge of firelight, on the fringe
   of torch, where the conquerors followed
     an image limned in quicksilver,
       some of those who sought this beast
       were mazled and confounded.

          Those
        who found —
      who drank glass
     drowned in a mind
    and are its dream still.

JUGGERNAUT

Grandfather of mammoths,
ancestor of wool and ivory,
   he contained the grasslands
   that might not contain him.

Pillars of cypresswood
   bore up a mount that might itself have
borne up a ziggurat
   beside the river's draught.

What strength was in his loins,
   lustihood in his navel — gristle
like iron plates, like pipes
   of bronze his body's bones!

Lakes have formed in his prints,
   as the fisherfolk well remember.
He has gone to the reeds
   which are thin and many.

KAMELOPARD

Say that the night was starred, the year not far
in advance of this, the sheik in his tent alone,
smoking his pipe. Outdoors the desert shone
in reflection of the moon that swung its arc
over the sweeping sands and the dunes' dark,
rolling shadows. Say the sound of a car

traveling the midnight highway sang its whine
the other side of the palms. The camels stirred.
The women on their pallets dreamed a bird,
perched on the ridgepole, sang a single note,
then fell to silence: They heard the motor float
upon its echo, taper to the fine

edge of a dream, and finally disappear.
A thin blue haze of hashish smoke was spread
in layers about the sheik who went to bed
with fleeting images moving behind his eyes
and dropped, among his coverlets and his sighs,
into a wadi deep as any mere.

Pretend he did not know when he awoke
hearing those sounds, sat up, the lingering fumes
of his journeys bemusing him with spumes
and ebbing fountains. Say that the moaning died,
that stillness took the desert back to its wide
waters beneath a sky like spangled smoke;

say he knew certainly at last, beneath
the fabric of his life, of his abode
striping the solitude of sand and road,
that he was alone forever with the reason why
the camel is, under a blank canopy of sky,
the only herbivore with a carnivore's teeth.

LEVIATHAN

    Morning touches the waves and breaks
        over the whitecaps where the ship cuts
through the waters turning an early blue.
        The wind is fresh in the east.
    Spume rinses the deck now and again.

    The light strengthens as the sun rides
        a high scud in rising flight.
Nothing moves to the horizon beyond
        susurruses of the sea.
    The ship rolls, and as she rolls she waits.

    Then sunlight touches a fountain
        rising from ocean abeam.
The ship shudders into pursuit at flank.
        A sharp sound shatters the wind.
    A coil of line unwinds, following

    its shaft over the combers. Stain
        tints the fluid of a wave,
and a great fluke rises into the air,
        then falls in an explosion
    of froth as Leviathan goes sounding.

The shallower waters glitter;
   with depth, they begin to dim.
Farther down, in the fathoms, there is night
   perpetual and cold; there
is darkness rising breathless and deep.

MINOTAUR

In my dream there is light
in the underground passage
turning between stone block walls.
The floor is a shallow stream.

How have I come to be
here in this place with my son,
not yet a yearling? Danger
waits nearby — one can feel it.

He must be preserved. At
the end of the passage there
is safety — another thing
I know, but cannot tell how.

The water moves slowly,
but it can bear him in this
frail shell in which I place him.
And he has been set afloat.

As he drifts through stone, through
light, he rises, leans upon
the rim to fathom water.
It is true: Pain is depthless.

My feet move to follow,
to seat my child again, but
the fluid drags at my flesh.
I call; he does not look back.

As he diminishes
in the curve of his passage,
I sense the beast I have feared
in the distance between us.

Nasnas

It must hop, having but one leg,
   but it does so swiftly.
   They say its flesh is sweet.
   It can give half a smile,
   but its laugh is grotesque,

so Nasnas snirtles instead, to
   keep its mouth as close as
   may be; thus, it tries to
   suppress its yawn as well.
   If it winks with one eye,

it is blind a moment and may
   be captured then. If one
   listens at its breast, to
   the half-beat of the heart's
   single chamber, one hears,

besides, the lone lung's suspiring.
   Its nostril flares in half-
   hearted anger. It can
   give but partial comfort.
   God knows how it makes love.

O DRADEK

    At first one might take it
      merely for another mathom:
a useless treasure such as may be found
      in a littered attic or lost
within a dim closet, toward the back —

    star-shaped, made of sticks, wrapped
      in thread-ends, knotted and tangled,
of many textures, thicknesses, colors.
      There is a small crossbar of wood
glued by an end to the star's center, and

    held to the rod, at right
      angles, another rod — a leg
on which, together with a starpoint, it
      stands upright. If you address it
on the stairs where often it lurks, it will

    tell its name, the tattered
      threads trembling, and then laugh like dry
leaves rustling. Look for Odradek and it
      will be absent for as long as
you remember. But in the fall, perhaps,

    a solemn wind wrapping
      the eaves, you will climb dusty stairs
into the garret, looking for — you know
      not what: A sheet of paper, sere
at the edges, on which your father wrote;

   a clock with a painted
     face, time run out of it. And there,
behind a chest, near the dry carcass of
   a moth, a fly, Odradek will
stand raveling. You will ask, "Where have you

   been?" But it will stand mute,
     spindling silence, draggling shadow.
You will shrug at last in the chill, droning
   afternoon, begin to rummage.
When you look up, Odradek will have gone.

PHOENIX AND SALAMANDER

None know how long the Phoenix lives,
but it is long — as long as forever,
  perhaps. As it was born of fire,
  to fire it must return, the gold
    and scarlet of its plumage

  molting in flame, reducing to
ore and ash. And it will burn a hundred
  years. Before it may again be
  born, while in its heat, it must mate:
    the chill salamander climbs

  into the aerie to live
within its host the century of love.
  The lizard dies with its embers,
  lies buried in ash, with the rains
    decays, becomes the rock's hollow

  heart. Out of this geology
the embryo is sprung at last, quaking,
  the mountain split, the fledgling bird
  shrieking in the clear air of dawn
    broken upon what now must be.

QUERULE

"Why?" it asks, and snivels.
I must get rid of it. It
makes me nervous, annoys me.
"Why?" it asks, a tear sliding down
its throat, making its whine slick as slime.

Its body reminds me
of gobbets. "But why?" it asks
again. It hangs around and
hangs around. It has no teeth, just
gums. It is a parasite, a sorn.

It sobs. "Why?" it cries. "Why?"
I pick it up, look at it
deeply, probe its mucous eyes.
Holding it, my hands feel cold and
sticky, like my stare. "Because," I say,

"just because. That's the way
it is. Enjoy it, why don't
you?" "I do," it moans, "I do, I do!"

ROC

    Stones are falling from the sky
      somewhere at sea. The clouds part,
  and a boulder edges through, slowly,
froths of vapor trailing from its edges.

    As it descends, behind it
      there is another, and yet
  another: A column of stones
dropping toward the cool blue mere below.

    They have always been falling,
      for how else would there be waves?
  The brown surface of a stone touches
the water, dimples it; a circle swells

    about its bulk like the lips
      of surprise. The mouth swallows.
  The astonished wave widens, begins
to roll toward the islands and the coast.

    It picks up substance and size,
      the fluid force moving through —
  not made of — water, this strength of stone.
Within the zero zone another grows.

    No one knows where the boulders
      fall to sea; no one has seen
  the bird, great beak filled with rocks, the cairn
of time piling upon the lost sea bed.

SASQUATCH
for John Ciardi

    After the wind-tempest, when
branches lie in crambles upon the clearings
  and neighbors at far distances phone
  down the foothills under the mountains

    to ask if all is well still,
the answer is "Yes" and, sometimes, "But have you
  seen anything of a shambling man
  dressed in furs running before the birds'

    chirming just before the sun
was wiped out of the slate sky and the rain erased
  the trees, made them slop and wiggle like
  pines in a finger painting?" And, "No,"

    is the answer, "not this time,
but now you mention it, last time we thought we
  saw a bear at the edge of the woods,
  and when we went to look there were prints

    "in the mud — footprints the shape
of a big man's, a huge man's bare feet. They put us
  in mind of the manse of the films,
  the girl in the chiffon gown walking

"down the hall to stop under
a portrait whose eyes move. And then, you know, it
　　slides aside, and a hairy arm comes
　　reaching out toward the maiden, and

　　"we scream, don't we, for the girl
in the white gown, but you know, what must it be
　　like to be the thing the arm belongs
　　to? What wouldn't we want, and wouldn't

　　"we hide in the walls and woods?
And if a storm blew up, wouldn't we wander some,
　　down from the timberline to where the
　　houses started, to look in windows

　　"at firelight and carpets,
to think about chiffon and wish the folk would
　　understand somehow, somewhen, that there's
　　a bit of hairy arm in everyone?"

TROGLODYTE

In the lowlands lie his reaches,
in the salt-queaches. Fogs and fens
he inhabits. Horrid by day
deep in his delvings where he sleeps
hard by his mother, by moongleam
he is most monstrous, most ugsome.
Night's eye closes as he clointers,
shambling through shallows to find food —
this scaly fiend, this feared foeman,
eater of carls, doomed damerel,
great gunsel. Why do his hungers
cause him to clamber from the deeps,
the tide's womb, to forbidden flesh,
the meat of men? It is not meet
he should hound us in the meadhall
under the alecask as we neeze
fleering in dream, noddles bobbing.
We whommel and wake — ah! the wight
has us in hand! The cumberworld
slobbers and slavers. Snithe his breath
upon our napes! His fingers prog;
his fangs are fastles on our flesh —
then home to mother through the mirk,
to the dark dens at the deep's verge,
there to drowse while the daylight lies
on barrow and beach and gull-buoy.

UROBOROS

    Some call him Uroboros:
"That-Which-Is-Its-Own-Sustenance."
He is the chemist's worm, things in a circle,
    air and fire, water, earth,
  a mouth of darkness devouring

    its own bright tail. Sarsens for
  his spine, scales of blue stones, he wheels
upon himself, and nothing is consumed. All
    wisdom and all matter: These
  are his. We may transmogrify

    his image in the dark glass
  of our minds — he may become the
worm in Eve's fruit, asp at the breast, Wyvern in
    the tower hissing out
  of Merlin's spell; nevertheless, he

    is the Hermetic dragon
  Uroboros: All things in one.
One may not transmute his elements unless
    he dies. Where shall one bleed him?
  How can we sever everness?

    He is the Worm Who Lives,
  each thing and All: Water of life,
torment's fire, wind-breath, stone and soil from which these
    green things spring. Uroboros.
  Look inward where he coils in blood.

VIELFRAS

He inhabits a precious pelt,
dogsize, but a hunger greater than he
    inhabits him. He is the gorger
        Vielfras, habitant of scrog

    and underbrush. All creatures grand
and minuscule are his prey. Upon his
    thick legs the long body moves, silent
        as snow, until his bright teeth close

    and rend. He will devour the roe,
the boar, the ox — anything greater than
    himself, his sac of fur swelling till
        it strains to split. Then, he will seek

    two close-standing saplings and squeeze
between them, head first, disburdening his
    swollen bowels of their freight. If he
        is captured somehow — stunned, perhaps,

    by blunt arrows so as not to
damage his variegated fur — when
    he wakes in a pit, he will attack
        mortar and stone, eat his way out,

    and noggle awkwardly into
the winter air toward his trees. If he
    is chased, the hunter behind will be
        pelted with half-digested rock.

The flesh of Vielfras, they say,
tastes like hunger. It will grow in the paunch,
and he who wears a coat of its skin
may never remove it again.

Werewind

    When she died she became a wind.
  Her body turned to dust, but her breath
expanded to fill the landscape of her mind
and to inhabit an old geography:
   the hills and plains of childhood and the vales
      of her despair. She looked down

    out of the cloudy air to see
   the house she had abandoned filling
with life again. She blew out of the maples,
eased to the windows, tried to filter under
   the sash to breathe through the familiar rooms.
      This she was denied, but when

   the children issued from the doors
    to play in the yard she bent the grass
before them, chilled their toes, whispered they were not
welcome in the place where she had never felt
  anything but a stranger, and stranger
      still in her body of air.

   Although they paused to listen, though
    they thought a voice was speaking to them
that they recognized from dreams from which they woke
with a vague sorrow born of midnight shadow,
   they soon were taken with another thought,
      or an image from the bright

world there before them. And at last,
grown weary even of couching in
the roots of nightshade, listening to the sounds
of ordinary passages of bone and blood,
she traveled north, moving against the grain
of the autumn flocks seeking

the climes and means of flesh. She came
where she belonged by temperament at
last. She recognized as part of her the floes
and washes of her life, the life she had made
out of thin air, and there she would remain,
feeding on herself and on

the white bones of the winter of her despair.

XOANON

    Its body is like that
of a buffalo, black and thick.
    It is ugsome as mud.
It depresses me to think of it,
    lying there in the corner
under a table of my study.

    It is best that I not
look at it, though its eyes are closed.
    I have fed it a root
of nightshade, and it is sleeping. It
    will not cast me one of its
killing glances for a while. It is

    content in its despair.
Its dreams fill that boarskull and spill
    out of the bristles, rank
as gorge, into lamplight. I try not
    to watch these visions in shades
of pallor and nocolor. Its neck

    querls about its body,
translucent as intestine. In
    it, slowly spiraling, the night
shade darkens and dissolves. If
    I rise, it will rise as well.
Its lids will open to slits, its neck

      uncoil; it will lumber
   after me, nearly stepping on
its chin, for I have tamed
Xoanon. I stop and stare it down.
   It moans, heaves beneath my bed
to watch me dream of it. The beast knows

   its master, knows that I
  will not think of it if I will,
that I can strike to its
heart with a look. And Xoanon knows
   as well parasite from host,
knows who shall cast the last glance at last —

who is the master's *bete noir*.

Yeti

We do not know whether the tales are true
nor, if they are, why he will not come down
out of the high slopes and the winter peaks
where he has lived, they say, since earth was new.
He is called Eldfather: The name bespeaks

ingle and hearth, perhaps, but he disdains
to take such comforts. So, from dawn to dimpse
he ranges his sterilities alone,
casting his shaggy glances to the plains
below the wind, taking nor giving rone.

And is he Adam, then, as some assume,
or Abel's line at least, rejecting Cain
with all his artifacts — the roaky skies
choking the murderous cities' palling doom
and piling scroil? Does he recall the lies

an uncle told, therefore seek out the screeve
of cloud along a ridge? It may be so.
And it may also be he is the beast
of solitude — merely that. Let him grieve
or joy and wander, coldly fast or feast

where blizzards rail and the planets hover.
Our crops are sown in blood upon the nover.

Zombie

Outside the door, the noises of the sleugh.
indoors, the tropic heat, the potted ferns,
a palm stuck in the corner near the couch.
She waits and picks at lint. Her fingers run
through her hair. "It's nerves, just nerves," she says,
but still she listens.
                    And then the sudden knock.
The potted palm sweats. Its leaves ripple.
She cannot speak. Then — "Yes, who is it?" She
gets up and smooths her skirt. Another knock.

She goes toward the door. The mirror there
beside the clock shows her what she must see:
a plain young woman with faded eyes, her hair
a neutral shade. "What does he want with me?"
she tells the glass.
                "Who's there?" she asks again.
"I've come," he says. She reaches for the knob.
Her palms are sweating: they slip as her fingers turn.
She pauses — pulls.
                He stands there on the stoop,
his eyes too bright and blank. His puffy skin
is white as mallow in the dimming light.
He has no hair. His body is too stiff.

His mouth gapes as he looks at her. She starts,
but catches herself. His hat is in one hand;
the other goes to his tie. He clears his throat.

"We'd better hurry," she says, "or we'll be late."
She turns off the light, picks up her coat, her purse,
and moves toward the door. He stands aside,
closes the door, and follows her into the night.

SEASONS OF THE BLOOD,
POEMS ON THE TAROT
1980

WHEEL OF FORTUNE

TAROT in the Wheel;
mercury, sulfur, water,
    salt. Mix well and turn.
The jackal-headed god bears
    up under the spin,
rising. The Garden's serpent
    slithers down the west.
The Sphinx in blue — a woman —
    squats atop it all,
holding a sword against her
    breast. Everything is
the same, despite the odd turns —
    so say the Fixed Signs,
each reading somebody's book:
    To the upper left,
Man with Wings; an Eagle to
    the right, a Lion
under. And a winged Bull there,
    lower left, scanning
his blank pages with the rest.
    His blank pages, which
he fills with hoofprints, hoping
    consciousness evolves
into Godhood somewhere, some
    when. Caught at this point
on the Mandala, the small

  bull confuses him-
self with Taurus, his Sign. It
  is expected, to
be forgiven. He is not
  affixed (nor is he
broken — not yet). He hopes that
  all is relative,

and complete; that there is choice,
  though all is finished;
that the smallest is the largest…;
  that some sure thing
is accomplished by means of
  these clumsy hooves, these
dull horns that turn to silence.

BANJO

It is the morning,
Brother Night. Put off your cowl.
Lay it on the sill.
Take up this banjo of strings.

Hear your paramour
sing among the taproots of oaks.
Willows chime as they lash her.

In this cell of shades,
at this table of boards whose
rosary of hours
lies telling itself to air,
there is a silence
repeating among crumbs, rinds.
*Shall we rise with this
friar, out of a lechery
of sheets, to go walking with
lilies and roses?*

There are blooms here, boles
and stems — the tempting garden.

FOLIAGE

*The carved elephant
in the shadowbox on the
    wall walks out of gold
leaf, settles into the air.*

*I hear him turning
my idea over in
    his mind. His trunk — like
a delicate snake — poises
    out of the shade of
his body above my eyes.*

*Behemoth, who shall
be mahout — myself or you?*

*It may be you will
ride me gently as petals
    unwound from the wind,
or as the quiet key of
fountains turning the sky's lock.*

*But, again, it may
be I will mount into that
    howdah billowing
like a garden out of the
black ocean-sea of your back.*

*We shall go, two halves
of a beautiful monster,
    silently among
the foliage of a rose.*

BONE

Am I in love? Birds are flying.
Do birds fly? I am in love.

   Why do these birds fly?
Where there is wind, there are wings.
Where there are wings, there is wind.

   *What is love? What is
wind?* The moon is a vessel
   of bone and of dust.
In her is conceived the dark.
   She is the night's womb.
Out of her, wind is gotten.
   Out of the night are
begotten all winds, each breath.

   Whenever one breathes
darkness, the dust of a moon,
   he must inhale light,
conceive of beginnings, ends:
Darkness, the dust of a moon.

   Whenever one breathes,
he breathes reflections: The moon
   lying in a lake.
Light touching water touches
our sight with sunlight's marrow.

   Darkness broods the moon.
The shell will break: Morning shall
   awaken to flight.

PENTACLES

The heart is a coin
of fire. *How shall we spend it?*
How is the sun spent?

THE DEVIL

He will have his will,
nonetheless — put to the torch
*   the man and woman*
chained to this Devil's-half-cube:
*   She has a tail of*
flowers; he, of flame. All three
*   are horned. The Old Goat*
has ramshorns. A pentacle
*   is inverted on*
his forehead. He is bearded,
*   glowering above*
his goatee. His loins are furred,
*   but we see his claws;*
we notice the mammal's wings.

*   As for the couple —*
well, they have the horns of fauns.
*   The chains are laid loose*
over their heads. Their bondage
*   is a willing one.*
They stand beneath the batwings
*   spread like parasols —*
to avoid the cold. Who would
*   blame them? If this is*
a wheel on which we stand, at
*   a moment not far*
along the Circle of the
*   Snake, when consciousness*
cannot merge with consciousness,
*   let what may merge, merge.*
Let there be heat if not light.

THE LOVERS

Was hers the blame? Blossoms flare.
Was his? The Garden is lost.

   When will it be found?
He must ascend the mountain;
   he looks toward her.
The mountain is between them.
   She looks to Raphael
hovering above the mount.
   She is searching Strength.
She will give what she must give.
   May she give gardens?
Blossoms flare in each meadow —
   They are reflections
of what is forever lost.

   Is it forever?
A moment lasts forever.
There is only the mountain.

TURN

    If you should waken
at the first turn of moonlight,

    would you please follow
the silver road, not the dark

at the first turn of moonlight?

FOXFIRE

*Does mallow whistle
in the yellow air? Foxfire
    burns the fox's eyes.*

*The land eats flesh, and
it gives up blossom. Hares root
    at the door. Lilies
turn tiger between sunfall
    and moonrise. Dusk comes
to cover, only to drown
    in deeper shade still.
Ash burns gray in the chord
of a music from the west.*

*   St. Elmo takes a
torch to green wood: His is a
    splayed breath edged darkly.*

*   The slug glisters in
a cupping of mud, in
    fern and bramble. The
world scutters at the snail's horn
    curling. A coin of
image silvers in the reeds.*

THE MOON

What has become of
these pincers of this creature
of the mother sea?
It has become the wolf's voice
raised beneath the Moon's lumen.

And what has become
of the sound of the wood's wolf
between the towers?
It has been transformed into
the howl of the hearthstone's dog.

What will become, then,
of the bark and the whine when
the towers must fall?
In the night's shadows there are
these words, and the Word beyond.

CUPS

    Moon takes the tide where
a tide must go: Light pierces
      the hardest crystal.

Stone shall be filled with water,
and dust will be filled with blood.

SWORDS

*Does this dark blade strike
my flesh?* Light is engrossed with
dust, and the organs of dust.

*Shall I not lament
in the night?* Mars shows his eye
when the heavens are darkest.

At whom does he wink?
You have shut your own eyelid.
It is mortal salt made you.

*To whom may I turn
in this anguish?* Blood lashes
the womb as seas beat the shore.

*Does this dark blade strike
all flesh?* The oceans wear rock
to dust, but the dust shall speak.

EPISTLES

I am writing you
from a pit. It is quite dark
here. I see little.
I am scratching this note on a stone.
Where are you? It has been long.

    Thank you for your note.
I do not know where I am.
    I believe I may
be with you. It is not dark
here. The light has blinded me.

SEASONS OF THE BLOOD

Is it winter? Blood is warm.
Is the blood warm? It is spring.

When is the wind warm?
The sun falls on wings moving
across the river valley.

In the water, fish
look for roads. Bridges extend
from mountain to hill.
Find your way. Look for the gate.

Walking this way, through
the air like crystal, like bells,
one neither moves nor
remains, but becomes what is,
the air like crystal, like bells.

The blood of a leaf
turns sunlight green when
the day is longest.
On a certain night, the wind
breathes blood into an oak leaf.

Life is an acorn
hidden in a cold valley.
The wind's blood is white.

DIALOGUE

*I am wearing blue
in honor of the sky. Shall
you wear green to honor earth?*

    I will don rainbows:
I will wear snow on my back —
white, allcolor forever.

PARADIGM

Why does the brook run?
The banks of the stream are green.

Why does the stream run?
The banks of the brook bloom
with roe and cup-moss, with rue.

The trees are filled with
cups. Grain in the fields, straw men
    talking with the wind.
Have you come far, water-
    borne, wind-born? Here are
hounds-tongue and mistletoe oak.

When the spears bend as
you walk through vervain or broom,
    call out to the brook —
it will swell in your veins as
you move through broom or vervain.

Have you spoken aloud? Here,
where the swallows' crewel-work
    sews the sky with mist?
You must cut the filament.
You must be the lone spider.

The bole is simple:
Twig and root like twin webs in
    air and earth like fire.

THE TEST

*It was a blue day
when he went out to test the
trees leaving for a day at
   the beach, curbs simmering
like snakes, the baseballs hanging
   in the air the way
   moons will hang waiting
for the sun to do something.*

*He found what he was
looking for, and then forgot,
or left it in a ragtag
   weedpatch down by the
tracks where an old billygoat
yard engine backed and snorted,
   butted some cars, woke
a 'bo in excelsior.*

*But before he could
remember the gift he'd found,
   the sun went down, and
   the moon rose in the
dark blue sky down by the tracks.*

That's the story. He
never found what he'd been given.
The trees marched back from
the seashore, the curbs
stopped hissing and slept as he
went home to think, as
perhaps he would, what test had
been passed, by whom, to what end?

FACETS

*Do you hear the voice
of the dog?* Use a wolf's ears.

The shadows cannot
bite, not even with stone teeth,
through there are marks in the wind.

*May I come along
like the aroma of moss?*
I will give you a forest.

There is nothing so
smooth as a dark ball rolling
    among sparks. There is
green hair in the lake's eye. *There
    will be hailstones soon
in your lungs. What may be made
    with frost of a sigh?*
Come away roaring, rainbow.

Who has seen circles?
*The stern season is a fire
    turning in nothing.*

THE RIVER

It was tidal. The
brackish eddies swirled with carp.
    Muskrats sneezed along
the mudbanks, and smoky cranes
    legged it among mists
as he poled over the flats.

    He was returning.
His journey was from the sea
    where coral had been
trackless, filled with cold lanterns.
His crew had been relentless.

    Now, the home shores loomed
out of cedar and pine; leaves
    fell out of a hill
full of maples. The river
ran at the whim of a moon.

    He poled over stone
and carp roe. The dark farms fell
    before him. Is this
your own place? There is
no other. Leaves fall, wind blows.
    There is no other.

CIRCLES

*A true October —
no winds lie with the season
at stake. Flocks revolve in sky.*

*Leaves burning below
cast no more light upward than
downward. It is a true fall.*

*Night sinks late, rises
early, stumbles over the
    lantern's cold corpse in
the morning doorway and shocks
    the last housecat out
of her warm contempt. Even
    So, what will keep the
world from turning winds to mild
dissemblance a few months hence?*
    Birds wheel the wind's wake.

*Snow, the snow running
the wind bleary and the grass
    rheumy in these long
meadows. Do you hear the chip
of the prairie dogs that we
    are, the burrowing
of winter in a tunnel
    of grass?* There is frost
in the moon's wake; there is a
comet snarling in the grass.

*Why do the weathers
of your waking smell like the
 evening? You talk to
earth with voices that dissolve,
melting in ponds of silence.*

There are rings of weed.
Why do the choirs of your eyes
 troll the dark bawd's glee?

THE HERMIT

The mountain of snows,
the lamp filled with starlight,
the staff and the beard.

*Graybeard in a gray
cloak, why do you gaze downward
out of the blue sky?*

Snow over stone, stone
in petrified cataracts,
falls to the valley.

*Who is that beneath,
looking upward into the hard
eyes, the Hermit's eyes?*

He is another
who would climb past the father,
out of the garden.

*What is to be found
on this bare ridge of winter,
on this chill summit?*

Would you have the eyes
of the one who has found all,
then you must wander
and climb. All is found below,
beneath all one's wandering.

DEATH

Who may withstand them,
the dark Rider and the Rose?
    On the blue river
a dragon ship sails under
stallion, Rider, and white Rose.

Who must go with them,
the dark Rider and the Rose?
    Ancient and infant,
Bishop and maiden await
the black banner of the Rose.

Where will they journey,
the dark Rider and the Rose?
    Between two towers
the sun shines. A white stallion
carries riders to the Rose.

TOAD

*Was there sense in that
flicker and swallow, silence
settling around its darkness?*

*Its skin is dry. Its
eyes are like lost volcanoes.
When touched, the sack of
its existence squirts a dark
    liquid hopelessly
upon the palm that would hold.
    It has swallowed light,
gives in exchange reflections
    of decay. Movement
is infirm. It halts, assumes
    the stance of fungus,
splits a quantum of daylight.*

*It does no ill? It
inhabits gardens? Quickness
arrested can be no good.*

*The lamps of fireflies
fall into its eyes. The mouth
    erupts with silence.*

THE HANGED MAN

Who is the Hanged Man? Golem.
Who is Golem? Ask Judas.

*Is he standing on
a Tau? on a toe? upon
a bough before a tree's bole?*

A rope suspends him
by an ankle, from a bar,
his legs crossed before the Tree.

*Does he think of Death?
Is this, then, the dance of blood,
the wind's breath shaking his bones?*

His arms are water
in a triangle, hands held
behind him. His eyes are clear.

*Who has hanged this man?
What does he see, how does he see it,
when will he tell how he sees?*

We have hanged him. We
gave him his aureole. Look.
He will tell us when we see.

THE CHARIOT

    Black sphinx, white sphinx, pull.
The Magician is riding,
riding between the castles.

    Which way, which way pull?
The canopy is bestarred.
The sphinxes have pendant breasts.

JUDGMENT

    The floating dead will
rise from their sarcophagi
      when the Sound falls out
of the horn, echoing from
the mountains, the hermit snows.

CORRESPONDENCE

*There is a black hole
in space, where the universe
    is disappearing.
This is what I have read.
The scientists frighten me.*

Have you never heard
of the hermetic dragon?
    Do not be afraid.
What disappears is not lost.
The snake is eating its tail.

THE TOWER

    They are falling out
of the Tower. And the crown
    is falling. Lightning
has struck it. There is fire.
The old forms are breaking
                              down

    with the descending
Yods.

      Where will they land — these folk?
    They are adrift in
the dark air.
          Who can see where
he will alight? At the base

    of the peak boulders,
grass, a solid cloud — ? Perhaps
    the mind is broken.

    Perhaps what the mind
made is diminished. Perhaps
there is a greater Tower.

THE FOOL

> *I have had little*
to do with all this nonsense.
> *He is the Fool, not*
I. He is about to step
> *over the edge of*
the precipice in this last
> *of the Tarot cards,*
a white rose in his left hand,
> *a wand and knapsack*
slung over his right shoulder.
> *Where is he looking? —*
up into the clouds, of course,
> *the abyss yawning*
at his feet, the white mountains
> *turning in their great*
circle around him, the sun
> *beaming. His dog is*
barking to warn him — no use.
> *A dumb animal*
has more sense than he has. Words.
> *Nothing but words. Oh,*
I admit that I have dropped
> *a few myself here*
and there. But my role has been
> *Devil's Advocate —*
not that I have been lying.
> *I merely desired*
to see how far he would go
> *with his sophistries:*

All this talk of gardens, moons,
    mountains to be climbed,
towers falling, the mute rock
    willing itself to
consciousness, the inchoate
    chaos evolving
Godhood out of its creatures:
    Things in a circle —
the serpent that eats its tail.
    I hope he falls far,
that air will not bear him up.
    All is relative.
There is no such thing as Truth.

    It has been a long
journey, though there is a way
    to go. He has been
a good companion. He is
    right — I am the Fool.
We have weathered the seasons
    together. Our blood
has run strongly in our veins
    as we have climbed out
of the valley past the wolf
    in moonlight, the toad
moulting by the tarn. Rivers
    have been forded. We
have found the pit, the garden,

    behemoth, lily,
serpent and rose together.
    He has used his sword,
and I have wielded my wand;
    he has spent his coin,
I have offered him my cup.
    We have walked beyond
the Emperor, we have kissed
    the Lovers, mounted into
the Chariot, climbed the mount
    of the gray Hermit
to find him with his starlit
    lamp on the whitest
peak. We have hanged by our heels,
    ridden Fortune's Wheel,
come at last together here
    to this precipice.
I, being the Fool, must walk
    on and leave him here
shaking his head. Yet, he
    is not left. He will
follow — by another route,
    perhaps. But all routes
are One. The rock cannot be
    cleft. We are ever
joined, though it may not appear
    so. There is this last
step, from ends to Beginnings.

Where will you go, Fool?
There is nowhere to be gone.
There is no Where, no Nowhere.

AMERICAN STILL LIFES
1981

I. TWELVE MOONS

COLD MOON

The lake drifts in the starfall,
    the father lake that will not freeze
        but hardens at its edges.

The earth has turned to stone
    beneath the stones
        upon the cold moon's shores.

Wind builds forts of ice
    crystal by crystal,
        and the pike go deep.

The grasses move in the air,
    some with dark plumes
        on stalks of shadow,

and where the trees begin
    darkness lies at the root
        hiding the trail.

SNOW MOON

Wind calls over the lake;
    snow rises to the voice of air
        falling and falling.

The deer circle and fold
    among the oaks of the forest,
        their eyes shining in the moon.

There is nothing but sifting
    among the maples
        and the sharp echo of a branch breaking.

The otchock is in its lair
    sleeping and listening in its sleep
        to hear if a shadow should fall above

or if a footfall should drift
    into its dream of roots
        fading into the wood —

but the men are in their villages
    dreaming themselves awake
        hearing the wind cry and the snow fall.

WORM MOON

The sky is a curtain of slate
    falling to the horizon,
        but behind it there is the sun.

The river flows north again
    into the gray lake
        splitting its skin of ice.

In the forest deer
    scrape velvet from their horns —
        blood on the bark.

The squnck leads her kits
    along the shore,
        tails cocked;

they follow the trail,
    then switch into the wood
        and the patches of old snow.

A robin listens for worms,
    hears instead footsteps in the earth
        and rises into the bare, bursting limbs.

SEED MOON

In the night there was a crescent
    thin as a breath
        floating in the sky.

Now the sun has quickened;
    it sprays the green meadows
        with drops of light.

Birds pierce the trees
    along the lake where grass
        thrusts through the bluff.

In the houses of the village
    there is the scent of savors —
        the women move and the men rise.

Soon the earth will fill with voices,
    the sounds of loam turning;
        the sun will stretch to fill the sky,

and in the woodland the deer
    will sample the air,
        lift their heads to listen.

FLOWER MOON

The sun blossoms in the sky,
    and the woodsflowers blossom.
        Herbs bloom in the gardens.

All day light falls
    until shadows fall
        with the failing west.

Then a yellow flare
    fires the clouds over the lake,
        sets the waves afire.

Upon the shore the boats lie
    among the voices of children
        skipping stones over the water;

the moon skims
    into the east
        washing silver into the wood,

shadow into the stone —
    and, beyond, the pike flash
        under the lip of shadow.

HOT MOON

The maize is shin high
    behind the fences
        of the village by the lake,

and in the blue haze
    above the mouth of the river
        seagulls call in the sun,

climb and fall
    where waters meet waters
        and fish lie over ledge.

BUCK MOON

The buck on the hill
    looks up over the high grass.
        A cicada sings of heat.

A man stands at the treeline
    where earth slopes under the wood.
        Nothing moves.

A grouse breaks cover
    calling and calling.
        In the grass a breath stirs,

a high cloud shadows it,
    moving northeast over the lake.
        Crickets chirr in the stalks.

The antlers of the buck
    spread like an oak
        over the brow of the hill,

and when he is gone
    the man begins to climb
        under the cloud and the bright song.

STURGEON MOON

As the boat rounds the river bend
    the great body of the fish
        breaks water like an arrow,

falls back into the spume.
    The prow of the boat
        slices through and past.

Maples and cedars
    follow the bank.
        A musquash climbs into the brush,

its coat shining.
    A turtle dives like a rock
        from a rock.

Below the rapids there is the lake
    spread to the horizon
        like a pond of blue light.

MAIZE MOON

The wind moves in the maize
    under a moon the shade of dust,
        shaking and rustling.

The corn's tassles
    are the colors of night;
        the cricket's song is the song of night,

of roots in dry earth
    and frost in the offing.
        The deer are restless in the wood,

waking to listen.
    An owl calls
        and a squirrel stirs,

dreaming of hiding.
    Out of the dark air
        a chestnut prepares to fall

from shadow to shadow,
    leaf to leaf,
        and the lake waits, biding.

TRAVELERS' MOON

The man's breath
    is a plume of steam
        too thin to see from the village

lying under the hill
    beside the lake
        among its straw gardens.

Evening is falling
    out of the horns
        of a bone moon

risen above the forest
    among the starpoints
        like beads of frost.

The trail is clear
    even by frostlight or bonelight,
        and the air is clear,

sharp as a blade,
    hard as a staff —
        as the path of the moon on the water.

BEAVER MOON

The sun through the clouds,
    high and thin,
        looks like a moon.

Beneath it the forest spreads
    from the lake to the south horizon,
        hard earth showing through the branches.

A brook with ice at its ledges
    flows barely through the trees
        toward a gray river.

A pond swells
    behind a dam,
        water racing over the logs

where a man appears
    walking quickly,
        then stops to listen.

Somewhere there is a sharp crack
    that ripples over the water,
        through the air and silence.

HUNTING MOON

Snow nearly hard as hail
    rustles through the bare branches
        and settles among the leaves

at the roots of the forest.
    In its den of earth
        a bear dreams of berries,

of fish gleaming in the shallows.
    A herd of deer
        shifts edgily in a clearing,

the young bucks shivering.
    From a distance
        a jay cries

across the gray air.
    They are in the wood,
        the band of men,

downwind and quiet.
    The wind begins to rise.
        The snow starts to flake and drift.

II. STILL LIFES

LANDSCAPE

Winter is hanging fire behind the sun.
Back of the eyes, a leaf grows its shadow.
Beyond that there are hills turning to fall,
and a river is disturbed by the sound —
like water cacading over the millsite
beside a road curling near the graveyard.
Earth is flesh lying upon ridges
of these falling places. Wind makes it move
as though it were a sleight of vetch or elm.
It is a hard thing to say where things stand.
The shadow lies beneath the leaf, beneath
clay and moss the colors of winterlight.
Silence is hanging fire behind the moon.

THE COLONY

Rising out of the summer woods
there is a column of smoke
beginning to fade into the sky where,
now and then, a tern or oriole

stitches stillness with a call
and emptiness with a curve of plumage.
The palisade stands open.
The living quarters yawn shadow

into the heat. The fires are cold,
their ash white and fine as snow
on the bare places in the grass.
The blacksmith's tongs lie where they were left;

a water barrel has rolled,
dry as the August wind,
into a corner of the compound.
The woods stand close,

but in them there is no echo —
only the needle rustle of the pines
moving inland.
The bark on the log paling

has not begun to show moss,
but one of the chief trees or posts
at the right side of the entrance
has the bark taken off,

and five feet from the ground
in fair capital letters is graven
CROATOAN without any cross
or sign of distress.

THE MAPLE WORKS

In the maple grove wind moves
and the snow grows heavy with water
in the footprints that approach the trunks

where, in each, a box cut collects the sap
that rises to the tap and seeps
heavily into a slat pail.

Over the forest an overcast lowers
and spreads east toward the sea.
The sound of an axe blade chips

at the solid hours filling the spaces
between bole and bole: each cut
is clear and a long way off.

If anything moves it is a naked branch,
its twigs scratching the wind or another limb,
creaking as though a door were opening

or closing between two places, each
unfamiliar and empty, isolate.
In the snow there is fire:

its heat races beneath a tripod
to lick the belly of copper swung there,
filled with the life that rose out of rock

and rises still, vaporous, to fill the grove
with a sweet scent, the steam
lifting past the stirring rod shaped

like an oar and propped against silence,
into the bleak sky blowing overhead
out of the unknown toward the forsaken.

THE MEETINGHOUSE

God is kept in this box of pine
beside the road of beaten earth.
A fence of stone holds off the new fields
thinly bitten by the share.

A crow on the limb of a hackmatack
hears his bleak word swallowed by the woods.
The wind from the east, carrying salt,
touches for chinks between the butted boards.

The altar is of oak, as is the table
that raises a pewter goblet to its Host.
Hard benches rest on a bare floor.

Sunlight as spare as the foliage of fall
descends through leaded glass,
illuminates the stillness of an hour
suspended beneath these beams that show their hewing,

beneath the roof that cannot vault,
but peaks and slopes under gray heaven.
The raven calls again, as old as dust,
spreads its shadow climbing through the air,

disappears between a gust and a breath.
The meadow grasses bend. A spate of rain
spatters the fence. A horse
whickers somewhere behind a screen of elms.

THE TAVERN

The path that passes is of mud.
Rain rattles over the rooftree,
and the wind rustles like a broom.

From the casks at the wall
there rise the scents of hops and apples.
Tables of rough wood and benches of wood

are staggered over the pine floor.
Through the gray windows the sky
lumbers over the forest and downlands,

scatters its March waters among
snow pockets and old furrows.
Now and then, as it passes over

the meetinghouse down the road,
the gale seems to catch a note of hymn
and bring it close. A stack

of fagots on the stone hearth
looks like bone in the shadows
standing at the mouth of darkness.

THE TRADING POST

Out of the weather, in the first room,
there are knives, blades lying on shelves.
The glinting lamplight slices shadow.

The river passing over the stones of the valley
does not quench with its voices
the flame on the hearth nor the dark fire
of the beads looping the pegs of the wall.

Beyond the logs of the building and its fire
are the boles of the forest bearing firs,
leaves and needles green and sere,
drinking the sun or the sounds of footfall,
light and leather.

In the second room there is a pallet
of pelts and sticks; a musket
lies beside it, its iron rusting.

The air is drowsy with musk and leather — the animals lie
flat or curl in bales
as though listening to the river, or the fire
among the beads and knives,
steel jaws and powder horns.

But the forest lies waking
beyond this frame of logs hewn
in the clearing against the river.
The animals wake listening
for fire and knives and the dark weather.

THE FORT

Was it the sound a blue spruce makes
in the wind at night, owls huge
among its needles —

or was it the echo of a footfall
springing among wet leaves and cedar boughs
on the riverbank? A light foot

in deer leathers, and the moon
lying like a quicksilver crosscurrent
on the water. The ghost-holes

of the fort on the point
make square spaces out of shadow, and the dark
bores of muskets forged of rust

aim into the sibilant wood.
There are fissures in the night,
dark eyes waking, time seeping

through the oak limbs and the maple limbs.
All the tribe shall gather
to make war paint out of the river

and its roots, their lips saying over and over,
it is time for war — let the children
and women take cover

in the pine copses while the men
storm shadow, while the fusillade
storms about them out of the stockade

like so many winds, and their arrows answer
as if the shafts were night birds
calling from spruce to spruce.

THE PHARMACY

The odor is of sulfur and autumn.
On the high bench at the back
there are pipettes and flasks,
a wooden mortar with its worn pestle,
alchemical spoons.

In the counter there are grooves
for rolling pills, a broken pill or two,
some powder, and honey in a jug.
On the shelves are tinted bottles
like gothic spires in small:

simples and decoctions,
extracts and infusions,
tinctures ink-labeled.
In drawers and bins pomander balls
roll out their round scents.

Ointments stand tinned
beside electuaries boxed,
and from the beams there depend
the sere leaves of lupine,
Indian root and lavender.

It is quiet among the cures.
The rumble of a cartwheel on the street
mutters barely through the door
to disturb ox-eye at blind gaze,
the ills of the world at bay.

THE COLLEGE

The wall is of brick. The buildings
are brick. Red brick flags underfoot.
Within these hallowed precincts
all is just, Divine.

The trees turn over a new leaf,
then another. They are rooted
in thin soil. Their shade
stubbles the grass, stipples cobbles.

Outside the compound drays
carry hay from the manger
to the town stable. A bell
peals the hour out of heaven.

A candle sheds small light
on the Word in a dusky room.
The portrait on the wall is robed,
its periwig haloing a hard stare.

Candles glow in the grate.
The shelves speak volumes:
the fatted calf has been slain
in order to bind them to order.

There shall be commerce
between earth and Heaven —
the steeple aspires over the cobbles,
ringing the changes on bell, brick and candle.

THE COURTHOUSE

The legal arm has reached up from the sea
along the estuary, past the straits
and narrows, negotiated rapids till
it has banked upon this plot among the pines.

The panes stare blindly at the dawn
that breaks across the bar, spills to the floor,
begins to ease enlightenment
upwards of the stairwell and the rail.

In the living quarters there are books,
calf-bound, upon the shelf.
The day's eye, falling through bull's-eye glass,
picks out in gilt the letters of the law.

THE FERRY

The cable bows downward,
touches the surface at midstream,
then curves to the far bank —

there, all is the same: the same woods
receding from the dock, squeezing the gravel track
to a certain point under the horizon.

The river is in flood, the water muddy.
Under the pier the pilings are in jeopardy.
Fish hug the eddy bottoms.

The barge pulls at its ties, strains the cable
running through eyes along the gunwale.
A smoky crane blows downstream

against its will, tacking westward
like the eroding light.
To the east dusk is breaking

along the road, submerging the forest,
touching toward a clearing where light
swims in a window, washes

into the dooryard: a pump, a trough,
a stack of wood, an axe,
its head glinting in a cleft.

The cable hums in the gale,
its fibers binding silence to silence.
The bell on the pier utters a note.

When its mate responds on the far crossing
night will fall in cataract,
the halves of earth be sundered and set adrift.

THE TOLLHOUSE

The bell rings once and then the woods are still.
Something startles and rustles in the shed.
In the dooryard the pump has not been primed.
The axe stands rusting in its cleft.

The mortar in the chimney turns to lime.
The fence is down beside the meadow;
nearby an apple tree stands knotted,
a woodchuck hole opening in its root.

A catbird in gray patrols the field
from limb to stump to lilac bush in bloom.
The wooden plow bleaches in a patch
of herbs and weeds: alumroot

and larkspur, thistle, trailing vetch.
The sun is warm and curling, warping shake
and shingle, the cord of peeling wood
that musts to lichen near the gate.

Toadstools like coins are spent beneath the elm.
The window glass is dusty, dusty webs
travel the breeze and catch in every gust.
The forest ponders at the door.

The road moves west through trees toward the river,
the crossing barge, the pier, toward the sun
beginning now to fall beyond the current.
The bell rings twice and then the woods are still.

THE MILL

The mill grinds the night
into dark flours which the river wind
blows among the trees along its bank

like pumice or mist. A coon
or some other animal stirs darkness
into leaves and underbrush

as it burrows along the mill wall.
The stream, cascading down from its pitch
and fall, turns the night sounds

like a great wheel, drowns the moon
in turbulence. It rises there, the building,
between those pine tips that spear midnight

in the gully — rises and disappears
and reappears as the villagers,
in mufflers and shawls, come in a long line

for sacks of umbra to make their bread.
The line wavers along the streambed down
almost to the river. Their hands,

extended out of frost,
accept the starlight. They turn to walk
back to town and home,

for they have shadow now to sustain shadow.
And as the wind comes up it blows them to earth —
blows the mill itself into mist, all

but the great stone
which rolls into the lichen and fern
along the stream to be still until tomorrow.

THE ICE HOUSE

The walls are of rough plank.
Time melts slowly in the straw
without reflection —
it is like dwale in glass.
A pole with a hook hangs from a spike.

In the room where the saws are kept
silence is finely honed.
Beneath the floor it is damp and cool.
The still lives of the riverbank,
summer-hunted, burrow there.

Upstream an eagle sweeps the river;
a trumpet-vine snows into a gully.
A boat, frozen against the current,
lies near the field where a sledge
turns its runners into loam.

Summer seeps toward falls
recollected in eddies along the brink.
The hazes of August turn to mist
when the door is opened and closed
where winter is in keeping.

THE ROPEWALK

The building is a telescope of wood,
the sea a glittering eye looking from the east
through dusk toward the hills.

Before the open door at either end
a stanchion rises, a great rope
spun and wound about, between.

Beside the wharves the vessels
lie among the screels of gulls.
The rope is undone; its splayed end
lies where it was laid upon the boards.
Bales of hemp are stacked along the walls.

Light falls backward through the scents
of salt and fiber.
Stillness ravels as the tide
siles along the keel, beside the hull.

The sun rolls down the rocks above the shore:
the flare of flint and steel,
and in the dark the coiling fuse of time.

THE SCHOONER

Even as she slides down the ways
alga begins to green her planks.
Sunlight strikes through the early haze
into the gray-blue water.
There are gulls, and a ruffled pelican
perched on a bollard.
In the bay there are shapes
tremulous among groves of weed and seagrass.

Rust begins to take the anchor
and climb the chain.
The canvas seems cloudy;
the sun's edges fray on the deck.
In the fissures of a ledge anemones bloom.

There is smoke on the horizon
as she moves toward open water,
and as she passes fields and pastures
the plowing stops,
the horses sag in their traces,
the white houses begin yellowing like fall.

THE HOUSE

Upstairs there is a bed
among the spiders and the moonlit chairs,
the loveseats made of shadow.

The book on the table has leaves
brown as the elm's.
Its cover is of moss.

A pair of trousers blows in the draft
as though the legs were filled
with nothing more than webs.

Tables, spindle-legged, stand in the corners.
The carpets are worn to threads.
In at the window the owl asks and asks,
and the swift answers from the chimney.

THE SILO

Two great elms. Hills beyond them;
fields and a white hillhouse.
Windrows filled with snow,
the rest, hay stubble.
Silence rustles along the road.

The trees are set to snarl the air just so,
their limbs stark in the morning,
and in them the redbird rouses.

Through the mist of limbs
there is a silo with its gray barn:
a swallow climbs up the still air
with straw in its beak,
and another dives down
through the haze and a flock of sparrows.

In the hills there are feldspar and quartz,
colors dull as the leaves the wind has used.
The clouds, white as whey,
skim the firs, small animals
concerned with windfalls,
and the hawk in the spiral currents.

THE COVERED BRIDGE

The snow is thin and wet
under the early winter clouds.
The wind has fallen.
The river is gray in reflection.

Only one horse-and-wagon has passed
along the road since dawn:
the hoofprints are small wells,
and the wheel tracks follow like canals —

they stop at the bridge, at the sill
flush with the brink. The roof
interposes shadow and gingerbread
between heaven and rapids.

There are the chance of echo for a space,
bare boards, a suspension.
Morning looks into the passage.
On the other side the tracks begin again.

THE TOBACCO SHED

September comes smoking over the hills
to lie on the fields smoldering.
Dust puffs among dry stalks and weeds.
The sun is old fire upon the clouds.

In the shed August hangs
sere and golden,
leaves browning among the slatted walls.
Shadow is thick in the heavy air.

Swallows sew the murk among the beams:
leaves and feathers, chittering and veins,
the harvest waiting to be consumed
in the waiting clay, waiting

to be snuffed like August, September,
like the lamps in the drawing rooms
or on the masts of the ships at anchor,
like the candles in the shanties in the pinewoods.

THE STABLE

The morning in the windows smells blue.
Over the great door a horseshoe has been nailed,
its open end up so its luck won't run out.
There is straw in the stalls.

The nails have rusted;
one has broken, and the shoe tilts.
Boards have been slatted across
the panes of some windows.

Dew mists off the lawns and meadows,
clover and ivy.
There are thunderheads to the south,
cold gusts out of the north.

Somewhere the roans and grays are running,
early sunlight turning the dust saffron,
alfalfa and cotton forgotten for the race —

but not here where harness flakes
against the planks, the pitchfork
grows splinter-brittle;
not here where the morning blurs
and runs to sable in the spider's corner.

THE DEPOT

The rails pause barely to tie the horizons
where the wheatfields curve into day and night.
A wooden cart, long-handled and iron-wheeled,
stands in shadow under the baggage sign.
Dust settles in the road on the other side.

The great hand hides the small
on the face of the town hall tower.
Behind the ticket window grill
there is small disagreement:
the railroad's time depends and seldom falters.

A valise lies on the green bench
upon the platform:
the planks show their weathers.
A cicada buzzes in a cindered elm.
The door blisters and stands ajar.

A hawk whose shadow crosses the tracks
can see the pigeon's lighter gray
against the slate, the iron flue.
The dirt track follows the rails,
then turns north among the fields.

Houses diminish; now and then
a silo pierces the yellows and rusts.
There may be a thunderhead
somewhere at the edge of things.
There may be smoke and a thin sound.

THE TRESTLE

The rails shine like new wire
in the moonlight; the beams and girders
are a fretwork holding the hills.
The gorge holds darkness in cascade.

If a whistle lies like an echo
upon the prairie, among the stones
of the rising ground, it is perhaps an owl
or a coyote among the pines.

The wind hums in the frame.
A rock clicks and splashes,
sharp as silence in the starlight.
Something touches the tall grass

and curves again into the air.
On the high bluff a hump shifts,
then another and another —

the rails begin to sing in the wind;
there is a lowing; there are sparks
among the stars. Then the earth moves:
it is a dune of shadow

that makes the trestle shudder,
that fills the gorge
with the sound of avalanche,
hair, horn, bone and blood.

THE HOMESTEAD

In the morning there is the east wind
carrying dust the color
of a darker sun
past the silo and the cribs.

At dead noon there is a pause.
The land bakes into its ruts and rows.

Then again the wind blows,
now from the west, taking soil back
over the cupola with its rusting cock,
past the screen porch, its door swinging.
The horned toads clamber into rock.

In the evening the house settles
down into the red dark.
The plains and fields crool
beneath the windows' oblongs of light.

When even the echoes of echoes cease,
beneath sensation
there is a strange sound
like wet things sliding:
the ghost of a comber, a slimming off,
then again a comber.

From far back and down deep
there is the scent of salt
and a falling off from the silent edge.

THE STOCKYARD

The lake that looks like a sea
fades into the descending sky:
there is no horizon.
It is just dawn.
The city smokes into the clouds.

In the snags of the pens' rails
tufts of hair bristle at morning.
The earth is pitted, partly ice, partly dung.
It is difficult to discern shapes
except for breath like fog
rising out of the darkness.

The rails make oblongs and oblongs.
Somewhere a bell wakens
among the sheds and alleys, along the streets.
Upon the ramps there is a memory
of slow passage; there are mallets
that stand, heads down, on floors
the color of rust.

THE OBSERVATION TOWER

It has a black throat,
iron stairs ascending.
The stars scatter above the park below:
the mirror lake is a tarn
swallowing night.
The air is edgy and warm.

In a car stopped among the trees
a radio plays the blues.
The tower breathes a vapor
of perfume and planets.
The wind gusts, and there is a scent
of damp stone rising.

The rock face falls away from the brink
into maple and elm.
Along the road in the near distance
streetlamps and nighthawks descend toward town.
To the east the hills break,
and beyond them is the sea combing sand.

THE CHURCH

In the basement it is cool
among the tables, the small chairs,
the folding screens and crayons.
The lavatory is damp, the water runs;
there is room for webs and fables.

The wooden stair ascends and turns
into heat settled among the pews.
The altar rises above the golden oak
which dark juice has stained.
Frayed wine runs down the center aisle
away from the electric keys,
the hymnals with the broken covers.

Summer lies upon the step before the door,
beneath the white clapboards,
the pictures peeling from the glass.
The gate of pipe and wire stands ajar.

Next door the parsonage is scaled to dolls.
It takes the corner,
facing another neighborhood.
Six garages stand by a gravel drive.
A pear tree withers there, and on the curb
an elm like a cathedral stays alive.

THE BARN

Behind the locked doors
swallows stitch shadow to make
a sampler of perpetual dusk.
Summer's hull tilts against the wall.

A gray car looms into rust,
its doors closed against silence.
A rain of motes slants to fall
upon an iron stove cast in hay.

Wind leans through the window
from the fields beyond where,
dimmed by the spider's cataract,
sunlight wanes into goldenrod.

The stumps of the two great elms
have colored themselves in the barn's reflection.
The road passes.
Under the bank the brown river ebbs.

PROTHALAMION

And in the morning it is a wedding
of starlight and winter. Over the mountains
the cold sun breaks pine-limb, hardwood bough,
touches the moss against the bark
where snow levels away toward the downlands.
It is a wedding, then, here among the houses
where drifts have fallen off from ridgeline
into meadow, into streets and glowing windows,
where men stand behind glass to gaze into glass,
to feel an edge of steel against hair and flesh,
where women lie dreaming awake in their
morning linen. It is a wedding, then,
of linen and steel, of starlight and winter.
It is a wedding of moss and streets.

III. AUTUMN'S TALES

THE NEIGHBORHOOD

The houses are settling into their foundations.
On this block, the houses are settling
into the heat of their furnaces.
The snow settles on the roofs,
into the eaves, onto window sills.

In the houses there is a settling:
the windows go hollow,
the doors set single irons
into their jambs.

The night settles on the houses,
but there is something that arises
to go out to walk in the starlight.
It will not settle,
not even under the moon's great weight.

THE YARD

This year's garden is a series of ridges
frozen against the hedge.
A tricycle, forgotten on the lawn,
stands in the arrest of the season:
it rusts among exploded milkweed
as a blue-jay melts out of the sky, alights,
encircles the handlebar with silence.
Not even a wingstroke breaks
the wind rising and descending
to trifle with playthings — husk, seed,
the rag end of dusk.

If the night should come now
it would pin snow to spokes,
to the feathers of the jay,
to the garden which would blossom
with darkness and trailing frost.

THE TREES

They stand there
as the first snow comes to lie
among their roots.
In the afternoon some bird, ruffle-voiced,
had told a blue story among them.
They had not answered.

The wind winds up silence
which will hang from the limbs
like a summer kite.

A kite, worn thin by scraping
against the sky, rustles
along the prow of night:

It is a figurehead of tissue,
of soft wood, its ragged tail
caught in shadow, pulling darkness.

THE AUTOMOBILES

The storm seems to gather
from within the steel.

Their fires curbed,
the autos stare down the avenue
as night hunches along its highway
somewhere over the trees
winding its horn.

THE STREET

In the street the wind gutters, moving papers
and leaves into heaps or sworls.
The scraps of the year make some kind of pattern,
some calligramme of their own,
beyond the imprint of new snow.

Lightly, on the flourishes of silence,
on the heaps of leaf,
the snow touches and explores.
Finally, in folds of stillness,
flakes begin to form wrinkles of crystal.

By the time dusk deepens,
the wrinkles will be pure streams
drowning whatever is old.
Then, in the night, in the darkest hours,
the road will be a river of snow
aiming toward morning, lost at either end
in the curbs of vision.

THE POND

The pond at the edge of town
looks straight up.
Its hard gaze sees little more
than a hard sky looking down.
A brow of old lilies
wavers at the edge of storm.
Then the first flakes
begin to build a cataract of crystal
across the eye of daylight;
the wind and the blind night
come touching through lily stalks.

THE FENCES

In the pastures the wind walks
browsing beside the fence.
Snow falls among the weeds
that talk together in an unknown language.
The fences parse this tongue.
The farmhouse lies beside the great barn,
ruminative in the early falling,
its chimney rolling up gray against gray.
The doors are closed,
the fields are closed and silent
except for rumors between siftings.
Soon the imprints of cattle hooves
will be small pools of white.

Later, the fences will cut through dusk
as though they were knives with white edges.

THE VALLEY

Seen from the side of this hill
the valley and the river go
together along the ridges into the woods
where the river disappears, where the forest
eats the river and the snow
comes blowing now out of the dusk whitely,
the valley turning white, the river gray
between the flakes falling, the snow and the blue,
hard blue of the river blending into gray,
eating the valley, its river,
eating the snow and, behind,
the night watching from a darkening hill.

THE VISTA

As the storm comes now like a cage of dark air,
the snowflakes fall before it:
they have been frightened by nothing
into their descent.

The trees are filled with small cries.
The avenue becomes a river of still forms.

The cars are trapped in frost fire;
the eye of a pond witnesses what it can
before the cataract steals its sight.
Houses settle into their yards,
farms into their fields and fences.
The hills rise over the valley,
and the river is lost.

The Compleat Melancholick
1985

Being a Sequence of

Found, Composite, and Composed

POEMS

based largely upon

Robert Burton's

The Anatomy of Melancholy

In order to avoid Melancholy, Robert Burton says in his *The Anatomy of Melancholy* (1628), one "May apply his mind, I say, to Heraldry, Antiquity, invent Impresses, Emblems; make Epithalamiums, Epitaphs, Elegies, Epigrams, Palindromes, Anagrams, Chronograms, Acrosticks upon his friends' names; or write a comment on Martianus Capella, Tertullian's Cloak, the Nubian Geography, or upon Aelia Laelia Crispis, as many idle fellows have assayed; and rather than do nothing, vary a verse a thousand ways with Putean, so torturing his wits, or as Rainnarius of Luneberg, 2,150 times in his Proteus Poeticus, or Scaliger, Chrysolithus, Cleppisius, and others, have in like sort done."

THE COMPLEAT MELANCHOLICK
out of Burton

"Of seasons of the year,
the Autumn is most melancholy."
Then lovers lie within their sheets,
thoughts winding among their separations,
dreaming of darknesses chill enough
"to refrigerate the heart —

"windy melancholy,"
cholick of leaves and limbs, of owlcry
and blue hound moaning at the sky.
"Some persons think that every star's a world,
and call this earth of ours an obscure
star, presided over by the least of

"gods." The lovers dream of
"phrenzy, ecstasy, revelations,
visions, enthusiasms," these
demons of the blood. "The Talmudists say
that Adam had a wife called Lilis,
before he married Eve, &

"of her he begat no
Thing but Dyvils. These unclean spirits
settled in our bodies, and now
mixed with our melancholy humours, do
triumph as it were, and sport themselves
as in another heaven.

"Cauls, kells, tunicles, creeks"
are their changelings for our desires. "By
their charms they can draw down the moon
from the heavens." The lovers? — they lie to
wish. "This humour of Melancholy
is called the Devil's Bath." You

least of Gods, this is
a petty Hell: These solitary
pallets beneath the falling moon.
I conjure you, with little charm, "Bring their
sweethearts to them by night, upon a
goat's back flying in the air."

ROOTS

So by little and little, by that shoeing-horn of idleness, and voluntary solitariness, Melancholy, this feral fiend, is drawn on & as far as it reaches its branches toward the heavens, so far does it plunge its roots to the depths beneath — Burton.

  The stars rattle the window
  like hailfire. I am smoking
brier. Nothing needs to be said.
    If I were a planet
  I would be hollow. Beetles

  would scutter in my skin. They
  would loosen sandgrains to fall through
my dry thoughts. Perhaps an ember
    out of my volcanic
  days, forgotten at the heart,

  would give off a puff of sharp
  vapor at the oddest moment.
I would roll. It would be enough
    to seek sleep, blind in my
  inwardness to the outward

  void, ignoring the faint tug
  of the star. I would describe my
circle not as a reflection
    in space, but as a dark
  sphere where I am contained, which

      I contain. At the center
    of what cannot be, I would live
giving dream. A corona should
         ripple like water in
a cavern; minerals would rise

    and descend like awls — like teeth
    of stone waiting for light to shine
them awake. Anything falling
        would echo forever
   like hailfire and glass.

THE MENU OF MELANCHOLY
out of Burton.

These do generally ingender gross humours
        and windy bile, fill "all those inward parts
    with obstructions: Beef, goat's flesh (a filthy beast,
and rammish); hart & red deer hath an evil name,
        it yields gross nutriment, next unto horse";

all venison is melancholy, and begets
        bad blood; hare breeds incubus; conies are
    of the like nature; pork "may breed a quartan
ague." All fish are discommended, for they breed
        "viscosities, slimy nutriment, lit-

"tle and humourous nutriment; eel, tench, lamprey,
        crawfish; all fish, that standing pools and lakes
    frequent, yield bad juice and nourishment, dried, soused,
indurate fish, as ling, fumadoes, red herrings,
        sprats, stockfish, haberdine, poor-John; all shell

"fish, conger, sturgeon, turbot, mackerel, skate. Amongst
        fowl, peacocks and pigeons, all fenny fowl
    are forbidden, as ducks, geese, swans, herns, cranes, coots,
waterhens, with all those teals, shel-
        drakes and peckled fowls." Among herbs: "Gourds, cow-

"cumbers, coleworts, melons, cabbage; all raw herbs and
              sallets breed melancholy blood; roots &
         sole food are windy and bad, or troublesome
to the head; as onions, garlick, scallions, turnips,
                 carrots, radishes, parsnips. All manner

"of fruits" are forbidden, "as pears, apples, cherries,
              plums, strawberries, nuts, medlers, 'serves, sweetings,
         pearmains, pippins, grapes & figs. All pulse are naught:
beans, pease, fitches, &c." — they fill the brain with gross
                 "fumes, breed black thick blood," cause troublous dreams. Of

"spices: Pepper, ginger, cinnamon, cloves, mace, dates,
              honey and sugar; all aromatics,
         all sharp & sour things, luscious & oversweet,
or fat, as oil, vinegar, verjuice, mustard, salt;
                 bread of baser grain, as pease, beans, oats, rye,

"or overhard baked, crusty & black, oats and corn.
              All black wines; overhot, compound, strong drinks,
         as Muscadine, Malmsey, Alicant, Rumney,
Brown Bastard, Metheglin, Cyder & Perry. Beer
                 overnew or over stale, over strong

"or not sod, that smells of the cask, sharp or sour —
              it frets and galls because of the hop." And
         compound strong dishes beyond these simples: "Puddings
stuffed with blood, baked meats, soused, indurate meats fried &
                 broiled; condite; milk, and all that comes of milk,

"—cheese, curds; all cakes, simnels, buns, cracknels, made with
    butter, &c.; fritters, pancakes.
pies, sausages, & those several sauces, sharp
or oversweet." And waters last: "Standing waters,
    thick & ill-colored, such as come forth of

"pools and moats, where hemp hath been steeped or fishes live,
    are most unwholesome, putrefied, full of
mites, creepers, slimy, muddy, unclean, corrupt,
impure." All are windy, full of melancholy.
    Shun them by dawn and dusk, by dark and light.

THE AUTHOR OF MELANCHOLY

...idleness, (the badge of gentry),..the bane of body and mind, the Nurse of Naughtiness, Stepmother of Discipline, the chief Author of all Mischief, one of the Seven Deadly Sins...the Devil's cushion, as Gualter calls it, his pillow and chief reposal. — Burton.

    I have put on my badge, and I repose me
upon this pillow beside my gross Familiar.
        My Nurse attends me — coffee, mead, or bile?
            I am in good Humour.

      The room grows close with folk: Stepmother waddles
among the lamps, tobacco thick as bats. Gualter
        and Burton hover above the Author,
            bid him take but little

    notice of the Nurse — or, better — none at all.
"Aquarius saddens the now turned year: The time
        requires, and the Autumn breeds it." One's arse
            begins to itch, digits

    cramp; Stepmother leaves the room. Burton suggests,
"They wear their brains in their bellies, and their guts in
        their heads," these revelers in idleness:
            "Who can drink most, and fox

    "his fellow soonest?" I belch and nudge my pen.
The Seven Sins dance slyly through my spheres. My tongue
        is thick, my ink stumbles among these leaves,
            "somniferous potions,

    "knots, amulets, words, philters. They that stutter
and are bald will be soonest melancholy, by
        reason of the dryness of their brains." I
            can no longer see, nor

    may I breathe, so thick has grown the air with these
bleak phantasms of the skull. "Circumforanean
        Rogues and Gipsies ride in the air upon
            a coulstaff out of a

    "Chimney-top." Enow! I will be idle hence,
though "the mind can never rest, but still meditates
        on one thing or other; except it be
            occupied about some

    "honest business" — one cannot be a common
Scrivener of Verse. "My mind of his own accord
        it rusheth into Melancholy." The
            Devil take his repose.

BLOOD DEEPER THAN NIGHT

...he is born naked, and falls a-whining at the very first, he is swaddled and bound up like a prisoner, cannot help himself, and so he continues to his life's end. —Pliny, as quoted by Burton.

Where have these strangers come from,
        those who cannot sleep?
    This is the bone of one
and the flesh of another.
    I hold them in my hand
like ivory and velvet.

They are clothed in blood deeper
        than night in the glass.
    They walk about, utter
what I cannot hear. They sink
    and rise. Their substance is
runic — parchment turned to smoke.

They chant in the vein; they tell
        lyrics out of plasm.
    The temple is groined where
they read without light. Under
    the palm they are silent
among their dark alphabets.

When will these strangers walk down
        into my waking?
    This is the word of one,
the silence of another.
    I hold them in my palm
like parchment and ivory.

THE MOON OF MELANCHOLY
...a silly country fellow...killed his ass for drinking up the moon, that he might restore the moon to the world. — Burton.

    It was late when they came in
       through the gate. He dismounted
beside the water trough, and the donkey
    dropped its nose into the moon to drink.

    He stood fatigued underneath
       the wind scudding high cloud. No
light beyond reflection lit the windows
    of the house. The barn soughed. The long grass

    of the fields grew longer in
       shadow laid over shadow.
The journey had taken forever. For
    as long as it takes to remember,

    he forgot where he had been,
       and then recalled again. He
closed his eyes, listened to the beast drinking,
    and was afraid, suspended

    in the stillness of his mind.
       When he looked again, when wind
had become too hollow against silence,
    he found his eyes were opened,

      but still he could not see. His
      animal had drunk the moon
out of the water. He tried to discern
    clouds, moon, sky, stars, the edge of the wind,

      but found there a well into
      which he felt himself to be
sinking. It was a vortex no world
    could withstand. In the morning he wept

      over the animal that
      had carried him home; he wept
in the sun that had risen with him. He
    remembered the image of

      bone, restored as the blade sank
      homing: The moon floating in
the trough of water and blood, and the wind
    not quite too hollow to bear.

THE SYMPTOMS OF MELANCHOLY
— *out of Burton*

    "Some signs are secret, some manifest, some
        in the body, some in the mind;
and diversely vary, according to the
    inward or outward causes: Some laugh,
            some weep, some sleep, some dance, some

    "sing, some howl, some drink, they are lean, withered,
        hollow-eyed, look old, wrinkled, harsh,
much troubled with wind, and a griping in their
    bellies, or belly-ache, belch often,
            dry bellies; hard, dejected

    "looks, flaggy beards, singing of the ears, ver-
        tigo, lightheaded, little or
no sleep, & that interrupt, terrible and
    fearful dreams — continual sharp &
            stinking belchings, as if their

    "meat in their stomack were putrefied, or
        that they had eaten fish; absurd
& interrupt dreams, phantasmal visions
    about their eyes, vertiginous, cold
            sweat, apt to tremble, & prone

"to venery; palpitation of the
 heart, a leaping in many parts
of the body, a kind of itching; fixed eyes
 and much twinkling of their eyes — they are
  very red-faced; they stutter

"most part; headache, a binding heaviness;
 much leaping of wind about
the skin, as well as stutting, or tripping in speech;
 hollow eyes, gross veins, & broad lips. To
  some too, if they be far gone,

"mimical gestures are too familiar,
 laughing, grinning, fleering, murmuring,
talking to themselves, with strange faces,
 inarticulate voices, excla-
  mations, &c. And

"though commonly lean, hirsute, uncheerful
 in countenance, withered, and not
so pleasant to behold — dull, heavy, restless,
 yet their memories are most part good, they
  have happy wits, excellent

    "apprehensions. They cannot sleep, they have
        mighty and awful watchings; they
do not eat much, yet they are lean, ill liking,
    troubled with costiveness, crudities,
            oppilations, spitting. Their

    "pulse is rare & slow, except it be of
        the 'carotides,' which is very
strong. Their urine is most part low colored &
    pale, not much in quantity, and their
            melanchooly excrements,

    "in some very much, in others little,
        as the spleen plays his part, and thence
proceeds wind, palpitation of the heart, short
    breath, plenty of humidity in
            the stomack, heaviness of

    "heart, & heartache, & intolerable
        stupidity and dulness of
spirits; their excrement or stool hard, black to
    some, & little. If the liver, heart,
            spleen, brain, be misaffected,

"as usually they are, diseases
        accompany, as Incubus,
Apoplexy, Epilepsy, Vertigo,
    those frequent wakings and terrible
                dreams, intempestive laughing,

"weeping, sighing, sobbing, bashfulness, blushing,
        trembling, sweating, swooning. All their
senses are troubled, they think they see, hear, smell
and touch that which they do not," as who
                does not, come dream or waking?

BALSAMUM APOPLECTICUM*

From John Quincy's Pharmacopoeia Officinalis Extemporanea, Or, A Complete English Dispensatory, in Four Parts. London: Thomas Longman, at the Ship in Paternoster Row, 1742, pp. 504-505.

"Take the distill'd Oil of Cinnamon,
    Cloves, Lavender, Lemons,
   Marjoram, Mint, Rue, Rosemary"
[if you would enjoy a calming down],

"Sage, Rhodium, and Wormwood, of each
    12 drops; of Amber, 6
   drops; Bitumen Judaicum,
2 drams; Oil of Nutmegs by Expression, 1

"ounce; Balsam of Peru, as much as
    is sufficient to make
   all together into a smooth
Balsam" [if you would enjoy a coming

down]. "This warms and enlivens the Nerves
    being either smell'd to
   or rubbed upon the Temples, or
any other convenient Part" [or

convening Part, unlike the Temples];
    "it does much good also
   to paralytic Limbs, by rubbing
them well with it. It has been in

"mighty Esteem and Fashion to wear
      it in little Ivory Boxes
   and Cane Heads; but it has in such
respects given place to more modish

"Contrivances" [couches, capsules]. "In
      Distempers of the Head
   and Nerves it is likewise directed
to be given inwardly from

"3 to 6 drops in a Bole or an
      Electuary." [If,
   indeed, after Visions, Love and
Hours, you would enjoy a common Down.]

---

*Apoplexy, in the sense used here, is a fit of violent rage. Balsam is any of various aromatic resins, including balsam of Peru, containing measurable quantities of cinnamic and / or benzoic acid, or the esters thereof. The recipe is for a sedative.

EMERALDA
*To any man who finds it equally easy to chop up a live dog and a live lettuce
I would recommend suicide at his earliest convenience.* — Konrad Lorenz.

       It was difficult. I was starved,
       of course, but still I found it hard,
       for I had raised her from a seed.
For moral reasons, I am a carnivore,
and in palmier days, before the game had gone,

       I shared my ample store with her.
       Before her germination was
       assured, I fed her one small fly.
Her roots ate gratefully into the carcass,
and she began to sprout. Later, she had a frog

       I carved for her. Such gratitude!
       Her tender leaves began to come
       to a head: I formed the humus
about her base and butchered her a guinea
pig, a cat, and then a dog — this latter at

       some risk, for it fought back. But at last
       I chopped it up and fed it to
       my pet, my greeny pet, my great
green love, my Emeralda, larger than life.
At last she grew so grand, importunate, nothing

would do except a chimpanzee.
I stalked one for hours, and it was
quite clever. It defecated
on me from the treetops. But I was cagey
too, and I cornered it at last. It did not fight,

but offered me its throat. It smiled.
I could not understand that smile,
yet I made it another one,
farther down, upon its throat. Emeralda
flourished, as did the bond between us. Then the game

began to grow scarce and scarcer.
The chimpanzees went first — the trees
were lorn at branch and root: dogs
raised their legs no longer. The cats prowled to search
for the dogs, the guinea pigs for the cats. The frogs

stopped grumping in the swamp. The flies
missed the sound — they went hunting for
the sticky tongues, and dearth came down
to settle on my plot. It was sorrowful —
but I was starving. I've managed to choke her down,

my Emeralda, may the Gods forgive me.

MELANCHOLY'S HERBAL

What a pother have authors made with Roses! What a racket they have kept! I shall add, red Roses are under Jupiter, damask under Venus, white under the Moon, and Provence under the King of France. — Culpepper.

There are others: Black Hellebore, being an herb of Saturn,
    (It is no marvel) is a sullen plant. If taken raw,
    it is safer to purify it "by the art of the
alchymist." It is specified against all Melancholies,
        quartan agues and madness. "The root consisteth
    of numberless black strings all united into one head."

Balm is an herb of Jupiter, under Cancer. Used as "an
    electuary with honey," it drives out "troublesome
    cares," thoughts blooming darkly out of Melanchly or black
choler. It "causeth the mind and heart to be merry," expels
        "those melancholy vapors from the spirits and
    blood which are in the heart and arteries," deep-rooted.

Hops are martial, under the dominion of Mars, that hot-blooded
    planet. They may be "profitably given in long and
    hot agues that rise in fever and blood." Despite its name,
Sow-Fennel (Mercury under Virgo) is indicated
        in cases of "lethargy, frenzy, giddiness
    of the head," its juice mixed with vinegar or rosewater.

Borage and Bugloss are Jupiter's, under Leo. "The leaves,
 flower, and seed," given as cordials, "expel pensiveness
 and Melancholy" if used green. How they strengthen Nature!
Endive is a "fine, cooling, cleansing, jovial plant." It is
 recommended for "faintings, swoonings, and passions
of the heart." It is conducive to the best of Humours.

But those Roses! — what a pother and racket! What elixirs
 and compounds: "Sugar of Roses, Syrup of dry Roses,
 and honey of Roses!" Rose vapor — rosewater cast on
a hot fireshovel and inhaled. Rose hips, rosepetals plucked
 or crushed, fit for all Melancholies: Provence spread
 like damask under Venus, tapestries beneath the Moon!

THE DESERT OF MELANCHOLY
They have myriads in their mouths. — Burton.

    It is not far from here to
nowhere. Merely across the furniture.
       We are experiencing
technical difficulties; please

    do not adjust. If there were
ink in this pen, it would be different.
       However, it is not. This,
then, is a poem written among

    furniture, on paper like
a glass screen, pen like a stainless steel steak
       knife. It is a poem made of
mirrors. In it you will see, if

    you look technically, small
creatures dancing on the head of a pin —
       any number of them: I
have myriads in my mouth. They

    do not know that they are there —
no more than we know they are watching us.
       Well, quite a charming place, this,
wherever: Chairs, tables, the smell

   of meat in the air. No one
will wonder at this devastation of
    syllables. Who is to be
  awed? It is my devastation,

   and I am past wonderment.
It is at this point precisely that the
   cactus must resume blossom.
  If it does not, words will have no

   point. Expect nothing. You will
be disappointed in other things. The
   desert does not flower.
  It is the flower that flowers.

THAT PARTICULAR AIR
How come they to dig up fish bones, shells, beams, iron-works, many fathoms under ground, & anchors in mountains far remote from all seas? — Burton.

      The hook has let go,
    and the Conestoga
has rolled down the cliff, along
with the television set. All
        the women sorrow,
      for their struggle has

        been for nothing, which
      they have achieved. The men
do not give up. They have yet
to understand that the wagon
        train will not get through.
        Of course, the wagon

      train will not follow
    the Tube, it will follow
the script; the prairie schooners
will reach California. There,
        the women will gaze
      at the Pacific

      Ocean; glance, with that
    particular air, at
each other, at their men; they
will lie down to have the children
        who sit on the shore:
      "You owe to yourself
      your own destruction."

WINTER IN MUSCOVY
In Muscovy...they live in stoves and hothouses all winter long. — Burton.

    Open any grate, any glass gate
    on a street of cast iron or glass,
and someone will say, "Hello," out from between
flames or fronds, white teeth smiling in a soot face:
A flowerchild, an elder or alderman,
        a young lady in pince-nez

    with a pot-belly, tendrils in her
    hair — "Hello, come in, enjoy, enjoy
'may-games, Wakes, and Whitsun-Ales!'" All winter long
in their stoves they make feast with "rare devices
to corrivate waters, musick instruments,
        & trisyllable Echoes,

"again, again, & again repea-
    ted [ted ted] with myriads of such."
But if ye be melancholick, enter not,
nor lay thine eyes longing on these revelers —
"Let them freely feast, sing and dance, have their Puppet-
        plays, Hobby-horses, Tabers,

    "Crowds, Bag-pipes, play at Ball, and Barley-
    breaks — an Index of Ignorance — let
them go as they are in the Catalogue of
Ignoramus, snorting on a bulk," although
"nothing can be more excellent and pleasant,
        so abstruse and recondite,

"so bewitching, so miraculous,
so ravishing, so easy withal
& full of delight" as these baubles of stove-
dwellers, inhabitants of glass houses,
these multifarious "Martian amulets,
    Weapon Salve, Universal

"Balsams, strange extracts, Elixirs of
Life," 'cause that's not where It's at; let one
take heed he do not overstretch his wits and
    make a skeleton of himself.

STONE AND SHADOW

...many cannot sleep for Witches and fascinations, which are too familiar in some places.... — Burton.

    It is as still as falling
        in this house of weathers.
Nothing but lamplight and the shadow of my hand
    lie along the page. The clock
        owns everything.

    I have been dreaming of the
        woman. She has faces
to burn. The day's fire is black upon the flagging.
    I listen for wind within
        the flue; there is

    only the dark sound of coals
        rising to enter night
smoking over the rooftree. Still, the woman is here
    under towels — or standing
        in a wardrobe

    among sleeves and lapels.
        I see her eyes clearly
between the strokes of an hour. She is of a size
    and a certain shape. She has
        loved me in time.

    Logs lie at the hearth between
        four dark chimes. I would know
her, for it is said, "She sees within the stone beneath
    the shadow." She is shadow.
        And I am stone.

FAILED FATHERS
On a theme by, and with apologies to, Greg Pape.

    Where do all the failed fathers
go? To Albuquerque? Cleveland?
After the slow slide down the drain,
    where do they go? After the last
lay-off, the class reunion where they're shown

    kissing the matronly Queen
of the Prom, where do they go. Where
do they go, these old young men, these
    paunchy guys with the eyes that squint
into the lens at the family picnic,

    the fishing expedition
near the falls, the baseball game where
they played second? After the fights,
    the money fights, the brief affair,
after the spree and the morning after,

    where do the failed fathers go?
Is there a bar where they gather,
is there a bus they all take,
    is there a line at the Bureau
where they talk over their sons and daughters,

  their Old Ladies turning cold,
  the milkmen they caught spending time
  drinking coffee in their kitchens?
  Is there a motel in Cleveland
full of fathers playing poker,

   smoking cigarettes, squinting
  at their hands, drinking beer? Is there,
  down in Albuquerque, some street
  full of walk-up rooms full of dreams
of mowing lawns, of paneling basements,

   propping children on their bikes,
  walking down the aisles of markets
  pushing shopping carts? Of course, we
  know what happens to our mothers,
but where oh where do the failed fathers go?

THE MANDARIN OF MELANCHOLY

Their Lau-sie, Mandarins, Literates, Licentiates, and such as have raised themselves by their worth, are their noblemen only,... — Burton.

    He is the Mandarin of silence:
  The wind, drawing through the trees, breathes easily,
though this is no light burden. Here, where mountains
        curl into forests; here, now,
                the wind rests, and mists twist
                    among the boulders.

    Half a bird sings in half a tree. A
  half stroke of rain runs down the mist, the cliff,
into what remains of any universe
        but this. Watching, there is no
                sight; listening, there is
                    no sound beyond this.

A FIN FOR THE MELANCHOLICK'S THOUGHTS

We are all prisoners. What is our life but a prison? We are all imprisoned in an island. — Burton.

      Denuded by the
      desert sea that swells
      and bowls these freshman
combers over inkwells, this winter beach
is clear now for a fortnight. The students
have washed home for the holidays. They swim
      within grottos and
      nets of motherly
      arms. Here and there, a

shell of an office lies stranded upon
the sand, inhabited by a hermit
crab or glued to silence by an eyeless
      jellyfish. Each of
      us — sea urchin or
      flounder — conjures dreams
of capes and codfish in the southern East;
boats and beaches we may never see, where
the sand is unlettered. Where dunes are not

                    cumbered with runes of
                    an Anglo-Saxon
                    origin. We smell
coastal forests whose heaps of leaf need no
correction. There, night spells daylight, and owls
wisely allow cotton mouths and copper
                    heads right of access
                    to marshland inlet,
                    swamp, and bog. Decay,

like a tidal stream, goes slowly there. There
is always new growth. Death wants no doctor
or master where life cures or kills and will
                    not cheat. There's a half-
                    moon-ebb till the fish
                    reschool. Let all old
seahorses squat back on scaling tails, mud
puppies scan aquarium shelves for leaks —
there's sand between our ears. And snakes, and owls.

THE GARDEN OF MELANCHOLY
What extraordinary virtues are ascribed unto plants! — Burton.

In the garden of odd seed, no
    weeds grow — or, if they do grow
        wild, row on row among
the blossoms of good plant and herb
    furrowed and furbelowed,

the beetles snub them. They crawl black,
    mandibles sawing among
        leaves, leaving speckled spoor
where they go. I care for them all —
    weed and beetle, poor old

plant, my trowel and hoe alive
    in the soil, sun drumming
        upon stone, rain in the
patch, wind quickening the nettle,
    lichen greying green moss,

everything springing, springing — "Priest
    Pintle and Rocket enliven
        the member; the Chaste-Tree
and Waterlily quench the sperm;
    some herbs provoke lust;

"others, as Chaste-Lamb, extinguish
	seed; Poppy causeth sleep, Cabbage
		resisteth drunkenness.
For the head, Aniseeds, Foalfoot,
	Betony, Calamint,

"Eye-bright, Lavender, Bays, Roses,
	Rue, Sage, Marjoram, Peony;
		for the lungs, Calamint,
Liquorice, Hyssop, Horehound,
	Water Germander; for

"the heart, Borage, Bugloss, Saffron,
	Balm, Basil, Rosemary,
		Violet, Roses; for
the stomack, Wormwood, Mints, Betony,
	Balm, Centaury, Sorel,

"Purslain; for the liver, Darthspine,
	Germander, Agrimony,
		Fennel, Endive, Succory,
Liverwort, Barberries; for the
	spleen, Maidenhair, Finger-

fern, Dodder of Thyme, Hop, the rind
	of Ash, Betony; for the
		kidnies, Grumel, Parsley,
Saxifrage, Plantain, Mallow; for the
	womb, Mugwort, Pennyroyal,

"Fetherfew, Savine; for the joints,
    Camomile, S. John's Wort, Rue,
      Organ, Centaury-the-
Less, Cowslips," each seedling and shoot
    finding roothold among

the darkling world's dark bones.

THE MELANCHOLICK ART

...no science, no school, no art, no degree; but, like a trade, every man in private is instructed of his master. — Burton.

I. The Conceit of Melancholy
      If your pen is a colt, freshly watered
    at the inkwell, and your pad of foolscap
lies before you like an undrawn map of open country;
      if you've fed your colt good provender:
  hay, oats, barley — a barnful of winter stores;

      if, I say, you've fed him well on what was
    raked and winnowed in the fall, likely you
will write some verses such as these. Outdoors, the pure meadows
      reach for the mountains. The colt can smell
  springtime, but you have him tethered just inside the

      barn. Will the yearling ride? No. Will he pull
    staidly at the phaeton? Not with grass
untasted in his world — not unbroken. Let the damn fool
      go! Let him whicker at clouds, let him
  moon and meander, then. He will be shod at last.

II. The Master of Melancholy
    It's like being haunted.
Something's in the air. I know it is.
I can almost feel it nip my nose,
    nibble my ear. If I reach out...,
        look! Tobacco smoke.

    Move a bit. There's a tree
on the lawn. I might write about that,
or the oriole nest hanging like
        Aphrodite's teat from one bough.
            That's not it, though. The

        lamp: Turn it off. Think hard
about shadows, shapes; the movement of
swamp ferns; how dinosaurs lie in mud
        but walk still. Nothing. Ideas
            rush for the nearest

        exit, but where's the flame?
There's a red engine clanging up the
next block. The hell with this. Perhaps I'll
        never write again. I'll go to
            bed. That always works.

A MEDICINE FOR MELANCHOLY

Tobacco divine, rare, superexcellent Tobacco, which goes far beyond all their panaceas, potable gold, and philosopher's stones, a sovereign remedy to all diseases. — Burton.

It ought to be a large old knot hole,
first of all, surrounded by most of the tree.
    Black inside, as though Hell had poked
    a smokestack out between your teeth.

Now, heave a wheeze downstem hard until
you've blown a beachful of igneous grains out
    into the bowl's bayou. Knock them
    onto your palm. Whistle them off

like a ruinous wind. The carpet
will thrive, grow lush as Virginia. Sit back.
    Knuckle off the roof of your root
    cellar where your tobacco, as

loamy as moss, masses and awaits
a spark's attack. Thumb up a balesworth; trammel
    it down deep into the devil's
    eye. Snatch up an eruption now

and spang! Puff a belly full of fumes.
Whoof! Off go angels and satyrs; clouds of them —
    furry thighs and messes of wings
    bearing you off like an orgy.

SOME FOOD FOR MELANCHOLY
Make a melancholy man fat, as Rhasis saith, and thou hast finished the cure.
— Burton.

Morning. The sun is a fried egg in a pastel
    spider.* Were it not for the fact that the world,
        today, is a summer meal, one might not
eat for a month. Seaweed: A garnishment for
the salad beach. Tongue of an ocean running
        gluttonously through teeth seemingly

reefs, ruining while renewing what it would chew.
    And Time, damn him, Time: The sadistic chef. He
        whose pendulum spatula flips our egg
over easy, never nicking the yolk, but
never truly serving it, either. You'd think
        it would burn. It does. Ogle it once:

It will turn the whites of your eyes to quicksilver.
    Let us not eat for a month. That old cook with
        a grimace of ice will not make gourmands
of gourmets. We can roast him first on the spit
of our minds. Imagination may make him
        howl with heat in his own oven, just

as Hansel and Gretel cindered the witch in her
    cookie house. We will savor, not salivate.
        But the hostel-mistress sea works her lewd
jowls with too much good humor, professional
of her lies. She and the chef run a public
        house. They know too well the public taste.

---

*A *spider* is a cast-iron skillet that stands on legs in the fireplace.

"I PRAY TO A GENITAL GOD"
A poem by Grace Schulman.

Such medicines are to be exploded that consist of words, characters, spells, and charms, which can do no good at all, but out of a strong conceit. — Burton.

    When I pointed out the pun
in her poem, she told me to be still.
It was no pun — in the panorama
of all her work there wasn't a single pun.
        She hated puns.

    She could no longer work, for
thinking of the pun. "Disruptive," she said,
"you're being quite disruptive." Rather than
rapture, she found but rupture now, a pun
        upon her page:

    "Cruel and inhuman pun-
ishment," she said, "to see where less was meant,"
but so much more than what I'd seen. She could
not write, not even punctuate. I must be
        more genital,

    compassionate, even blind
to the printed word, for what she meant was
holy — "My god!" she cried, "can't you at least
be a gentleman? The god I meant was Pan!"
        I bowed my head.

"I'm sorry," I said, "I saw
    you paging what was not there. I've caused you
        pain. I did not mean to pan the poem
you thought you wrote, nor even the one I saw.
            I shall be more

    "genteel in future, and if
        I see a pomegranate where you meant
        only a poem, granite I'll not see
on Shakespeare's tomb, the punography between
            his poignant lines.

    "I shall note the inscription only,
        done by the chiseler's hand when he was dead.
        To hell with language. I shall bear my soul
tiptoe among the tombs, hope to fall prey to
            a genital god."

THE AGE OF AQUARIUS

It is the age of Aquarius;
    Taurus is quit of it.
"Aquarius is the butlere of goddes
    and yeuyth them a water potte."
The bull is drowning in his labyrinth —

the sea has returned. The servant pours
    Earth's primal blood into
the earth. There is no way out. The Pleiades hiss
    like dying snakes in the libation.
"Thro' scudding drifts the rainy Hyades

vext the dim sea," and now the old Ocean
    swallows the little pigs
like sausages; Taurus gores the tide: "The butler
    done it." This is the age of waiters.
In the roaring kitchen there is much mirth:

The butler is making the maid. They
    have sacked the winecellar.
Aldebaran, the old baron, lies buried in
    the ooze under his castle. The bull
is afloat and cannot paw the black mud

      where glory lies buried. The Seven
          brilliant Sisters ride on
Taurus' back, weeping for darkness as the waters
          rise to his horns. Electra is lost.
      Atlas, the father, has grown old, and he

      has fallen. The world is adrift. Where
          is Pleione? — locked in
a turret, railing at her skies. The Water-
          Bearer has finished with the upstairs
      wench. He has eaten and drunk. He pisses

      down a drain hole, and the maid giggles.
          Urine mingles below-
stairs with the bull's last spuming breath. At last the house
          Is theirs — the butler takes another
      snort. He winks. "Shall we 'ave at 'er agyne?"

      The castle is adrift among the stars.

TAURUS SIRES AQUARIUS
For Christopher Cameron Turco, b. 23 January 1973, with reference to Burton.

It is anomaly and paradox: Somehow,
    Taurus has sired Aquarius, long,
        lank and fair. He has the father's mouth,
            the same chin, different color,
the original blood born into its own age
        in the first Decan of its Sign.

As "The Soul is an alien to the Body,
    a Nightingale to the air, a Swallow
        in an old house, and Ganymede in
            Heaven, an Elephant at Rome,
a Phoenix in India," just so are Father
        and Son — magnetic opposites.

For blushing "It is good overnight to anoint
    the face with Hare's blood, and in the morning
        to wash it with strawberry and cow-
            slip-water, the juice of distill'd
Lemons, juice of Cowcumbers, or to use the seeds
        of Melons, or the kernels of

"Peaches beaten small, or the roots of arum, and
    mixt with wheat bran to bake it in an oven,
        and to crumble it in strawberry-
            water, or to put fresh cheese curds
to a red face." This child is a nugget out of
        middle age, discovered against

odds and medicine; "digg'd out of that broody hill,
    belike, this goodly golden stone is, where
        the ridiculous mouse was brought to
            birth." Perhaps the Bull may drink now,
out of the Water-Bearer's cooling urn. "In the
    belly of a swallow there is

"a stone found called Chelidonius which, if it
    be lapped in fair cloth, and tied to the
        right arm, will cure lunaticks, mad men,
        make them amiable and merry."
Come, Bearer of Water, of Consciousness and God.
    On my arm, bear up your father.

MELANCHOLY LOVE
Every Lover admires his Mistress, though she be very deformed of her self,...
— Burton.

"...ill-favored, wrinkled, pimpled, pale,
red, yellow, tanned, tallow-faced,
have a swollen Juggler's platter-face, or a thin,
lean, chitty-face, have clouds in her face,
be crooked, dry, bald, goggle-ey'd, blear-ey'd,

"or with staring eyes, she looks like
a squis'd cat, hold her head still
awry, heavy, dull, hollow-eyed, black or yel-
low about the eyes, or squint-eyed, spar-
row-mouthed, Persean hook-nosed, have a sharp Fox

"nose, a red nose, China flat great
nose, snub-nose with wide nostrils,
a nose like a promontory, gubber-tushed,
rotten teeth, black, uneven, brown teeth,
beetle-browed, a Witch's beard, her breath stink

"all over the room, her nose drop
winter and summer, with a
Bavarian poke under her chin, lave eared,
with a long crane's neck, which stands awry
too, with hanging breasts, dugs like two double

"jugs, or else no dugs, bloody-fain
fingers, filthy long unpared
nails, scabbed hands or wrists, a tanned skin, a rotten
carkass, crooked back, she stoops, is lame,
splay-footed, as slender in the middle

"as a Cow in the waist, gouty
legs, her ankles hang over
her shoes, her feet stink, she breeds lice, a mere change-
ling, a very monster, an auf, im-
perfect, her whole complexion savours, an

"harsh voice, incondite gesture, vile
gait, a vast virago, or
an ugly Tit, a slugg, a fat fustilugs,
a long lean rawbone, a skeleton,
a truss," and though she look to another

"like a merd in a lanthorn, whom
thou hatest, loathest, and wouldest
have blown thy nose in her bosom, a dowdy,
a slut, a scold, a nasty, rammy,
rank, beastly, quean, obscene, bare, beggarly

"antidote to love," it would seem,
yet withal to her Lover
is she rather Mother-of-Pearl, not the grey
clam in brine; the sphere, never the neck;
she is stinking Venus on the half-shell.

THE MISTRESS OF MELANCHOLY

Let her head be from Prague, paps out of Austria, belly from France, back from Brabant, hands out of England, feet from Rhine, buttocks from Switzerland, let her have the Spanish gait, the Venetian tire, Italian compliment and endowments. — Burton.

    I have waited so long for all the mails to come —
    one box Tuesday, another Friday parcel post —
at last I can begin. My screwdriver at *en garde*,
        my mistress first shall get a head: Those perfect
Czechoslovak eyes, Dresden blue, staring up out of

    excelsior. Like so, the China throat upon
    the Athenian shoulders, soldered without seam.
Now the paps hung, tinkling Bach, upon the Gold Coast chest,
        coasting neatly down to the Riviera.
The thighs from Thailand, smooth as ivory; the Mound of

    Venus, straight from Pompeii, sloping invitingly
    between Scylla and Charybdis...the Spanish gate.
The kneecaps imported from Hanoi, shins from Vientiane;
        those Aryan toes they floated down the Rhine!
Turn her around to get at the Queensland calves: Clockwork

    bums stupendous in their art — one's heart goes running
    down to think of the chimes we'll have! Let me get your
back up, honey, this model from Brabant. And now these
        English hands go here, these Wedgewood hands upon
the Remington arms from the good old U. S. of A. —

O Leonardo! Thou shouldst be living at this hour!
My mistress hath 'tire to strike the Venetians blind!

"A SQUIS'D CAT" — BURTON

Louis Wain (1860-1939), a British artist, was internationally known for his drawings of cats, characterized by their almost human expressions and antics. In 1921 Mr. Wain suffered a brain injury in a motor accident, from which he never fully recovered. From that time — possibly as a result of his injury, possibly as an artistic experiment — his cats were transformed from recognizable household pets to creatures one might see in a nightmare. — Consuelo Reed.

         Melancholy kitty, nice pussy,
sweet pussy. Purr in a corner; lap up your
            milk. Swish your tail, lie on a rug.
    Pretty cat in a kitchen. Fur and nice
        eyes winking slowly, slowly. Go to

            sleep. Wake up, cat, your eyes are too bright,
a little. What dream was it that made your back
    curve that way around a queer corner? Your
            ears perk like crooked peaks. Hackles
        up, cat; scratch the wall of your saucer.

         Squis'd cat, electrical kitten,
symmetrics and fall apart. The paper
room will hold you in place. Triangular tongue
        sharp, not rough: Rakes the eyes, laps blackness
           from a spoon. Where do your whiskers

go? Now, cat, pussy in
a pail, snarl lines and sparks into my ear. My
    eyes wail all your pins and dots, my
tail does flash, flails behind thy riven head.
    My bowels dissolve,
                  dissolve bad puss;

    see, Fyre Catte,
                drink thy
                      nice
                          Night.

THE GOD OF MELANCHOLY: A RELIGIOUS TREATISE

...he is a rammy, fulsome fellow, a goblin-faced fellow, he smells, he stinks, he belches onion and garlic, how like a dizzard, a fool, an ass he looks, how like a clown he behaves himself! — Burton.

    His feet point inward at
90° angles. The world spins
       between His big toes. He squats
above it all so that the tallest peaks
       just barely miss His ass-

    hole. He waits. That's His job,
partly — waiting. And while He waits, things
       get better between His thick
toenails, perhaps. The President goes to
       China; Muhammad goes

    to the mountain, conquers
the ultimate crag, never even
       glimpses a hemorrhoid; Dick
puts it to Jane: His wife doesn't suspect
       a thing. But at last it's

    time. Deep in His bowels,
Melanchole senses the thin movement
       of gas. There is a small cramp
beneath His duodenum. A tremor
       passes along the San

Andreas Fault. Pressures
build. It is time: There is Agony
    in the Cosmic Expression.
Slowly, our nostrils in the blithe air, we
    begin to understand

    the essence of sulphur,
the quintessence of hopes digested.
    Along our valleys, brown fog
seeps out of the hills. China gags, believes
    it is the President's

    western odor. Boulders
dump Muhammad, and Dick's wife finds out.
    Were we not blinded, we would
understand Joy; were we without noses,
    we would serve no Purpose;

    could we but see beyond
our noses, we would relish delight
    between the toes, under His
cheek — for our Keeper is smiling; nay, He
    is laughing in Relief!

FAREWELL TO MELANCHOLY

It is most true, the style proclaims the man, our style bewrays us, & as hunters find their game by the trace, so is a man descried by his writings. I have laid myself open (I know it) in the Treatise, and shall be censured I doubt not, yet this is some comfort: our censures are as various as our palates. If I be taxed, exploded by some, I shall happily be as much approved & commended by others. — Burton.

If night is staining the window,
let the streetlight take care of it,
  washing it into the road
    with the neighbors' dreams.
It is March, unseasonably warm

in this garret where my clothes hang
about my shoulders. Music is
  sneaking out of the books and
    writhing in the last
cactus. The gerbil has died, but I

hear his wheel looming something in
and out of shadow. My father,
  whom the mouse has followed, casts
    a hard stare askance
out of his frame. He is young and

will not forgive me. I can feel
my words crinkle among his ash.
  The new Christbearer under
    me sleeps; the aging
wife, the pubescent girl. I have looked

    into the window and seen what
    the streetlamp can do with plain glass,
        quicksilver, the image of
          a human life, with
night and the past stored in beds, rooms, books,

        in words and silence.

NEW POEMS FROM THE SHIFTING WEB
1989

REFLECTIONS AT FORTY-NINE
for Jean

    Nothing is to be seen
in the pond water except alga
        and weed. The breeze is stiff,
    too stiff. The last leaves of summer
        float in ripple and eddy.

    In the dusty window
of the summer place the sun of dusk
        glimmers. But behind it
in the glass a shade passes, light
        trumps the eye. The sight winks out.

    The bedroom is deckled with moon.
Shadow undresses in the mirror —
        the heft of a thick man
in a thin frame. Night is sparing.
        The alarm keeps track of it.

    But there is your dark eye.
The image there is clear. The leaves turn
        on the iris, the lash
flickers. Yet no mistaking what
        we two see stealing away.

THE HABITATION

There is no way out.
Now the windows have begun
to cloud over: cobwebs, dust.
The stairs and floors are unstable —
the hours nibble the foundations.

In the bedrooms, sheets
have begun to yellow, spreads
to fray. Coverlets have worn
to the colors of late autumn,
thin as a draft sifting at the sill.

On the kitchen floor
crumbs and rinds lie recalling
the old feasts. In the larder
preserves rust among speckled jars;
the bins yawn; shadow sates the cupboards.

The fire has been damped
at the hearth: its bed of ash
sinks in pit-holes over brick.
The ceiling snows on the carpet —
Rejoice! Rejoice! The house is failing!

VIGILANCE

You stand waiting. You listen.
At your back the house is still,
between the tickings of clocks and timbers.
Beneath the rough soles of your feet
you can feel the cellar stretching to its foundations —
silence in the stone, the furnace brooding.

Shades are partly drawn against
the night. The panes are harder
than ice and as cold. Were you to touch them
they would shatter or seal you in.
The scent of dust is scattered in the air. The breathing
of the stairwell is a deep cascade. Now.

It will happen now: The knob
will turn, the tooth of the lock
take a strain in the cheek of the door where
it is set. You do not ask, "Who
is it?" It makes no mind; it is the wind of autumn,
the winterchase, the sky of change. The hours

flatten on the walls where you
have pinned them; you sense their weight
dragging in their frames against the wire.
A flake of plaster sifts onto
the carpet stretching like a lane of leaves along the
hall. You listen to the respiring rooms

        where youth is dreaming age, where
            aging sleeps. And you patrol,
       you walk the hours listening to nibs scraping,
            paper rattling, clocks marking. You
    watch the knobs revolve, the windows shake, and in the flue
        you hear the cinders rustling to the grate.

THE GIRL YOU THOUGHT YOU LOVED

    Open the trunk: She is there,
  breathing — the girl you thought you loved.
These are her eyes, a pair of opals
      in a twist of tissue.

    This is her heart, this dogged
  valentine knocking at the chest.
Who is she — who have you been, and where,
      and when? The spider locks

    its web across this clock, this
  pendulum moving in the lace
billowing like her hair. The ticking
      of her bones on a bed

    is ragged in the skull. Here
  is her scent: Dust in an attic,
a wasp buzzing. A sack of marbles
      rolls out the times of love.

ATTIC POEM

This is already old. When you find these pages
they will be brown as autumn. The ink
will look like bottled shadow etched
on a leaf. The attic room in which I write

will stand in these words only, if it stands, if it
ever stood. I see myself as I am now
as through an hourglass telescope reversed,
the falling sand turning the sight grainy

as a curled photograph: The man writes
in his house by the lake, in rainy weather,
his family asleep below — the two crones
and the ancient boy, his trucks scaled to rust.

That love is dead; all the trees are leaving.
It is spring, it is the fifth spring
since I was that other
not dreaming of a son:

It was as though he were a hollow fang
filled with midwinter and night. The bed was sweaty.
The ache was solid, without a sharp center.
He marveled that so much pain could keep him alive.

Sand is filling the attic room.
Leaves are turning in the night.
That love is dead, twice dead.
Darken it now. Close the book.

A DAUGHTER MOVES OUT
for Melora.

    She has left
her posters on the wall.
The phone lies overextended on
    the floor, humming: its
      black panel is gone;
        it shows its coils.

    There are dust
bunnies under the bed.
The books on the yellow shelves study
    the color brown — an
      uncertain shade tilts
        against the sun

    falling down
into the winter lake.
Who, though, is this in the closet, hung
    from a rack, his slit
      eyes lidded in the
        gloaming? Is it

    the specter
of the prom-watcher, ghost
of the dawn-waiter, the hanger-on?
    Yes, it is he who
      clutches at glass, sand
        siling out from

                beneath his
           feet, between his dry toes
        into the lower cone. Let him wear
              shadow, let him hang
                 on for a while.

CANCER
for John, in memoriam.

We did not know, then, what the wen
   was on his heel. The gulls wheeled
in the summer sun, the combers
     broke and broke; the sand siled.
   On the beach the grandchild ran
   and stopped, dug wells, ran again

while the old man slept in a round
   shadow cast against the light.
The old wife dreamed beside his dream,
     wound in a shawl, as shade
   fretted the edge of waking.
   But all the while, as the tide

pulsed, moving by moments toward
   the drying seaweed of high
water, through the web of his veins
     the crab sidled, stalking.
   The day was perfect, then. Now
   a sea-change has taken it;

rather, it has become two days,
   that fair one and another
in which sandworms rise from the child's wells,
     segmented, mandibled.
   The beach umbrella sends its shade
   casting over the rising surf

to meet the east wind. The seabed
   is calm and murderous with
life. The boats toss like dreams, their nets
      seining the undertow.
   Now the ocean is almost
   upon us — our eyes are stars

   with spines; our minds are eight-armed; they
grope and coil in the darkness of the sun.

THE RECURRING DREAM
for Luigi, in memoriam.

I seek my father — that minister
of the deep — among the furniture
    of my childhood. I step out of waking
  into this room and know
that time has passed. The windows are webbed
  and moonstreaked. A lamp with a glass shade,

  green and saffron, burns
on a brass stem. The bookcases hold sermons
    and silence. My aquaria
  stand among tumbled
tomes and testaments. The dust rises
  into the amber darkness.

  I disturb a desert of hours,
search for the fish that glide
    in musty waters — blue scales
  glint under my glance,
their eyes are corals budding
  among rusty blades of sea grass

and swordplants. I remove the glass lids
and dip my hand into the water —
    it is what I have feared:
  shadow of a shadow, dim air
flowing from corner to corner.
  The fish rise along the curtains

to swim about me in the air,
their black fins wavering.
    I dig in the gravel stranded
   among the shelving,
the decaying books. I dig,
   and here, in the root

   of the largest plant, blooming
from a socket of bone, I find my father
   where he has scuttled,
at last to be brought back, smiling.

CORRAL
for Christopher

   When you were small I lay awake at night
      and dreamt of how I loved you
sleeping beyond the wall of lath and plaster,
      flesh and bone and blood that lay between us.

   Now you're grown. Now, in half a year, you've gone
      from spore to weed taller than
the man who fathered you, the sire who lies
      dreaming his waking fictions of the dark —

   that hobby horse of old, the rearing roan,
      the sorrel nag of nightmare
held at bay by words, and words alone like love
      that leap the wall to find the yearling flown.

CONCEIT

If I were you, I wouldn't listen
to me. If I stood there in your shoes,
staring at this graying man writing
in an attic late at night, a motor snoring
and music trickling from speakers
to seep through a sleeping house,

I would turn away, thinking of dreams
I have had, wondering if I'd have more
someday, some night, some winter morning,
the blue of the lake dripping out of its ice, wind
sniffing at the window. But spring
will have come by then. If you

were I you would be grateful. You'd say,
"Listen to that nib scratching, the grass
struggling up through drifts of sleep, these words
forming themselves as though they meant something to me."
You would say, "Over the chimney
of this house night is lifting

beneath the wings of geese returning
to their old haunts." And I would reply,
"They have never been away. All is
as it was, as it will always be." Then, shaking
your head, you would turn your back, you
would leave me here just as I

would leave you, if I were you walking
down the stairs, yellow light cascading
out of the ceiling, along the eaves,
into the rooms full of sleeping people whose love
will wash through our dreams of waking
when we shall lie down at last.

THE SHIFTING WEB

It is time to write a poem.
You have spun out the string of hours —
    it winds down the road, across
  people's lawns; it tangles itself
in the bushes of the park, catches
  in the lower limbs of a horse

  chestnut, and there, now, it lifts to
a kite, a blue kite against the gray
    sky. You must shinny after
  it. When you've caught it, hauled it down
by its rag tail, you see your poem
  scrawled on the tissue wrinkling in

  your hand. You feel the balsa rib
bow. Windcaught, the kite whispers free, sweeps
    across the street, blowing like
  the spiders that ride the air as
voyagers: you have read that somewhere;
  the kite spins out its line. You can

  not now follow. Your hands stop. No
longer do they climb and circle. You
    have seen the poem. The day
  freezes in its frame. The words squirm
out from beneath your hand. The wind is
  solid air, the clouds the color

   of waiting. Only the kite moves
above the still neighbors in their rooms,
      on their lawns, amid their sounds
   turned to rosedust hovering in
a blank white square of world: When that is
   done, things will move again. The kite

   will be somewhere in the center
of the shifting web it is weaving.
      You will follow it, follow
   the filament from pause to pause,
poem to poem. It is almost
   done. You can feel the wind stirring.

A SAMPLER OF HOURS
*Poems and Centos
from Lines in
Emily Dickinson's Letters*
1993

Proem:

CLOTH OF DREAMS

In what shall I be clothed today?
    Sack cloth and ashes?
    Or has that feeling died —
shall I wear crepe for it?

Perhaps I ought to choose a chintz
    to prance about in,
    or dolor of linen
in a nice winding sheet,

such as Emerson's Aunt Mary
    Moody chose to wear
    on social occasions
in her native Concord.

But no, this is Amherst. We wear
    no shrouds in this town.
    Love, like the cloth of dreams,
cheapens other fabrics.

THE HARPER OF STILLNESS

    The lawn is full of south
    and the odors tangle,
and I hear today for the first
    the river in the tree.

    The cricket in the root
    has found a note to cast
upon the pool of eventide,
    of shadow welling from

    a coast of pines. Swiftly
    now he comes, the harper
of stillness, lifting up his strings
    to net the western fire

    shoaling the upper limbs,
    the rooves of our houses
swept by a wave of daylight lost
    in the depths of summer.

CRIMSON CHILDREN

Tonight the crimson children
    are playing in the west.
They do not hear the stars call
    down the burning sky
that time has passed, is passing
    under clouds afire,
tumultuous with ash.

THE EAR OF SILENCE

Not what the stars have done,
but what they are to do
is what detains the sky,

keeps it from failing us
now when the children sleep
in rooms of dream's keeping.

What does darkness confide
in the ear of silence,
vessel of the hollows? —

echo of a sunken
bell ranging the far fields
of light, the well of chimes

that takes us awake now
in our waiting for night
and the starlight falling.

EPITHALAMION

The moon rides like a girl
    through a topaz town,

her steed the beast of air,
    the mound of the wind.

We see her riding there
    where the desert knocks

against the horizon,
    cactus burning like

silver on seas of ore.
    But our doors are shut —

they are studded and barred,
    and if we are still

she will pass in our streets
    blind to our whispers,

deaf to our lingering.
    The sand will take her,

this girl who comes riding,
    this bride of the night.

THE MOWER

The mower is tuning his scythe
in the long meadow
looking for a voice.

A MEMOIR OF EVENING

The book is fair and lonely,
like a memoir of evening —

sunlight spills from its pages,
the note of a dusky bird;
a glass stands on the table,
    and a bowl of fruit,

but these are no miracles,
companions of the twilight.
Something is among the crickets
still as the sky that closes —

not one word comes back to me
    from that silent West.

SCARLET EXPECTATIONS

Second of March and the crow
and snow high as the spire,
and scarlet expectations
   of things that never come,
   because forever here:

the cardinal in carmine
on the sacrament of snow
whistles to the wind his fruitful prayer;

the nut-hatch and chickadee
confess their want of winter
alms in the cathedral pine:
   New England has none to spare,
   you think, in its season?

Perhaps you think I have no bird,
   and this is rhetoric —
pray...what is that upon the cherry tree?

MANSIONS OF MIRAGE

    I live in mansions of mirage
        where seeming turns to Be.
The leaves of summer near the winter glass
            etch themselves in frost;
the busts in the conservatory nod

    in shadow — I am not less wise
        for that marble story.
The many households clad in black attire
            are where others live.
I come in flakes...the bright inhabitants

    of the white home where strange blooms
        arise on many stalks
and trees receive their tenants. On the stair
            that falls like water
I meet my voice in amber speaking of

    the undertow of the organ —
        a similar mirage
of thought, a woe of ecstasy in white:
            she will pirouette
in a paper room, not in the parlor

>   among the guests; they do not know
>   the blood is more gaudy
>   than the breath but cannot dance as well. I
>   will raise the lid to
>   my box of phantoms. There I will not find
>
>   among my souvenirs in season one
>   to startle, to cry
>   a cold yet parched alarm that chills and sears.

A DAINTY SUM

One is a dainty sum!
One bird, one cage, one flight;
one song in those far woods

where mandrake likes to dream,
where dragonfly patrols
its image in the stream;

one song out of the limb
of juniper or fir
moving across the field

where primrose tries to snare
the note of solitude,
the message from the air.

MARBLE ROOMS

    The rooms were marble
        even to the flies
that trod the noses of those stony folk

    who stood in the hall,
        their words like agates
rolling from their lips, clicking and skirling.

    What was it they said,
        those heroic folk?
When they turned an ear, did the voice crack,

    the fair brow take a stain?
        The vine came rapping
at the windowpane, the sunlight coiled

    round about the pillars,
        rubbed the ridges smooth.
The shadows hid beneath the furniture

    like creatures caught in time,
        lichens in the dust;
the mortar turned to powder on the floor.

AN OLD TALE

I hear the wind blow the wide way
in the orchard, snaring itself
    in the April limbs,

telling its story to the lymph
rising to Spring. It is an old
    tale, forever fresh,

and in it one can nearly hear,
diminuendo, the first lines
    of Autumn's legend:

the bloom and the fading away,
the sere blossom, the petal pressed
    between the ancient leaves.

MORNING MUSIC

Where is the morning music,
    the song played at the sill?
    I cannot remember

how it went in its feathers,
    only that it went well
    preening and disporting

against the window casement.
    The garden enjoyed it,
    I recollect, nodding

and nodding. The melody
    went this way and went that
    to the twigs tapping glass.

One day I will recall how
    only the pines sang tunes, now
    the birds are absent.

TWILIGHT TOUCHES AMHERST

    Now the grass is glass
and the meadow stucco.
Twilight touches Amherst

    with his yellow glove.
Do you recall Summer
with its meadows in bloom,

    gardens full of light
settling in bright petals
upon the flower stalks?

    Nothing has been changed
but the season — all things
have been changed but the mind,

    which is change itself.
When will you come again
to see the springtime fall?

    Miss me sometimes — not
on most occasions, but
the seldoms of the mind.

THE GIFT

A one-armed man conveyed the flowers.
I gave him half a smile.

HOME

    The forests are at home —
the mountains intimate at night
    and arrogant at noon.

    I am at home as well —
there are meadows in my parlor,
    and in the bedrooms, vales.

SAMPLER

Many an angel, with its needle,
      toils beneath the snow
    making a sampler of hours
      that fades with the sun

just as the snowfall fades to reveal
      a green alphabet
    written in the script of flowers
      bordered in lilac:

the arbutus is a rosy boast
      adrift in morning;
    zinnia, an ochre brag
      along the far fence.

What is there between them but waiting
      for the sky to rise,
    lifted by the seraphim
      who ply their stitching?

THE CAGE

This morning sang at the windowpane
    and asked to come in — I let it
        fly in the halls a little;

it went sweeping out when you arrived.
    The sun perched on the roof listening
        to the gift of tongues you bore,

but after a short while it felt faint.
    A colloquium of shadows
        fell to discussion of it.

After you went, a low wind warbled
    through the house like a spacious bird,
        making it high but lonely.

FOUR SMALL SONGS

The sun came out when you were gone.
    I chid him for delay —
he said we had not needed him.
        Oh prying sun!

What lethargies of loneliness
your letters brought. I read them in
the garret, and the rafters moaned.

The clock purrs and the kitten ticks.
    She catches dandelions,
mistaking them for topaz mice.

    I am going to sleep
    if the rat permit me —
    I hear him singing now
    to the tune of a nut.

THE DEEP STRANGER

Sometimes as I am drifting
    toward my sleep, I dream
    I am the deep stranger
    smoking his pipe, looking
    through his reading glasses,
and sometimes I look out and see
        I am not dreaming.

BROWN STUDY

His son's dinosaurs surround me.
Overhead in his attic study
      antique maps slant away
      between me and the stars.

The knee-wall set into the eaves
is sated with books. Down the garret,
      charts and prints cascade from
      the eastern wall — its slit

window — to the western
door with a panel of glass stained
      green and faint lavender,
      the *fleur-de-lis* aqua

in a field of frost. The gable
end displays portraits of him, the boy
      whose ancient animals
      walk this landscape of books,

that pause of space which we call 'Father!'

NOCTURNE

This is the world that opens and shuts
    like the eye of the wax doll
        lying in a box
of castoff things. I hear its breath
    in the wind of evening,

in the darkness between planets
    and the shining of the stars,
        even the whistle
of a boy passing late at night,
    or the low of a bird.

THE AMHERST FIRE

    I sprang to the window and each
side of the curtain saw that awful
sun. The moon was shining high and the birds

    singing like trumpets, and so much
brighter than day was it that I saw
a caterpillar measure a leaf far

    down in the orchard. The innocent
dew was falling and sweet frogs prattling
in the dark pools as if there were no earth.

    What, indeed, is Earth but a nest
from whose rim we are all falling?

A PEARL JAIL

    This is a stern Winter,
        and in my pearl jail
the cricket and I keep house
    for the frost. No event
of wind or bird breaks the spell

    of steel. I think of sun
        and of Summer as
visages unknown: those were
    the nosegays of twilight
and these — the nosegays of dawn.

    Though it is many nights,
        my mind never comes home.
I find you with dusk, for day
    is tired and lays its
antediluvian cheek

    to the hill like a child.
        Therefore I give you
good night with fictitious lips,
for to me you have no face.

MAY, MERELY

       The weeds pant
like the center of summer.
       I follow my nose
to the dogwood in bloom:

       it is May
merely, but Amherst blossoms
       in its early heat,
sap oozes from the bark,

       and the limbs
are heavy with what may be:
       phantom fruit, the seed
in the dusty pollen.

AN AMHERST HAIKU

   Will you bring me a
jacinth for every finger,
    and an onyx shoe?

THE MILLER'S TALE

    I am saving a miller moth.
It laid six eggs on the window sill and
      I thought it was getting tired,
          so I killed it.

    Death obtains the rose, but the news
goes no further than the breeze.
      The ear is the last face. Today
         I slew a mushroom.

THE NAKED EYE

      The chickens grow very fast —
  I am afraid they will be so large
      that you cannot perceive them
with the naked eye when you get home.

      The flowers have reached the eaves
  and are heaving against the roof
      which has begun to buckle —
you will have to do something I fear.

      We had eggs for breakfast or,
  rather, an egg — the yellow yolk
      ran under the sideboard, and
it stayed there, refusing to come out.

      The cat walking down the stair
  makes a great noise — the banister
      bulges out as she descends.
The trees in the yard block out the sun —

      we are not sure that the sun
  still regards us in our small world
      with a great eye fully clothed
in the raiment of its rays and beams.

      We stumble in the shadows.
  The candles speak so slightly that
      we can hardly hear their words,
and the moss — the moss is at the door.

A MORNING PICTURE

    A shadow falls upon my
morning picture. The dust falls
on the bureau in your deserted room,

    and gay, frivolous spiders
    spin away in the corners.
I don't go there after dark, for the twilight

    seems to pause there. I weave for
    the lamp of evening a kind
of twilight before the moon is seen.

PASSING

Autumn is coming on
along the country street.
Chestnut husks lie cloven
 along the walk,
 one and another.

The sun is lost. The sky
wears masks of smoke on gray,
and there is moss showing
 upon the oaks,
 one and another,
 one and another.

The walk is made of slate,
and roots have buckled it.
The child rides, wagoning,
 up and over —
 one and another,
 one and another,
 how we pass away!

THEME AND VARIATION

The orchestra of winds performs
its strange, sad music.
I hear it fretting the window-ledge
where the frozen starling sings.

A NEW YEAR

Who is approaching?
Oh, arctic February
    wading through snowdrifts.

I have heard birds sing,
but I fear their bills will be
    frozen closed before

their songs are finished.
Not yet has old King Frost had
    the cold pleasure of

snatching them in his
frigid embrace. Would that we
    might spend this year, now

fleeting swiftly by,
better than the one that we
    cannot now recall.

SUMMER'S CHARIOT

    Summer is past and gone;
Autumn with the sere and yellow leaf
    is already upon us.

    Someone must have oiled
his chariot wheels, for I did not
    hear him pass. And what report

    has he borne to heaven
of misspent time and wasted hours?
    Each moment in its season —

    now we wear our golden
    tresses done up in net-caps.

SMALL VICTORY

At noon I heard a well-known rap.
A friend I love so dearly came
and asked me to ride in the woods,
    the sweet, still woods.

I said I could not go; he said
he wanted me very much. Oh,
I struggled with great temptation.
    It cost me much

of denial, but in the end
I conquered — not a glorious
triumph, where you hear the rolling
    drum, but a kind

of helpless victory which comes
of itself, not faintest music,
weary soldiers, nor a waving
    flag, nor a long,

loud shout, only a small silence,
a pause, a stillness at the heart.

HOUSEKEEPING

    The sun has barely
  risen, and I am in
mourning, for the house is being
    cleaned — I prefer pestilence: that

    is more classic and
  less fell. I wear my cap
awry to frighten the spiders
    a-dangle in the corners.

    I have been at work
  scaring the timorous dust,
being obedient and kind.
    I am the Queen of the Court,

    if regalia be
  dust and dirt. I have three
loyal subjects; like a martyr,
    I serve and sweep before them

    in bonds of despair.
  I survey my kitchen
and pray for kind deliverance.
    My kitchen, I called it! God

keep me in His Majesty
    from what they call households!

AMONG THE STONES

    Tonight it is cool and quiet,
the toil of the feverish day forgotten.
        Some of my friends are gone,
and some of my friends are sleeping —
      sleeping the churchyard sleep.

    I have walked there sweet summer
evenings and read the names on the stones, wondered
      who would come and give me
the like memorial. There will be
      no sun or singing birds

    in the coming spring. I shall
look for an early June then, when the grass is
      growing green; I shall love
to call the bird there if it has
      a gentle music; the

    meekest-eyed wildflowers,
and the low, plaintive insect. How precious is
      the grave when aught we love
is laid there, and affection would
go too, if the lost were lonely.

FIRST SNOW

   A thousand little winds wafted
to me this morning an air
fragrant with forest leaves and bright

   autumnal berries. Now and then
a gray leaf fell. Crickets sang
all day long. High in a crimson

   tree a belated bird trembled —
there must be many moments
in an eternal day. Alas!

   I remember the leaves were falling,
and now there are falling snows.
Are not leaves the brethren of snows?

   I dream of being a grandam
and binding my silver hairs,
the children dancing around me.

DELAY

I have tried to delay the frosts,
I have coaxed the fading flowers,
I thought I would detain a few
   of the crimson leaves,

but their companions call them — they
cannot stay away. You will find
blue hills with autumnal shadows
   silently sleeping

on them: there will be a glory
lingering round the day. You will know
autumn has come and gone his way
   through the acorn wood

wrapping his faded cloak about him.

COMPANY

How I love to see them, a beautiful company
   coming down the hill crusted with snow,
      wearing its blue mantilla,
   which men call the future. Their hearts are
   full of joy, and their hands of gladness.

The bouquet was not withered, nor was the bottle cracked
   when they arrived singing, but the wind
      whispered so violently,
   and it grew so cold, that we gathered
   all the quinces in, put up the stove

in the sitting-room, and bade the world good-by. These brief,
   imperfect meetings have their own tales
      to tell — we shall hear them
   when the nails hang full of coats again,
   and the chairs hang full of hats, and I

can count the slippers under the kitchen chair.

AN AMHERST PASTORAL

Today is very beautiful —
just as bright, just as blue, just as green
      and as white and as crimson

as the cherry trees full in bloom,
and the half-opening peach blossoms,
      and the grass just as waving,

and the sky and hill and cloud can
make it, if they try. When the west
      wind blows, the pines lift their light

leaves and make sweet music. You will
awaken in dust, in the ceaseless
      din of the untiring

city. Wouldn't you change your dwelling
      for my palace in the dew?

DEATH

There is a subject on which
we never touch. Ignorance
of its pageantries does not deter me.
I too went out to meet the dust

early in the morning. I
too in daisy mounds possess
hid treasure. I write you from the summer,
and frogs sincerer than our own

splash in their Maker's pools. Oh,
dew upon the bloom fall yet again
upon a summer's night! Of such have been
the frauds which have vanquished faces,

sown plant of flesh the church-yard
plats, and occasioned angels.
When you hear the new violet sucking
her way among the sods, shall you

be resolute? Many can
boast a hollyhock, but few
can bear a rose. Distinctly sweet your face
stands in its phantom niche. How brief,

from vineyards and the sun — for
in the merriest flower there is
a pensive air, but fairer colors than
mine are twined while stars are shining.

ASEA

    I am pleasantly located
in the deep sea. The shore is safer,
        but I love to buffet Ocean —

    I can count the little wrecks here
in these still depths, hear the murmuring winds.
        Oh! I love the danger! Love will row

    you out, if her hands are strong. Don't wait
until I land where you stand peering
        into the humming gale, for I

am going ashore on the other side.

JUST GOD

Who writes these funny accidents
        where railroads meet each other
quite unexpectedly, and gentlemen
    in factories get their heads cut off
        quite informally? The Author

    relates them in such a sprightly
            way, they are quite attractive.
If prayers had any answers to them,
    I should not know the question, for I
        seek and I don't find and knock and

        it is not opened. I wonder
            if God is just — presume that
He is, and 'twas only a blunder of
    Matthew's. Heaven is large, isn't it?
        Then when one is done, is there not

        another, and — then — if God
        is willing, we are neighbors then.

A DREAM OF ROSES

I thought I would write again.
　　I write many letters
　　with pens which are not seen —

do you receive them? I think
　　of you today, and dreamed
　　of you all last night. When

father rapped upon my door
　　to wake me this morning,
　　I was walking with you

in a wonderful garden,
　　and helping you to pick —
　　roses, and although we

gathered them with all our might,
　　the basket was never
　　full. Therefore, all day I

pray that I may walk with you,
　　gather roses again,
　　and as the night draws on,

it pleases me, and I count
　　impatiently the hours
　　between me and darkness,

the dream of you and roses,
　　and the basket never full.

LAMPS

    I love to have the lamps shine
    on the evening table,
    but I am out with lanterns
    looking for myself — and now
this falling snow sternly and silently

    lifts up its hand between. While
    I sit among the snows, that
    summer day — on which the bees
    came and the south wind — turns to
phantoms and vanishes slow away. How

    many years, I wonder, will
    sow the moss upon them till
    we bind again? As many
    as the suns that shine between
our lives and loss, and violets — not last

    year's, but having the mother's
    eyes. I often wish that I
    were grass, whom all these problems
of the dust might not terrify. What is

    this carnal chill, zero at
    the bone? Sometimes I wonder
    if I ever dreamed, then if
I am dreaming now, then if I always

    dreamed, and there is not a world.

FADING THINGS

   If roses had not faded,
      and frosts had never come,
   and one had not fallen here
and there whom I could not waken,

   there were no need of Heaven
      other than this below.
   I love these fading things — where
they go when summer's done, only

   the thyme knows, and the robin
      who, when the west winds come,
   winks and away forever
till the next eternity.

AN ORATOR OF FEATHER

Summer? Was there a summer?
I saw the fields go — dancer and floor
and cadence gathered away,
and I — a phantom — rehearse the story!
an orator of feather unto

an audience of fuzz. I
found a bird this morning — down — down — on
a little bush at the foot
of the garden. "And wherefore sing," I said,
"since nobody hears?" But he replied,

"My business it is to sing,
for the supper of the heart is when
the guest is gone. Pardon
my sanity in a world insane." He
puffed his feathers out and lofted song,

but he left me with a quill.

THE WINTER GARDEN

It is November. The noons are more
laconic and the sundowns sterner.
    November always seemed to me
the Norway of the year. A neighbor

put her child into an ice nest last
Monday forenoon. Sharper than dying
    is the death for the dying's sake.
I cannot stoop to strut in a world

where bells toll — frost is no respecter
of persons, and yet the wind blows gay
    today; jays bark like blue terriers.
My heart is red as February

and purple as March, for I taste life —
it is a vast morsel. If we knew
    how deep the crocus lay, we should
never let her go. The gentian is

a greedy flower, and overtakes
us all. Although death grasps the proudest
    zinnia from my purple garden,
blossoms belong to the bee. I would

eat evanescence slowly — my winter
flowers are near and foreign. I have
    only to cross the floor to stand
among the Isles of Spice and Summer.

ADVENTURE

    A circus passed the house this morning —
        I followed it along the street
beneath the summer oaks, among the folk

      staring at Africa on parade.
         When I came to myself and saw
how far I had come away, how many

      of us were strangers, I turned and ran.
        I have just shot past the corner,
now the wayside houses, and the gate flies

      open to see me coming home. Still
         I feel the red in my mind — though
the drums are out — the echo of the flags.

WINTER BOUQUET

    It storms in Amherst five days —
it snows, and then it rains, and then
soft fogs like veils hang on all the houses,
    and then the days turn topaz

    like a lady's pin. The hills
take off their purple frocks and dress
in long white nightgowns. The men were
    mowing the second hay not

    long since — the cocks were smaller
than the first, and spicier. I
would distill a cup, bear it to my friends,
    drinking to summer no more

    astir, make a balloon of
a dandelion, but the fields
are gone where children walked the tangled road,
    some of them to the end, some

    but a little way, even
as far as the fork. Remembrance
is more sweet than robins in May orchards.
    Today is very cold, yet

    I have much bouquet upon
the window pane — of moss and fern.
I call them saints' flowers, because they do
    not romp as other flowers

do, but stand so still and white.
   I enjoy much with a precious
fly, not one of your blue monsters, but a
      timid creature that hops from

      pane to pane of her white house
   so very cheerfully, and hums
and thrums — a sort of speck piano. I
      have one new bird and several

      trees of old ones. A snow slide
   from the roof dispelled the sweetbrier.
There are as yet no streets, though the sun is
      riper. This is a landscape

      of frost and zeros. I wish
   "the faith of the fathers" didn't
wear brogans and carry blue umbrellas.
      The doubt, like the mosquito,

      buzzes round my faith. My heart
   has flown before, my breaking voice
follows — that bareheaded life under grass
      worries me like a wasp — life

      of flowers lain in flowers —
   what a home of dew to come to!
We reckon by the fruit. When the grape gets
      by, and the pippin and the

    chestnut — when the days are a
  little short by the clock, and a
little long by the lack — when the sky has
    new red gowns and a purple

    bonnet, I am glad that kind
  of time goes by. Twilight is but
the short bridge, and the moon stands at the end.
    With Nature in my ruche, I

shall not miss the spring, the seasons falling
and the leaves — the molting goldfinch singing.

FLOWERS IN SEASON

    i. *Spring*

Such a purple morning, even to
the morning-glory that climbs the cherry tree.
   Crocuses came up, in the garden
off the dining room, and a fuchsia
     like willowy strawberries —

   primroses, and heliotrope by
the aprons full — the mountain-colored one — and
   a jessamine bud with an odor
like lupine — gilliflowers, magenta,
     a few mignonette, and sweet

   alyssum bountiful — carnation
buds. The ice-house is filled to make tumblers cool
   next summer, and now and then a cream.
   I spent some moments profitably
     with the South Sea rose. I have

   removed a geranium leaf or
two, supplied a lily in the parlor vase.
   The sweet-peas are unchanged, and the fields
   give brawny promise of haycocks by
     and by.

ii. *Fall*

North Wind has arrived —

the trees stand right up straight when they hear
his boots, and will bear crockery wares
    instead of fruit, I fear. He hasn't
    starched the geraniums yet, but will
        have ample time. I pick up

tufts of mignonette, and the sweet
alyssum for winter — these red and
    gold and ribbon days seem as dim as
    winter. Faded petals proffer me
        colors from the vault of Earth —

nothing has happened but loneliness,
perhaps too daily to relate. With love for
    supper — if deferred it will fade like
    ice cream — the moon is morning's memoir.
        Take the key to the lily

now, and I will lock the rose.

LATE SUMMER

In the dooryard a stand of milkweed
    draws the gorging honeybees,
      and in the oak a squirrel
treads, nattering of the impending

fall. The skies are blue and yellow, and
    there's a purple craft or so
      in which a friend could sail. I
feel as the band does before it makes

its first shout — a catbird clothed in gray
    patrols the goldenrod, drops
      over the sod bank toward
the road — he stops now and then to cry

his ownership. Pray, what does he keep
    of the sweet season beyond
      the shape of the maple leaf,
and the swift, waning sun? I could play

    in the woods till dark — till you
    take me where sundowns cannot find us.

LATE FALL

The stove is singing the merry song
of the wood — it is sweet and antique
   as birds — not a flake assaults
   them but it freezes me. Though

the sailor cannot see the north, he
knows the needle can. I dreamed last night
   I heard bees fight for pond-
   lily stamens, and I waked

with a fly in my room making grim
ado of death — 'twas much of a mob
   as I could master. This is
   a mighty morning. Too few

the mornings be, too scant the nights — how
long the days that make the flesh afraid.

AMHERST NEIGHBORS

Do you recall old Mrs. Ay,
   with the nose of a hawk?
   Last Monday-week she fledged
her antique wings and soared
   to her nest in Heaven.

Bee and Cee are closest comrades
   still. Together they walk,
   talk, eat — vote together!
They intend to be Jonathan
   and David, or Damon

and Pythias, or what's better,
   the United States of
   America! Mrs.
Dee grows larger, rolls down the lane
   to church like a marble.

I found Miss Ea in our garden
   peering at a purloined lily —
   bats think foxes have no
eyes. It comforts the criminal
   little to know the law

expires with him. Father feels ill —
   the straightest engine has
   its leaning hour. Madame
Gee goes tattling still. Her yard needs
   combing — no one can keep

a sumach and a secret too.
   And there is Aitch, of course —
   she looks a little tart,
but makes excellent pies after
   one gets acquainted. I

tend house and to a quiet hour.
   Miss Jaye grows so thin
   in her cottage of slats,
I could fancy that skeleton
   cats caught specter

rats in dim old nooks and corners.
   Mr. Kaye is less lively
   than he was wont, if one might
discern it — there are those in the
   morgue that bewitch us with

sweetness, but that which is dead must
   go with the ground. To speak
   of wings yet again — sweet
Mrs. Elle comes with the robins.
   Robins have wings. Mrs.

Elle has wings. A society
for the prevention of wings would
be of benefit to us all.

PASSAGES

i.

The crocuses are with us
and several other colored friends.
There is a tree in the woods
that shivers. I am afraid it is
cold. I am going to make it a little

coat. I must make several,
because it is tall as the barn, and
put them on as the circus
men stand on each other's shoulders. I
hear robins a great way off, and wagons a

great way off, and rivers a
great way off, and all appear to be
hurrying somewhere undisclosed
to me. Even the wren upon her nest
knows more than daisy dares — we must be careful

what we say. No bird resumes
its egg.

ii.

       The colors quiver upon
   the pastures and day goes gay
to the northwest. Oh that beloved
witch-hazel! It looks like tinsel fringe combined

    with staider fringes, witch and
   witching too. It haunts me like childhood's
      Indian pipe, or ecstatic
  puff-balls, or that mysterious apple
that sometimes comes on river-pinks — and a dim

    suggestion of dandelion,
 if her hair were raveled and she grew
    upon a twig rather than
a tube.

iii.

   What an exchange of awe! I
suppose the wild flowers encourage themselves

   by the dim woods. Two or three
  finches in plush teams reined nearer to
   the window, but the bird that
 is bruised limps to his house in silence.
We will miss the nasturtiums, but we will meet

the chestnuts.

iv.

I open my
window and it fills my chamber with
white dirt. I think God must be
dusting. Slips of the last rose repose
in kindred soil with waning bees. How softly

summer shuts without the creaking of a door.

EPISTLE

    Evening called with a twilight of you.
The men were picking up the apples today,
    and the pretty boarders left the trees,
birds and ants and bees. I heard the chipper say
    "Dee" six times in disapprobation.

    His bombazine reproof falls still on
the twilight, and checks the softer uproars of
    departing day, for how should we like
to have our privileges wheeled away in
    a barrel? We had two hurricanes

    within as many hours, one of which
came near enough to untie my apron — but
    this moment the hens are warbling.
A man of anonymous wits is making
    a garden in the lane to set out

slips of bluebird — the moon grows from the seed. I
    send you a robin who is eating
a remnant oat upon the sill of the barn.

AN AMHERST CHRISTMAS

Atmospherically, it was the most
        beautiful Christmas. The hens
    came to the door with Santa Claus,
the pussies washed themselves in the air
without chilling their tongues. Visitors

from the chimney were a new dismay,
        and the friends at the barn were
    so happy! Maggie gave the hens
a check for potatoes, each cat had
a gilt-edged bone, and the horse had new

blankets from Boston. Will the sweet child
        who sent me the butterflies,
    herself a member of the same
ethereal nation, accept a
rustic kiss flavored, we trust, with clover?

POETRY

Memory's fog is rising: I had a terror
    I could tell to none — and so I sing,
    as the boy does in the burying-ground,
because I am afraid. When a sudden light
on the orchards, or a new fashion in the wind

troubled my attention, I felt a palsy,
    here, the verses just relieve.

                    I am
small, like the wren, and my hair is bold,
like the chestnut burr, and my eyes like sherry
in the glass the guest leaves. There is always one

thing to be grateful for — that one is one's self
    and not somebody else. "We thank thee,
    oh loving Father," for these strange minds
that enamor us against Thee.

                    If I read
a book, and it makes my body so cold no

fire can ever warm me, I know that is
    poetry. If I feel physically
    as if the top of my head were
taken off, I know that is poetry. These are
the only ways I know it. Is there any

other way?
	How does the poet learn to grow,
  or is it unconveyed, like witchcraft
  or melody? I had no monarch
in my life and cannot rule myself. When I
try to organize, my little force explodes,

leaves me bare and charred. I marked a line in one
  verse, because I met it after I
  made it and never consciously touch
a paint mixed by another person. I do
not let go of it, because it is mine.

Two editors of journals came and asked me
  for my mind. When I asked them, "Why?" they
  said I was penurious — they'd use it
for the world. I could not weigh my self myself —
my size felt small to me. One hears of Mister

Whitman — I never read his book, but was told
  he is disgraceful. To my thought, "To
  publish" is foreign as firmament
to fin. My barefoot rank is better. If fame
belonged to me, I could not escape her — if

she did not, the longest day would pass me on
   the chase.
               There seems a spectral power
   in thought that walks alone. I find
ecstasy in living — the mere sense of life
is joy enough. The chestnut hit my notice

suddenly, and I thought the skies in blossom!

AN AMHERST CALENDAR

January
The vane defies the wind.

February
                            It is warm now.
  A mellow rain is falling.
It won't be ripe till April. How luscious
is the dripping of February eaves!
      It makes our thinking pink.

It antedates the robin.

March
                  Who would be
  ill a-bed in March, that month
of proclamations? Sleigh-bells and blue-jays
contend in my matinee, and the North
      surrenders instead of

the South — a reverse of bugles.

April
                     And now
  arbutus is knitting pink
clothes.

May
The apple-blossoms yesterday were
slightly disheartened by a snow-storm, but
   the birds encouraged them

all that they could, and how fortunate that
   the little ones had come to
cheer their damask brethren! We have inland
buttercups, as out-of-door flowers are
   still at sea. The seed sown

in the lake bears the liquid flower.

June
                    There is
   a circus here, and Farmers'
Commencement, boys and girls from Tripoli,
and Governors and swords parade the streets.
   They lean upon the fence

that guards the quiet churchyard ground, and jar
   the grass, now warm and soft as
a tropic nest.

July
       Sweet-peas stand in carmine
sheaves. The fuchsia is a bliss of sorrow.

August
                In the garden scarlet

carnations with a witching suggestion,
    and hyacinths covered with
promises, nod and beckon, beckon and
nod.

        September
    The red leaves take the green leaves' place, and
        the landscape yields. We go

to sleep with the peach and wake with the stone,
    yet the stone is the pledge of
summers to come.

       October
                My garden vanished with
beautiful reluctance, like an evening star.
    There are sticks of rowan

for the stove — chopped by bees — and butterflies
    stacked the cords on Saturday
afternoons. I am kept busy picking
up stems and stamens, as the hollyhocks
    have left their clothes around.

November
I had the luxury of a mother
   until November. She slipped
from our fingers like a flake gathered by
the wind. The anguish was also granted
      me to see the first snow

fall next day upon her grave.

December
                I have no
letter from the dead, yet daily love them
    more. Instead, a jay drops me a note —
blue on white. He asks me to begin again,
that bleeding beginning every mourner knows.

THE CLOCK

      i.
The geese make a sound like vee in the air
    as they pass homing to the South.
        'Tis not long since the fields
        could not remember frost.

I grope through drifts of awe as I settle
    into Autumn, reflecting that
        the grapes were big and fresh,
        tasting like emerald dew.

The Summer's picture is not yet mottled
    by the snow. My window frames it —
        the orchard recalling
        its dream of sweet burden

against a sky that is falling to Earth.
    Time seeps from the clock behind me —
        I hear it splash like glass
        melting in mists of breath.

      ii.
Except for the tapping of the clock,
it is quiet in the room. The floor
    has a paisley skin on oaken
        bones. Along the walls, books
        walk the shelves, stop

at casements where a wan sun falls in
on pools of shadow. I am sitting
    in an arm-chair considering
        this flow of moments, drift
            of hours. Each rap

of the pendulum laboring here,
in this quarry of silence, transmutes
    itself, becomes its own echo,
        a retracing between
            wood and crystal

of what comes to pass. The quarry fills
with emptiness seeping through the chinks
    of sound, between tick and tick — there
        are droplets falling from
            the tap of time.

        iii.

    I study the clock, regard
    its face — it is my own, my hands
    that swing their arcs through numerals
        that mark me at my meals,
the funerals of friends, the pillow sighs
        that summon sleep from dream,

that take me down to verges
beyond which I may just discern
the figures of the lost, the shades
      that bide and wake. It is
the face of the familiar and the strange —
    my image lurks upon

    the glass, sinks through, and travels
with the moon of brass in its pace
and shining pause, the falling and
      ascension — eyes and mouth,
lips, brow and cheeks caught swinging in the bright
    machinery of time.

iv.

It is as near as though
I can see it — the river
    of time flowing out
    of the clock —

a clear stream, like air, but
more crystalline. It is as
    though a cataract
    made of sun

and shadow spills into
the room among the tables
    and chairs, begins to
        wash against

    the claws of the divan,
the leg of the candle-stand —
        begins to deepen
        over the dim

    design of the carpet.
It is a tide rising to
        fathom the corners
        of my space.

    v.

    There are voices in the flow
of time cascading down the wall,
    out of the clock. It is hard
        for me to discern shapes
caught in the quick crystal river

    deepening about my feet,
lifting to my ankles, my knees.
    But as the fluid air moves
        to the level of my breast,
as the river slows and deepens,

    becoming instead a tarn,
I make out the little figures
      at last — floating and drowning,
          flailing and calling out.
They are naked. Their eyes are bright,

    their skins glisten. I feel the suck
of the undertow on my flesh.
      In the center of the room
          a vortex is forming —
they are all being drawn into

    the whirlpool — it is taking
them down, these people caught in time.
      They grasp at my shoulders, now
          awash, attempt to claw
ashore — I must try to save them!

        vi.

I lift my hands out of time. I stand.
I stare hard at the clear ocean stream.
Stop I cry, and *Stop* again — all stops.
    Time freezes in its wash.

Like insects caught in amber, the folk
lie jeweled in their eddies. Shadow
and lamplight deckle them. Sunset glows
    in the dark window-pane.

The ice of time engulfs golden oak,
mahogany and teak, warp and weft
of fabric — drape, couch, and carpet. On
    the wall the paper scrolls.

In its cradle the globe floats. The hands
of the clock mark the Apocalypse —
it is of no moment at long last.
    The vortex vanishes.

No chime begins its song, no stroke ends.
The chain is weightless. Eternity
is now and only now. Let it go —
    go with it — let them go.

vii.

    I wind the clock and time begins
    to wind. Life begins to windle.
The room becomes the room in which I dwell.
    All is as it was and cannot

    be again — no part of mind is
    permanent. Though this may startle
the happy, it assists the sad. I will
    make do, then — I will make time do

those things it would have done at any rate.

PHOBIAMANIA
An Expanded Version of
A BOOK OF FEARS
1998

PROEM

ERATOPHOBIA: *The Fear of Poetry*
for Linda Sardella Boucher

Dear Cousin, she wrote, *Thanks
for the books of poems. I must admit
that I haven't opened them. It's a source
of pride to me to have a poet in the family,
but I'm afraid I won't understand*

*the poems and I'd feel stupid.
I fear I haven't opened them.
I must admit I fear what lies in wait
between the covers: words that writhe,
that hiss at me off the page,*

*words that wriggle and won't hold still
to let me understand them.
Weird, huh? I'll work at it. I'll work
to get beneath the covers, to open one
in bed beneath the covers — they lie in wait*

*beside me on the nightstand. I'll reach out
one night and grab one, pull it underneath
the covers of my bed and, with a flashlight,
open it and see the poems writhing,
hissing at me on the page I fear.*

PAPYROPHOBIA: *The Fear of Paper*

It stares back at him, a blank white sheet
of winter lying on his desk. They hypnotize
each other. He shakes his head and blinks his eyes,
takes up a pen and puts its nib upon
a random spot. He stops and stares some more,

lifts the pen and looks — a single dot
of darkness blooms like an iris off the slope
of winter. It does not help...it makes it worse.
He takes the sheet in his fist and crumples it,
throws it to the floor. He shakes his head

and takes another leaf out of the drawer,
takes up the pen and puts it down, leans back.
A field of frost lies waiting on his desk.
He feels its chill blooming off the slope
of his escritoire. When he shuts his eyes,

there it is again, blooming now
behind his irises, hypnotizing him
with sheets of winter desolation turning
slowly into dots of darkness spreading
downward from the alpine pinnacles.

MONOPHOBIA: *The Fear of Loneliness*

She sits by herself at a table, not the bar,
slowly stirring her warming cocktail, listening
to the buzz of conversation — the softball chat,
who dumped whom and when and why and where.
A cirrus of smoke is suspended in the air.

She smiles at him. He passes by. Another
takes his place. She smiles again and sips
her warming cocktail. "May I sit down?" he asks.
She nods, he sits. "Buy you a drink?" "Okay."
While he is gone she drinks her warming cocktail.

When he returns he says, "So, what's your name?
Mine's...." She doesn't catch it. What's the difference,
anyway? But she tells him hers. They add
to the buzz of conversation — who knows whom
and where and when and why. But no one knows

any other, she thinks and does not think.
She stirs her warming cocktail now and then,
and when it's time to go she takes her bag
and follows him through the buzz of conversation,
the cirrus of smoke suspended in the air.

ZELOPHOBIA: *The Fear of Jealousy*

Jealous beyond love or hate, he walks
past an armless Venus, helpless as
her marble passion. Down by the fountain, near
the wood, wild pigeons pitch and pander under
the leaves of the sycamore. With both hands

he scatters his crumbs of sorrow. They lie
upon the loam like lost thoughts until
the birds and squirrels, so like his fears,
partake of his personal disaster — or so
it seems, down by the fountain, near the wood

where, hour on hour he avoids the sun,
encounters merely sprinkles of light to work
together, if he can, into the whole
puzzle, filling in the dark and blind spots
with the dreams of wretched intellect. Upon

the harlot moss he lies at last and presses
his body down upon its sweet green flesh
to let his being wander past the fountain
into the wood beyond the armless Venus,
and be at one with love in her blue womb.

ABANDOPHOBIA: *The Fear of Divorce*

She heard her mother say the word that struck
a knife of ice into her heart; she heard her father say,
"All right, if that's the way you want it, fine. Let's do it now!"
and then stalk out of the house, slamming the door
on them, slamming the panel door

on all the past, on everything she loved,
mother and father, home. She heard her mother scream,
"Fine!" saw her turn away with an ugly face.
She began to cry, she ran upstairs to her room and slammed
the door on all the ugliness, the hate, the ruin

of every dream she'd ever had. She hid
among her dolls in the closet, and when her mother came
into the room and called, she wouldn't answer.
Not even her dolls could comfort her. She felt
the icy knife searing her insides, slicing her up

into small bits and pieces of fear. Even when her mom
opened the closet door and found her there
she wouldn't look up. She curled herself into a ball
of snow and cringed away from the open arms
of the person that now she knew she could never trust.

CHOROPHOBIA: *The Fear of Dancing*

He watches the dancers skimming across the floor
holding one another, letting go,
falling away and coming together,
approaching and passing. "Come on, let's dance,"
she says. He shakes his head,

and as he does so the ballroom wobbles,
the dancers shift and shimmer
holding one another, letting go,
falling away and down because the floor
is a firmament of whirling dots of light —

he watches the dancers skimming across a floor
insubstantial as a summer sky.
The music murmurs among the whirling lights
like zephyrs beneath the stars, falling away,
approaching and passing. He shuts his eyes

because the floor is a firmament of shadow
deckled with dots of light spinning away.
The dancers shift and shimmer, begin to fall
through the spaces between the dots of light,
begin to fall holding one another.

PARTURIPHOBIA: *The Fear of Childbirth*

He's not for her, no matter who he is.
It's all his fault — the blood, the pain, the mess.
She's not responsible for the stocking of the planet —
let someone else do that. Too many people
anyway as it is. She looks at him

and shudders — the tremor begins about waist high
and travels down her hips, along her thighs,
ends at her knees. She feels her stomach turn
and looks away. He's not for her, no matter
what. She doesn't need the mess, the pain,

the blood, the squalling brat for the rest of her life.
She recalls her younger brother and what he did —
he's responsible for what happened to
their mother, he and her father — she's well out
of that; she'll never see either of them

the rest of her life. Let someone else do that,
go see the murderers in their jackals' lair.
She smooths her hair, looks up and sees another
coming in the door. She almost stares,
but he is not for her, never for her.

HOMOPHOBIA: *The Fear of Homosexuality*

He wanted him to shake his hand? No way!
No telling where that hand had been, what it had done,
what it would do if he should take it, shake it there
where everyone could see. He'd just as soon
go down to Hell on pony-back as take

that puffy hand, that flabby, puffy hand
limp at the wrist, and shake it. Oh, see him smile —
no, not a smile, a smirk! A simple smirk...,
a simper, really. As though he knew some secret
they shared together, just the two of them,

among this crowd of people in the room, this crowd
of who knew what? How many of them were there here?
Were all the women females? Would any drag
him into phony conversations just to feel him out?
No way he'd shake their hands, no way at all

they'd trick him into giving anything at all away,
he'd sooner go to Hell on pony-back!
How to avoid that hand he's holding out, limp at the wrist,
that dangling hand, how to avoid those eyes
that saw something in his that wasn't there?

CLAUSTROPHOBIA: *The Fear of Narrow Spaces*

She wakens gasping, feeling as though her throat
were stopped up tight. She'd dreamt that she'd been nailed
into a narrow box and couldn't breathe, her heart
pounding in her chest, knocking against her ribs, trying to burst
out of its cage of bone, of blood and flesh —

she opens her eyes and looks across the counterpane
toward her bedroom bureau. The mirror there reflects
only the dark, the shadows lying along the floor
beneath the night light. She begins to feel
again as though her throat were stopped up tight,

and so she rises, unclutches her nightclothes, stumbles
across the room to the window. She lifts the shade and sees
lying across the lawn the streetlamp's glow. She begins to breathe
again. The air begins to move
across her lips and tongue and down her throat.

She raises the window to feel the cooling air
stirring her nightclothes, wrapping her body in distances
sensuous as the dawn that begins to break
over the horizon there, beyond the trees,
beyond the closed-in houses along the street.

GAMOPHOBIA: *The Fear of Marriage*

What could he have been thinking? He'd thought he could
go through with it, and she is waiting there,
waiting there for him right now, down at the church,
expecting him to be standing with his best man
as she starts down the aisle. But where is he?

Driving around the town, beads of sweat
rolling off his nose, down his cheeks, down his sides
beneath the monkey suit. He'll smell like hell
when she takes his arm, when he leans to kiss
the lips he loves to kiss. What could he have been thinking

when he asked her to be his wife? What's that sign say?
I-95 — he's heading out of town! And she is waiting,
expecting him to be a better man
than his old man had been when he took off
when he was five years old. He, not his dad! he means....

His monkey suit is soaked. His hair's a mess.
How can he show up looking, smelling like this? Where is he now?
What's that? The church! How'd he get here? The cars
parked up and down the street — can he get out?
His legs are shaking so, he can hardly walk.

NOMATOPHOBIA: *The Fear of Names*

What shall she name it? She cannot bear to think —
Prudence, Penelope, Phyllis, Faith, Frenosia?
Oh, what will happen if she conjures up
a demon with these names? What if her child
turns out to be a monster? Beelzebub,

Old Ned himself, Scratch, Murgatroyd or Mabel —
Worms on the page that wriggle and writhe and wrine?
She cannot bear to think of what to name it:
Blister and Bore, Bumjohn, Barticle, Bruce,
Antichrist, Jesus! Bessy, Blossom, Livelong,

Love-in-a-Mist. Surely she must be mad —
Don't call her Shirley, Sherryl, Shunaboy, Suze,
what's in a name? A Rose by any other
anagram would be as Sore. She drops
the dictionary upon the floor. She weeps

and strikes her brow with the hardel of her hand:
Horace and Hosmer, Hokestraw, Wellington, Widge,
Trifosa after great grandma, Luigi, Drew....
Knute the Unlucky, Erik the Dreadful, Alice,
Alas and Alack! What in the world will she do?

PEDOPHOBIA: *The Fear of Children*

He sees them on the sidewalk before his doorway
and begins to sweat. What can he do? How
can he negotiate those laughing voices,
those whirling arms, the quizzing eyes, how
get into his apartment and be safe

behind the dusty windows closed against
the nasty games, the screams, the dirty faces?
He crosses the street and keeps on walking. He
goes slowly as he can around the block,
keeping watch against another clot

of children or a lone minute assassin.
When he approaches home again carrying his bag
of groceries he sees them still before his door.
He bites his lip. He walks quickly among
the laughing voices, whirling arms, dirty

faces, the screams, the staring eyes. He walks
stumbling up the stairs and through the door,
drops his burden on the couch, reaches
trembling for the shade, pulls it down
over the dusty panes, the life, the laughter.

AMATHOPHOBIA: *The Fear of Dust*

If she closes her eyes, before she can drop
off the edge of silence into sleep
she imagines the dust beneath her bed
clumping itself, sending out strands of hair
to gather more dust, become a ball of fuzz,

and then begin to search for other balls of dust
with which to copulate and reproduce.
If it is a daylight nap she tries to steal,
her eyes spring open to see the noontide sun
slipping through the blinds in laddered beams

down which the motes of dust climb one by one —
she feels them landing on her chest, her face,
she feels them searching underneath her bed
to be caught in strands of hair, become a ball
of fuzz. She sneezes. She coughs. She begins to wheeze.

She throws off her coverlet to rise,
cover her mouth, walk to the kitchen through
the laddered beams of light and dust to find
the mop, the rag, the vacuum cleaner she
put away before she lay down to nap.

PHALACROPHOBIA: *The Fear of Balding*

He washes his hair carefully in the shower,
massaging his scalp as gently as he can,
lathering twice, then working in conditioner,
rinsing at last. He sees it there afterward,
lying in the bottom of the tub —

a single strand of anguish, a filament
of rue. He picks it up and looks at it
accusingly. He turns the water off
and reaches for a towel. He dries himself
carefully, massaging his scalp as lightly

as he can. He looks into the mirror
over the sink and sees what he despairs
to see: the youngish man whose hairline even
in steam recedes almost from day to day,
whose eyes are wide with anguish and with rue.

He's washed his hair as carefully as he can,
lathering gently twice, rinsing at last
as though the man were father to the boy
he sees disappearing in steam and dream,
strand by strand, day by rueful day.

AELUROPHOBIA: *The Fear of Cats*

She cannot stand their eyes, the way they stare
at her across the room, those lazy oval
pupils and the sleepy lids, the noisy purr
that sounds like a muted roar to her, as though
they waited slyly for the perfect time to pounce,

yawning to show the diminutive scimitars
that are their fangs. They like to toy with their prey —
the way they stare across the room purring.
How can people pet them? She shudders to think
of the smooth, soft, sleek, dissembling fur

beneath her fingers, the little knives hidden
in their sheaths like diminutive scimitars, the roar
in the dissembling purr. And when they walk!
the tail like a lashing snake, the soundless paws,
the grinning mouth hiding those little fangs....

How can people pet them? How can they touch
the dissembling fur, how can they stand the eyes
staring across the room with their oval pupils,
the yellow eyes, the eyes that know her soul
cringing in her breast, in its hollow place.

ARACHNOPHOBIA: *The Fear of Spiders*

He sees that the night is a dark web
and that the stars have come flying.
He hears the weasel sidling under the hill
where the long grasses are coarse.
The wind strikes a dim note, for the moon

is a dead eye beneath the stars struggling
over the hill where the owl ranges, the leaves
lie rustling in the coarse grasses. He hears
the wind as a dim note beneath the stars
trembling. On the hill a fox barks,

the spiders come floating upon the wind.
The blue stars lie quivering over the hill
as a weasel sidles through the grass. His fire
is a catamount hissing in the darkness
beneath the stars' keening. He hears the mole

listening to silence like a fog as the stars
come quaking, the weasel sidles under the hill.
The owl ranges the dead eye of the moon
while he sits at his fire listening for the spiders
floating in the blue wind, hissing in the darkness.

BRONTOPHOBIA: *The Fear of Thunder*

The first time she could remember hearing thunder
she'd been sitting on her grandma's lap
in the formal parlor of the big old house where she
was visiting. She flinched and shuddered. "What's that,
grandma?" She'd asked. "That is the voice of God,"

the old woman said, and then they heard it again
rolling out of the clouds, across the sky
and into the formal parlor hung with drapes
where the portrait of her dead grandfather hung above
the mantel and stared at her

as though with the eyes of God. She blanched and shuddered,
and had been shuddering ever since, whenever
the great dark clouds rolled over the deep blue sky,
shutting all the earth into into a parlor
hung with mists and rain, where a dead old man

stared down at them out of the roaring heavens
and told them what he thought without a word,
with only the sound of warning, the sound of dread,
the clap resounding out of admonition
and into the parlor in which they were entombed.

HOMILOPHOBIA: *The Fear of Sermons*
for David A. Casagrande

When he was young they'd called him "preacher's kid,"
"P.K." for short. "He's a heller on wheels, for sure,"
he knew they whispered behind their hymnals.
And every Sunday he'd had to sit and listen
to his old man up there in the pulpit, praying

and spewing on about God. "God" this, "God" that —
if you can believe it, his dad had wanted him to be
a preacher, too! Fat chance. He'd given God his shot:
prayed, read the Book, tried hard to hear the voice
his pop had told him would ring in his brain one day

and wring his heart. Nothing. By the time he was twelve
he knew the only voices he would hear
would be the pulings of hypocrites and fools
or choirs spouting out of their open hymnals
every Sunday until he could get out.

Not a week between his high school graduation
and joining the Navy. He'd gotten out
and stayed away, not gone home again
except on liberty. The only voice
that had wrung his heart had screamed, "Get out, P. K."

APOCALYPTOPHOBIA: *Fear of the Apocalypse*

It was only six weeks away, and then it would be
the end of the world for her, according to
the pastor of her church. She wasn't saved,
she didn't suppose, and when Y2K arrived
the earth would yawn at her feet and the Devil's claws

reach out for her ankles to drag her down to Hell
where the flames would eat her soul and the mouths of Baal
drink her blood from the Grail. The talons of Satan
would hold the holy cup for his evil minions
to sip in a ritual of dark communion,

she was sure. She'd tried to be one of the Good, a Chosen One,
but always she fell, always she was sure that she
was damned eternally. And now, six weeks away,
when the millennium fell upon us all,
she knew there was no hope, she knew that she

was one of the Lost, one of those who had
been cast aside by the Lord, the King of Kings
who took his drink from the Grail, Blood of the Lamb,
and tossed the Lost into the yawning earth
that gaped and disgorged the nails of the Devil's claws.

APEIROPHOBIA: *The Fear of Infinity*

He lies awake in his bed
in the pit of night, gazing into the infinite
reaches of his mind. Stars whistle there
in the vacuum; shadow fades
into shadow, and he is falling —

he is disappearing into himself.
He peers into the well without bottom,
feels compelled to drink the black water,
slake his thirst in the liquid
that stands among the stars holding his eyes.

He lies awake in the dark of night
lost in the reaches of his mind,
disappearing into himself, into the well
of shadow, falling, hearing the stars whistle
in the vacuum filled with the water that holds his eyes.

Water rises in his throat. He sees himself
drowning in the well, in the infinite
reaches of his mind. He hears himself whistle
among the stars, shadow fading
into shadow, fading and falling.

ACOUSTICOPHOBIA: *The Fear of Noise*

She loved her son, but oh! the blare they made —
that band of his. He'd wanted them to practice
in the garage, but that would never work. They'd tried it
once: the pounding in her skull
was quite incredible. She'd barely managed to stop them,

to send them home before she collapsed in bed
with a migraine tall as Everest and as broad
as the Mississippi River. And what was she to do
when he turned his stereo up loud as it would go?
She bought a pair of earplugs, but even that

would hardly do. She'd leave the house, if she could,
it wouldn't do to keep on saying "No!" No to the blare,
the pounding in her brain, the Everest of noise.
And what would she say when he asked her to go to hear
them play in the School Revue? Could she say "No!"

again to her loving son, or would she wear her plugs,
put on her earmuffs too and clap her hands
over her pounding ears to keep out the blare,
the unholy blare that hammered in her head
and gave her a migraine the size of Everest?

QUIESCOPHOBIA: *The Fear of Silence*
For, and on a line by, John Gilgun

He awakens in the darkness hearing
nothing — does this silence
hold a secret at its center? There is
not a timber creaking nor the ticking
of a timepiece, only stillness

at the center of awareness,
only emptiness and shadow. He
turns on the light and listens — still
there's little in the quiet but his
breathing, so he holds his breath to listen

to the dancing of his nerve-ends, to the straining
of his throat, the tongue as dry as fever.
Can this silence hold the secret
at the center of the dance?
And the dance...the dance, what is it?

What's that noise? He startles — only stillness
rushing through his veins, the surge of blood
within his eardrums, in his arteries
the whirling of his hours, of his being
in the silence at the center of the dance.

CATOPTROPHOBIA: *The Fear of Mirrors*

If she looks into the mirror she will see
no one she knows. The image there,
standing in a room of roses on the wall,
will be a stranger's; it will wear
the eyes of an assassin, the face

of the treacherous unknown. A wrinkle here,
a freckle on the cheek or near the nostril
might appear familiar — she does not dare
to turn about, confront no one she knows
standing in a sheet of wintry glass. The mere

of memory, the tarn that must accept
those cataracts of time, darken there
among the fading roses of the walls.
She does not dare turn and approach the mirror,
for she will meet a stranger, in the hall

of receding years, smoothing familiar hair
grown wintry among the roses on the wall.
The image will be a stranger's. She will stare
into those treacherous eyes and begin to drown
in the gaze of glass, in the tarn of memory there.

ENNUIOPHOBIA: *The Fear of Boredom*

He starts to worry. The job is almost done.
Is anything lined up? He looks ahead
even as he's concentrating on
the work in hand. The weekend's coming up.
His family will want him to do some things

with them: his wife will want to shop, the kids
will pull him around while she goes into stores
to try on this or that. He starts to worry,
tries to concentrate upon the work
he has in hand, but the weekend's coming up.

"T.G.I.F." somebody calls. He laughs, says "Yeah,"
but doesn't mean it. He looks ahead and sees,
with a touch of panic, two days of empty time
filled with nothing to do except putter
around the house, cut the grass, trim the hedge,

play with the kids while all this work goes begging —
how can he beg off? Can he bring some home?
His worry concentrates itself and he notices
he's not enjoying the work he's doing now,
still doing, the work in hand.

SABBATIPHOBIA: *The Fear of Holidays*

The calendar is her nemesis. The days drip off
the edge of the month bringing the holidays closer,
closer, ever so much closer. The pots and pans
that hang from pegs on the kitchen wall reflect
her dread, her consternation in shining copper

and stainless steel. Goodwill and jollity approach,
family values, thoughtfulness — she begins to suffocate
in the sea of expectations. The days drip off
her nemesis the calendar, begin to form a tide
of time that washes against the kitchen walls,

begins to rise to knees, to breast, to chin. She gasps.
So many things to do, shopping for gifts, for the tree,
for ornaments, baking, decorating,
sending the tastefully selected cards, displaying those
the mailman brings as the holidays come closer,

closer, ever so much closer. She can hardly breathe.
She loathes the calendar, her nemesis, the days that drip
off the edge of the month onto her kitchen floor,
turning the copper bottoms of her pans on the walls
a sickening green she remembers from childhood dreams.

MELANCHOPHOBIA: *The Fear of Depression*

He feels it first in his belly: a dying fall,
a slide and a lurching stop
at the brink of a pit that has opened in his mind.
He begins to whistle, then quits — that does no good;
breathes deep ten times. He hyperventilates:

oxygen saturates his blood, makes him dizzy,
nearly — lightheaded. He believes he's beaten it
and sighs with relief. Ten minutes later,
there it is again, the worm of despond
gnawing at his bowels, the dying fall,

the skid and lurching stop,
psychic heels dug in, at the brink
of the sinkhole of causeless sorrow.
He tries to read — that makes it worse. Music
seems to help a while, and then he turns

to television: the flittering images
ghost across the glass — he sees them through
a veil of descending mist. He goes out to run
the streets of his neighborhood, to slide and lurch
over the curbs and cobbles of his dread.

NEBULAPHOBIA: *The Fear of Fog*

The fog is rising...but not like Lazarus,
she hopes and prays, nothing like Lazarus —
more like the head of a fungus
rising to top out a summer morning.
She knows there's no reason to go into mourning,

none at all. So why is it she's in mourning
over the risen sun set on adorning
a mushroom here and there as the clouds disperse
across the blowsy sky, rush to disburse
scraps of storm across the universe? —

for now at least. There's a glamour in the air
and water-prisms whistling a liquid air
with eclat amounting to a flare
for causing one of a gloom-beridden cast
to lift her lids and seek the light at last.

Instead, she feels as though her livingroom
is full of webs of fog left over from
the morningful of summer morning gloom,
for the disappearing fog, like a slug or snail,
has touched the light and left a slimy trail.

MNEMOPHOBIA: *The Fear of Memory*

He's walked these halls for nearly thirty years:
they used to house the school his kids attended,
now they hold his office. How has he stopped
thinking of picking them up in the afternoons
from the lot he parks in all day now?

Has he mislaid those memories? He recalls
seeing his daughter run down the corridor
toward him walking up the passage; his son
stopped in traffic to shoot a car along
the wall outside his office. How can it be

he never thinks of these when he comes to work?
And with the question come recollections borne
upon a tide of loss; waves of pain
wash down the halls. He nearly drowns in them.
His stomach fills and turns as his daughter jumps

into his arms — he pushes her aside,
blocks out his son, stops to raise the dikes
that kept him safe. He retches for air, then walks
again down the familiar corridor
where pools of memory eddy in every door.

GERASCOPHOBIA: *The Fear of Aging*

Somewhere within these houses a woman looks
into a mirror and wonders why, or who
or when today has turned to mist and the sky
to leaves. Wherever else one looks a squirrel
seems to have a small request, but it

will still be weeks before the oaks manage
the feat of acorns. For now, the sun has gone
to earth, the trees brood in a pall of breathless
forenoon along the early summer streets,
among the late-arising neighbors. Here and there

a car coughs and begins to idle. The morning
papers materialize upon the verandas.
A schoolbus turns the corner saffron and then
disappears in a puff of smoke and gas.
In her room a woman wears a sapphire.

She looks into a mirror. Perhaps she lacks
that certain blue capacity, if she's lucky.
And if she's not, well, still she has the day,
the mist, the oaks, the squirrels, the mooning night
and the long dream of what is forever lost.

CHRONOPHOBIA: *The Fear of Time*

He hears his timepiece ticking in the night
beside the bed. Down the shadowed hall
each ponderous hour is rung by the standing clock.
He jerks awake and wonders why he has
these instruments of torment in his home.

He lies awake and hears the sandgrains fall
between the walls. The deathwatch beetle marks
behind his bed the moments of his life —
will daylight never dawn? Is all the world
forever lost in labyrinthine gloom?

He comes awake, rises and leaves his room
to wander down the hall. He hears the hour
rung by the standing clock. Its pendulum
swings through the moon, describing a silver arc
sixty times a minute — he hears the chatter

as though the sounds were rising from his brain.
Is all the world forever lost in sand
falling between the walls, deserts composed
of the moments of his life? He returns to bed
and hears his timepiece ticking in the night.

ONEIROPHOBIA: *The Fear of Dreams*

Her eyelids will not close. She stares awake
into the darkness lying upon her chest,
pressing upon her face — she feels the night
breathing beside her in the double bed.
Although she cannot see them, still she knows

the images lurk among the shapes of the room,
waiting their chance to enter through her ears,
to insinuate themselves into her mind
through the apertures of her nostrils, of her mouth,
her eyelids that will not close. She stares, aware

of the images in the darkness, of the darkness,
creatures of shadow lying upon her chest,
pressing upon her face, breathing her breath,
absorbing her life like fear into their own
insubstantial masses.

They bide their time, those creatures of the night,
those images of shadow, they wait their turn
to enter her mind and begin their naked dance
in the starlit berth of nightfall lying behind
her eyes and the lifeline of her constricted breath.

MUNDANOPHOBIA: *The Fear of the Ordinary*

The maple across the street says something deeply
red; the one nearby, something green.
The speakers spill Mozart across the floor.
Along the walls the shelves of books attempt
to speak. The sun is taut between the limbs,

brittle upon the moving leaves. What's
to be done with such a day? What should one
be doing? How many days like this can anyone
count on?... That was yesterday. Today
rain spills across the trees like Gershwin.

The colors of the leaves trend to mist;
therefore, there is no boundary between
earth and sky, only a confusion of shifting
tones of gray settled over the city.
What a relief! One knows what one must do

on such a day — tend to business. If there were
no such things as mist, Mondays and rain
what would one look forward to? Chores
in the sun, the churning mower, softball in the park,
smoke rising through the sizzle of afternoon.

ALLIUMPHOBIA: *The Fear of Garlic*

He thought she was a vampire, she felt sure — a witch at least,
for when she saw him coming she'd turn aside
and cross the road, or turn into a doorway and hope he'd pass
her by unnoticed. The few times she
had met him, shaken his hand, said hello,

she'd nearly choked on the stench. She was told
he ate whole cloves, several times a day! And she could believe
he did. One time she'd had to stand
and talk with him for some time at a gathering —
she couldn't get away. She'd nearly fainted as he said,

"It's great for colds. I've never had the flu!" The words flew by
filled with winds of odor, tornadoes of fetor, hurricanes of stench.
She'd nearly fainted before she got away, staggered away
on the arms of her snickering husband. And now she could
no longer bear to have garlic near

her anywhere, not even faintly in her food. She nearly choked
at the scent, she turned away, she crossed the room,
she staggered to the Ladies' to avoid the cloven hooves
of the evil herb, the vampire shield of stench
that gagged her if she even caught a whiff.

ARACHIBUTYROPHOBIA: *The Fear of Peanut Butter*

He opened the door of the fridge, and there it was:
the jar of peanut butter urging him in — "Come on,
grab me and spin my top, open me up,
stick in a finger and take a nice big dollop!"
He wanted to — oh! how he wanted to! But if he did,

he knew what would happen: the luscious stuff would stick
to the top of his mouth! He'd feel gummed up,
no matter how he sucked, no matter how he scraped
away with his tongue, the brown, delicious stuff
would cling to his palate like oils to an artist's palette,

and he'd have to stick a finger in his mouth to scrape it away,
and then he'd have to swallow and take a chance
that it would happen again. No, no, there'd be no dollop
for him...why did he keep the stuff around?
Why did he let it seduce him as though it were

a trollop on the corner of the square? A square of bread,
urging him on, "Come on, grab me and spin
my top, open me up, stick a finger in
and suck me down!" Oh, how he wanted to,
but if he did he knew what would surely happen.

ARITHMOPHOBIA: *The Fear of Numbers*

Onetwothreefourfivesixseveneightnineten
run through her brain tennineeightsevensixfive
fourthreetwoonenothing nothing nothing
can stop the drab cascade she goes to sleep
dreaming of numbers they indundate her dreams

and when she wakes the numbers on the clock
break upon her eyes she closes them
again and then the alarm goes off it shrieks
"It's six o'clock get up get up get up"
and so she does but in the shower the drops

cascade in avalanches down her body
in hundredsthousandsmillions a billion drops
too many to add they multiply divide
in rivulets of steam torrents of water
what can she do how can she escape

in numbers there is strength divide and conquer
sine and cosine no one can calculate
the drab cascades that multiply in her brain
waking or sleeping the terrifying ones
digits and tens fingers nose and toes.

IDEOPHOBIA: *The Fear of Ideas*
for George W. Bush

What good were they? The only thing they did
for him was make his poor head hurt like hell,
batting about between his ears, back and forth,
bounding off the walls of his skull, making his eyes
go spinning in circles like some cartoon of Elmer

Fudd after he'd been hit with a hammer. If he had wanted
to study stars he'd have become an astronomer…
or was it *astrologer?* He didn't know. Who cares?
He'd hated high school where they tried to make
you actually remember some of that stuff,

like economics and current affairs. College was great!
Beer and pot, girls and games, parties and brawls
until you woke in the morning, your poor head hurting
like hell, bells bounding off the walls of your skull,
batting about between your ears, back and forth

until the day he had to go to class
or get kicked out. But what the hell — no pain, no gain,
is what they say. As little as possible, though,
that's his motto. "Make love, not war," but do it smart,
don't stand for anything, just do it, get it done.

AMBIGUPHOBIA: *The Fear of Puns*

Neither hear nor dare to utter them:
that is her mutter as she walks the lane
between her home and work. No other theme
keeps her intention. Shakespeare is her bane
of contortion — all those double entendres,

wierd ploys, warble chokes. How can one stand
a language that sniggles like string, snags in the tongue?
A word should mean what it means and not demean
the person who speaks it, cause her demeanor to alter,
native good humor to melt in the foyer,

or before the altar, of the Laughing God.
She works the line between her ham and wok
when she pre-pares a meal. What is amiss? Better
to walk a mile than think of puns; sooner
choke on Oklahoma dust and walk a mule

than have as motto, "Neither hare nor deer
to otter dam." Better emigrate
to Rotterdam and get in Dutch
than stumble over meanings, double over,
wretched upon the quaking worth of words.

ALEKTROPHOBIA: *The Fear of Chickens*

He couldn't eat them, the dopey birds, not even
to shut up his friends when they called him a dumb cluck
and laughed and laughed. He wouldn't date "chicks" — the thought
of a hen party turned him off. His "pecker" wouldn't rise
to such an occasion. And all because

when he was a kid he'd lived in a house that stood
beside a chicken farm. There were what his uncle called
"hen dressin's" everywhere: the lawn, the walk, the porch,
and the stench suffused the air. There were rotten eggs
lying everywhere in the tall grass — Lord help you

if you stepped on one! Talk about stench! The smell of Hell,
sulfurous as the odor of the smoke that night
when the firetrucks woke them up, parked on the lawn,
the men snaking the hoses to the roaring flames
and the biggest barbecue in town! He'd never eaten

another of the dopey birds his whole life long,
the disgusting clucks, wattle-eye dewdrops on their beaks,
chicken fixin's and Colonel Sanders notwithstanding,
for the thought of it stopped his throat up as though with feathers,
and his nose with rotting sulfur in the grass.

METEOROPHOBIA: *The Fear of Weather*

She looks at the calendar. It's February now,
and it is snowing. It started snowing back in bleak
November, and it's kept on snowing all through cold
December. But that was nothing. In January
flowing snow came riding bareback on the blowing

Wild west wind. She couldn't recollect
a colder month or a more arctic winter. She
shakes her head — it's still that way. If anything,
it's growing worse and worse. Halfway through the month,
And nothing's getting better. The world is still

buried in the deep-freeze.
She leans her forehead against the pane and feels
the out-of-doors stab through the glass into
her deepest drifts of thought. She hears the wind
whipping and whining through the empty trees.

She thinks, *Borealis, it takes some skill
to be a tyrant. Call yourself a mensch?
This isn't cruelty, it's overkill.* She shudders
at her joke...or something. The calendar again:
still February, no matter how often she looks.

AMNESIOPHOBIA: *The Fear of Forgetting*

For a moment he forgot to be afraid.
When he recalled his fear, his eyes
widened in disbelief. His hand
rose to touch the taut cords of his throat;
beneath the heel of his palm his heart

battered his chest. It was beginning —
he was beginning to forget himself,
his past, who he was and is. Whom will he be
should he forget? His eyes widened
in disbelief when he recalled his fear,

and he was afraid —
Beneath the heel of his palm his heart
battered his chest from within. How can he
be sure he is who he is now that he has forgotten
to be afraid? His eyes widen in wonder,

and he forgets again, forgets his fear
in disbelief, recalls it again. His hand
rises again to touch the cords of his throat
and he knows that he has killed the man he knew
to find the lethal stranger he must be.

SOMNOPHOBIA: *The Fear of Sleep*

At first she jerks awake time after time,
but then at last her muscles lose their tension
and she begins to drift. On its pleated wings
her sleepless mind descends
the staircase of dream; its coils encircle the sounds

of evening seeping through windowpanes.
The hounds of midnight bay along the trail
of winds. The reptile brain creeps through fens
of solitary thought. She sees no bounds
to these morasses, these domains of dream.

As dread advances solitude impends
and swallows her at last. She remembers nothing
till morning tints the windowpane at last.
The mind begins to tear away
from fantasy's dim hordes.

The moat of night has finally been passed,
and she awakes, bathed in perspiration. She'll stay
awake till oblivion throws another coil around
intellect and dulls it in the vast
abyss of nonentity that sleep affords.

ACROPHOBIA: *The Fear of Heights*

When he was young he thought nothing of climbing
onto a roof and working there all day, the warm spring sun
falling across his back, making him feel
as easy as a chick in its nest in an airy oak.
Then came the day when, halfway up a ladder,

he happened to look down at the ground where the other men
were working, but what he saw
was his body lying broken among the lumber. He felt his hands
freeze on a rung, his knees begin to tremble, the sweat
break on his brow. The ground began to spin

in a lazy loop beneath his shaking legs. He tried to make
himself look up at the sky with its warm spring sun
riding the flying clouds but couldn't tear his eyes
away from the looping earth riding the sky
about his broken body lying among

the timbers and boards there on the ground
beneath the bones
as brittle as sticks. He didn't know
how at last he came to be standing on solid earth,
his hands still clenched as though frozen on a rung.

MORTOPHOBIA: *The Fear of Death*

She sees that he rides a dark stallion.
He holds a vermilion banner.
His hand is a hand of bone, white bone,
ivory upon the rein,
and he rides alone.

She knows he rides a dim stallion.
At his side is a blade of steel.
His brow is a brow of bone, white bone
beneath the iron helm,
and he rides alone.

She fears he rides a black stallion.
On his chest is a corselet of rust.
Through the mail one can see the bone, white bone
clasping a cage of air,
and he rides alone.

Lost is the name of the stallion,
And the name of his blade is Hours.
His pace is the gait of bone, white bone.
He hums like the wind as he wanders,
and he rides alone.

AGORAPHOBIA: *The Fear of Open Spaces*

If he goes out they'll see his fly is open,
perhaps, or something will occur to make them laugh
at him — his pants will rip on a passing nail
and he will have forgotten to wear his briefs. Or maybe he'll
merely meet someone he ought to know

and forget the name, forget the occasion, the place —
forget it! He'll stay at home. There are too many
possibilities for disaster there, among the streets,
among the people, among the dogs and cats
that roam the alleys waiting to make him fall,

to bite or claw him, and then...to cross those streets,
the autos whipping past, the confusing lights: Walk!
Don't Walk! Men at work! Open your fly! Close it! Beware of men
in hard hats working here. The open manhole there!
He holds no brief for going out today. At home the worst

that might occur — perhaps he'll chip a nail
passing a chair. No one around to see him split a hair,
but there — out there! They'd all be watching him
to see the latest stupid thing he'll do
to make them giggle, to make them laugh at him.

DEMENTOPHOBIA: *The Fear of Madness*
"Sometimes our connection is frayed, it is in danger, it seems almost lost. Views and streets deny knowledge of us, the air grows thin." Alice Munro, "The Albanian Virgin."

It was such a day. The gulls in the park
wove their patterns in the wind above the lake,
but nothing came of them. The young lovers
stood holding hands or speaking in low voices
beneath the trees, but who could tell them

what it was they meant, their voices falling
into the shadows beneath the leaves? Falling
and disappearing. Perhaps the sun fell
as well into the dark column of a cloud.
Nor could she be certain of the city

that lay about the park, along the lake.
Were children there as well upon the streets,
fathers in shirtsleeves working in the warmth
of summer, or early fall, or late spring? She
felt a sense of danger, a worn place here

or there in the afternoon. A child fell
and hurt its knee. No one offered to help it.
Perhaps she was merely uneasy, perhaps she
was afraid...perhaps she didn't care. Perhaps
nothing, no one, mattered any more.

AMBIVOPHOBIA: *The Fear of Decisions*

He will go to the valleys of Andorra; *He will stay
in his brown room, the dark sunlight seeping
through the blinds.* He will live in a cabin
on the lip of a gorge, listen in the chill wakening
to a river crying among the forests. *Tomorrow

his eyes will open to the sounds of a thin child
calling news of war.* The birds of the wood will weave
through clouds rising from the chimney.
The smell of labor will smother the city.
In the mountains of Andorra folk speak with the echoing

stone. *Listen — walls eat his voice. In the alleys
old men cough. Death is visible
in the phlegm speckling the curb.* He will go
to Andorra's valleys to live on a thin edge
which the blood hones and the bone grinds finely

as it moves beneath the skin. *He will stay
in this brown room, on a bed snarled by night's
restless passage, hearing the Christmas bells
rattling upon the street corners, watching
the sunlight seep feebly through the blinds.*

BIBLIOPHOBIA: *The Fear of Books*

In her New England house as old as moss
winter whistles up a stony flue,
seeps through clapboards, windles on the shelving
where leaves of ancient books in their calfskin covers
ruminate upon the approaching spring.

Three centuries have settled graying moss
under the eaves where the white winters flew
to seep through clapboards, windle on the shelving,
riffling the leaves of volumes in leather bindings
praying the seasons out — fall, winter, spring,

summer and starlight settling like moss,
smothering her life gone up the flue
like smoke, rustling in the shelving,
turning the pages of books in vellum covers
seasoned with the scent of another spring

in this New England house as young as moss,
under these eaves, wind whistling down the flue,
between these clapboards, here upon this shelving,
in books with vellum bindings, calfskin covers,
waiting the winter out, looking for spring.

SENILOPHOBIA: *The Fear of Senility*

He looks at the bottles on his shelf —
gingko-biloba, that's the ticket,
extras of those. And for the arteries,
anti-oxidants: vitamin E, alpha-lipoic
acid. What had he forgotten?

He breaks into a sweat. Did he forget
something? And if he did, was it a "senior moment,"
a harbinger of things to come? He wracks his brain
and tries to concentrate. The thought
slips his mind. He won't become a thing,

a zombie in a chair — ginko-biloba,
that's the ticket. And exercise: crossword
puzzles, acrostics, word-games, talking
backward — he breaks into a sweat
looking at the bottles on the shelf,

feeling the wattles on his chin atremble.
He walks to the living room, he takes a book
and tries to concentrate upon the words
sliding about under his eyes,
staring like those of a zombie from his chair.

THE GREEN MACES OF AUTUMN,
VOICES IN AN OLD MAINE HOUSE
2002

ALBUMS

        The ancient albums lie
    behind the parlor door spinning fine
tintype fables between plush covers: straight stares
    line out over handlebars and whalebone

        stays. They were familiars,
    once; now the summer eyes of the old
farm run through evenings of conjecture, try names
    against heydays, trace the features of these

        generations peering
    over collars and boas. A jowl
sags here, beneath this rafter. An eye is gray,
    like the sky over the hill. A fire

        flickers at the grate, flares
    and settles. Someone lights a pipe. Now
the pictures come to life and walk the halls: this
    bone is the old lady's, that tooth the man's.

        Whose child is this that sits
    in the dusty shadows — whose dust, whose
shade? Who made the bed of webs above the ell?
    Who sleeps, who wakes, whose footfall on the floor

        disturbs the carpet beetle in its lair?

JOHN BOURNE
1698-1761

There was no house here when I came
up the Kennebec from the coast
through Merrymeeting Bay, its mouths
emptying the forests of their waters.

The pines and cedars pressed in close
along the banks. Loons dove and laughed,
their voices echoing like men
gone mad, like demons or savages.

Yet here I would plant myself, my
crops, build my mill, raise barn and house
among the hardwoods whispering
their secrets into the ear of the wind

winding up the dark passages
from the sea, the riding ocean.
I cleared the land, my sons and I.
We built the house, and we laid in the seed.

We took root in the clay and stone.
The sun shone and the snow fell down
through the smoke of our fires rising
out of the valley. Where are you now, flesh

of my flesh, blood, bone of my seed?
You have fallen down through the mist
of years rising from the Eastern,
its tides riding and siling with the sea.

PRISCILLA BOURNE
1705-1772

There was time until there was no time.
I made them bread with little leaven.
I split wood and I carried water.
I bore them all — men, burdens, the hard years

and the easy weather. I weathered them
and I withered, doing what women
do. Did I regret it? No. These were
mine. I would do it again if I could

flesh that bone lying in the churchyard
under the dying elms. I throve while
I could, and I watched my children thrive —
two of them. We made the halls of the house

echo and the bare fields yield. We throve
and we died. Now our voices murmur
in the dusty corners when the wind
rides up the valley bearing on its back

a siege of storm. We discuss the hours
lying muffled in the dark eaves.
Wasps humming in the summer attic
are our neighbors now. All, all has fallen

away into the lath and plaster
that covers the first boards I scoured,
into the clocks muttering upon
the mantels. Now, at last, there is no time.

PAUL PULLEN
1719-1743

She cannot hear me now, but once she could.
    This never was my home, I merely
        wooed her here — a short courtship
    before I took her coasting down East

and wed her on the strand where lay my ship.
    I laid her down and gave her seed,
        then shipped aboard a doomed vessel.
    I fought the fathoms to rise

from off the bottom where my shipmates slept
    scattered in galley and forecastle, on the bridge,
        between decks, dreaming of storms
    and pearls; I fought the gales

across seas and lanes of sky until I came to rest
    here, beached and dumb, among these dry walls.
        Here have I remained, speechless,
    while my son grew into a man,

then into a relic long in the tooth,
    older than I had ever been. Nor could I
        speak his name until he joined
    me here within this cold bonehall.

Now we watch as our seed washes thinner
    with each generation, as the sea
        sends its message upriver
    with the tides twice each day forever.

HESTER PULLEN
1723-1795

I was the eldest, the oldest daughter.
    I was married once, and widowed.
My husbandman was a man from the sea,
    and it was the sea that claimed him

with the Narwhal out of Bath and all hands.
    I was but a bride at the time.
He left me with child and little beside
    in my cottage upon the rocks

looking toward the horizon as blank
    as stone, or no horizon — fog
settling upon the ledge by the sea.
    My father came for me one day,

down river in a skiff, and brought me home.
    My son was born here in this house
creaking in the wind, and here I remained
    the rest of my days. My life was preserved

in crock and root cellar. Winter ate it,
    summer renewed it, and the child
consumed my hours. The wind filled the elms
    like sails over the dooryard blooms,

and in it his voice grew ever fainter,
    as though he were sailing farther
over the water, till I could hear it
    no longer — never a whisper

among these walls where time siled and settled.
    I made old bones as my son made
young ones — they were his, and his the face
    that rose and fell in the long tide

at last that claimed me. I became
    the shell of the hermit on the strand.
Emptiness inhabits me still. I am
    the silence that invests these walls.

JOHN BOURNE, JR.
1724-1740

    If you walk these acres today,
      back of the house, look carefully
and you may find an arrowhead lying
among the furrows, in the blue clay soil.

    It was one of these that took me
      as I was plowing on a bright
day of spring, the snow in rare patches still
among the boles of the near woods. I lay

    looking into the earth that I
      would enter soon as my blood would
richen it enough. At last they found me
and rolled me over to stare at the sky

    with an eye of reflection. When
      I woke from my brown study,
I was here in these joists, listening to
the years working the fields, the crops growing

where I had let my boyhood seep away.

HENRY BOURNE
1726-1726

    I remember, briefly,
        a light flickering —
a candle or a taper, perhaps,

    clouds bending above me,
        then silence, darkness,
and the smell of small lives about me.

THOMAS BOURNE
1730-1811

   And I was the last of the old man's sons,
the only one to survive the deep winters
      into the deeper springs. I remember
         my brothers not at all — they were ghosts
before ever I was born between these walls.

   Though they were never spoken of in my
hearing, yet I heard them speaking for themselves
      in the lath. I knew who they were. At night
         they came into my dreams to play their
strange games with me. I loved them and feared them both.

   Now I have joined them, I am the elder —
old enough to be their father now, aye, and
      grandparent as well. Time in these walls is
         a strange place and yet a stranger
feeling. We are a single generation

      made of all generations. History
is a telescope. We dwell upon our crushed
      existence here amid our descendants.
         They have draped the flesh of our future
upon the musty skeleton of their past.

FRANCIS PULLEN
1744-1779

At the age of thirty-one I left Gardiner
      with Arnold to trudge the Kennebec
   and take Quebec. The march was terrible hard.
    We carried the greenwood boats farther
       than they carried us, it seemed.

In the bitter weather of northern November
      we found the city had been forewarned.
We waited for Montgomery from Montreal
    a freezing month and more. Christmas came
     and went. Then, on New Year's Eve

we tried to overcome the garrison but took
      only losses, I regret to say,
including my left leg. They carried me home,
    more dead than alive when I arrived
     and was laid upon my bed,

but I did indeed live to tell the tale over
     and again to my fellow townsmen
or anyone who would listen, till they tired
    of the bloody words and the thumping
     of my crutch on the floorboards.

I studied books a while, took to me a helpmeet,
    and practiced law as the case arose
  at Pownalborough Courthouse on the river.
    Now I read the tracks made in the dust
      by mice on joist and rafter.

But not all of it is bad, as we used to say,
  for I can tell my tale forever
    here, and no one will complain, and I can walk
  again upon my leg of shadow,
    for we are reunited.

PATIENCE COBB PULLEN
1749-1780

    You mustn't listen to him.
    To hear him talk you would think
he did nothing but brag. That is far

    from the case. None hereabouts
    practiced better country law.
None was a better son or husband.

    When he passed away from me
    I waited a decent year
then came to join him here. Although we

    are insubstantial as drafts,
    our voices dim as a trace
of mist upon the millbrook coursing

    through the dell below the hill,
    we are two portions of one
person, and his is the better half.

THOMAS BOURNE, JR.
1750-1823

When the call came, I was ready.
We rode or walked until we found the place
   where the recruits were being mustered,
       and from there we were shipped

   to Massachusetts for training,
such as it was. The winter killed many
   of us — more than were lost in battle.
       And when it was over

   we returned to our homes heroes.
Nothing in my life ever came near it
   again. It was as though my living
       had ended before it

   ended. And now endless is
my death. Glory is a fly caught in a
   web; the drum is the death-watch beetle
       rattling among these walls.

CALEB PULLEN
1765-1834

    I was the odd one, the merchant.
I ran the store overstreet, on the track
      from Wiscasset to Augusta, nigh
         the tollhouse. I enjoyed commerce —
         with goods, with people. What I miss

      most here in my corner of the old
farmstead is the bustle and the hum
      of life passing through my shop and hands —
         not the coin, for I amassed no fortune,
         nor ever wished to do.

      The goods, the goods! They were only
for getting on with it, for use, for pleasure.
      It was the talk and the activity,
         the gossip and the goings-on.
         Ah, I miss it, I miss it all!

      I hope some day I'll find that this
is just some sort of penance we put in
      here amongst these boards and droppings,
         to pay for...only God knows what,
         ere we are worldly-born again.

TIMOTHY BOURNE
1778-1839

There was an animal in the sun
    and he was black. He was the cat
    who lived with us here, in this house.

There is no danger in blackness, in
    the darkness itself, except that
    it hides itself well in shadow

and in the night so that we cannot
    find it among the trees, among
    the roots of the woods and the weeds.

There were no children here, no offspring,
    no legacy of the springtime
    for the cat to play with or my

wife to fondle, or myself to heft,
    feeling the weight of the future.
    The cat was all for each of us,

his blackness the blacker for the love
    we bore him and for the shadows
    we knew he loved more deeply than

he loved us. We knew the cat would go
    some night. Came the morning we did
    not find him seeking sun. My wife

wept for a while. The house felt weightless
    and plundered. Dark had bolted dark,
    and blackness had contained itself.

MARGARET BOURNE
1795-1847

    White and yellow, its flight
outlined in black, the butterfly
    cut a trace among lilies
    of the valley and a hedge

    of lilac. The falling
sun touched its eyes to prisms
    refracting light and air. First
    cousin to twilight, vagrant

    weightlessness of shadow
or breeze, its motion was silent
    as evening fading among
    silhouettes. I captured it,

    preserved it in a book
amid fathomless lines whose
    point is lost. All wings stutter
    against this pressing darkness.

EPHRAIM BOURNE
1800-1836

      When the angels came to fetch me
        there was a slim white burst of feet
   upon the stair where worn wood glanced up
          between spread toes. I said, "At last,
quietly but with thunder, you have come.

      "The firmament has struggled. Out
        of clouds my smoky mistress' womb
   has fashioned feathers and a soul which
          sunder, bearing you — platinum,
brass, incense and sinew." The family

      was relieved to see me go; they
        did not believe I saw you, nor
   the things I said in my ecstasy —
          no more than they did in my life.
But out of the dust there was sustenance.

      The angels' hair was wheat, it was
        bread broken, visions made of sun!
   Light swirling through the valley! Levels
          of blue — the latitudes of their eyes!
Complexions: mauve, purple — shades within which

      crouched the burned feet — mother wings with
        the strength of gnarled tree roots clutching
   infinities of cliffs, bringing green
      gifts, winds and voids from which angels
spring. Eternal and immortal Cosmos,

      glide backward into time with me,
      soar forward into time! Hover
   slowly within your perfect circle
      where boundlessness eternally
must occur! Create the ever-welling

      fount, the phoenix forever blue
      and calm and fire: Life, which is
   Light, which motivates the vehicle
      I once propelled down wooden stairs
to greet with joyful blood death's bright angels

sprung gently but with thunder from my brow.

WENDELL PULLEN
1825-1907

    My cousin James showed me how to skate
        the winter ice of the Eastern.
    And when it was time to harvest cold,
we went together to the Kennebec. There
        the cutters gathered beneath

    the great ice houses where winter would
        be stored until the schooners came
in the dead of summer to haul
crystal New England to the China Sea. We
        scored the ice and sliced it;

    we cut it with saws as the horses hauled,
        steaming, across the still river.
    I did not see Thomas fall, but when
I heard his cry, I followed. It was I who
        pulled him back to life — but not

    for long. It was not the river that
        took him down where he could not breathe,
but the long haul of winter in his
lungs. I heard him rasping like a saw
        in the dark hours of night, and I heard

    the stillness come upon him at dawn.
        Then, in the darkness that followed,
  I thought I could hear him again where
the mice scuttered. I was right. Again
           he has taught me, this time how

    to breathe in the dust and how to sound
        now like an October draft; now
  like a zephyr of May in clover;
again, like a last gust of August caught
           in the milkweed of September.

JEREMY CARR
1840-1861

      At the first blare of the Federal trumpet
    I rose up out of the breast of my family,
left my beloved wife standing in the doorway
      in the late April wind of 'sixty-one, one arm
          bearing our child, the other waving. We sons

      of Dresden walked down the dusty road singing.
    You can't call what we got "training." We could hardly
march in good order when we arrived at Bull Run late
      in July. We fought the rebel rag-tags for a while,
          and then our ranks broke and ran. I tried to run

      as well, to my shame, but a musket ball fired
    by a boy from Tennessee broke my back. I lay
there in the dirt, unable to move, as the Grays rushed
      over me yelling, but feebly. If we could have
          stood our ground just a little longer we

      might have won instead of they. When finally
    I made my way home through the strange night of first death,
through the reek and stench of battle, the dark tents teeming
      with men grateful to be alive, but some dying
          and many others to join me soon enough,

      I found myself my niche here in the bosom
    of my family again. Here have I stayed, here
I have been counted a hero. But heroism
      is a matter of luck, ill or good, and I would
          rather have had none of it and a long life.

MICHAEL PULLEN
1861-1919

   Hours accumulate.
Dust sifts down between these laths
    in drifts of white time.

THOMAS CARR
1870-1936

      Smoke Hole, Coeur d'Alene —
the names of these places and the houses
  of the streets, the trees walking along
    the curbs: shrub-faces, lilac
        ears pressed against houses

    listening to the night
coming over the lawns, overcoming
  gullies as the moon arises, screels
    into the sky to touch up
        darkness; bodies wound in

    sheets, touching the dim
scent of earth wheeling in some barrow
  among forests and coils of water,
    stars riding the falls as dream
        drinks us down wherever.

PATIENCE PULLEN
1880-1885

This is the way I played with my dolls,
my children of rag among these walls —
    upsy-daisy and down we go
    lullaby baby, and sleep, sleep.

This is the way that I sang my songs,
the songs I made up of hours alone —
    sleep, baby, sleep, away we go,
    lullaby baby and good night.

This is the way I lay down to rest
never to wake in my bed again —
    dream, baby, dream and here we go,
    lullaby now, good night, good night.

RANDALL BOURNE
1885-1973

    Once upon a blue moon, legend has it,
we boys ran the river to the Atlantic
        in a small boat, avoiding the rocks
    and rapids, passing beneath the bridges,

    and it was so. We stared into gardens
where young women waited, growing their flowers.
        The day was blue then, the river brown.
    There were the summers always. This house was

    set in the fields above the fallen mill,
the brook, the waterfall. I remember this:
        the raspberries passing in a dream
    after a day of pressing through the thorns.

    Those were the summers of events hanging
in the imagination like thunderheads
        glimpsed through the attic window during
    a hunt in the heat for linen or frames;

    like the northern lights that woke the household
to walk out onto the black dew in bare feet;
        the snapping turtle like a stone
    on the lawn. Here in my gallery of webs

    and timbers I recollect the summer
an enormous hive burst the church steeple, poured
        honey down the clapboard spire
    in a viscous cataract. But what may these be

    beside the presences? — the grandfather
in the tractor, the falling stalks. There was once
        a morning of coffee as the rain fell,
    the grandmother at her dishes

    and the stench of kerosene in an iron stove.
There were always the spiders hanging brown
        and great in their drapery about the porch —
    familiars of the old woman

    who kept them there, not to be molested,
for their veils swallowed up a plague of flies.
        And they are there still, numberless
    in their generations, as are we, caught

    in the toils of time among these walls, these alcoves
of remembrance from which nostalgia's icons
        peer out into the dim air flowing
    down the stairwell, swirling into corners,

    and rising again through the great brick throat
of the chimney into the dusk falling
        in moments and starlight onto roofs
    and the slumbers of the dwellers.

JULIA PULLEN
1885-1965

      I was the aunt who made the collection
of vials filled with sand. I remember
standing beside the sea on a day lambent
with haze, the surf moving in from Madagascar.
      I stooped to sample the world. Later, in

      this house, in a room faint with lavender
and shadow, I labeled the vial and laid
it in batting, interred it in my bureau
drawer with the others. I would exhume them from time
      to time, perhaps, when the sky closed in and

      the season. I enjoyed recollecting
the day I trod on Number Twelve; Number Three
was a fine blue afternoon, the combers like
white roosters coming to take my seed, sand smoothing
      against my nail. The dark, as some child slides

      my drawer to now, closes over these strands.
The conch of stillness echoes among these hours
sequestered against the day when, in a fine
riptide of shattered glass, all my being shall come
      together in a dune of years and I

shall be lost at last in the siling sands of time.

AMANDA PULLEN
1887-1980

Destitute of sound, I rely upon the room
to resolve my silences harmonically.
        The chandelier's highlights set the tone.
      The stillness is crystalline. It has been
a thousand separate moments since I sank

into this drift of time. Before me, in the brick
flue, something small but live seems constricted. Not flame —
        no heat swells the throat of solitude.
     No phoenix nests here. Listen. The sharp hour
sprinkles daylight through the windows like quarter

notes or — no — like the feathers of an arctic tern.
How long has it been since there was a touch, or a
        taste, even of smoke, in this white air?
     Something binds but does not span these moments.
Something hovers: it spirals and hovers like

an eagle somewhere near the ceiling of stilled time.

HARRIET BOURNE
1890-1985

As the summer was gathering to its end
        all the clan gathered to feed
     on lobsters in the swimming heat.
We considered the season and the gathering
       at the white house with its field spread
  to the river and the brook, to the falls,

the mill site lying stony below the bank,
          willows for axles. The claws
      were spiked with wedges of wood,
and golden ears lay steaming before them. We laughed
       at ourselves, at them. A car passed.
    A bowl of steamers yawned and raised vapors.

The butter was drawn. Thus it was that we fell
        to in celebration, for
     the weathers of winter and of
spring had been weathered like the yard of stones near
       at hand. We devoured August,
  cracked the shells like frost breathing in granite,

savoring the meat and the flesh. When we were done
         we had raised a monument
    of spent bodies in our very
midst — we were those who had survived. We offered
       ourselves wishes for the coming
    fall, leaves and cobs, rime and shell. This is as

I recall it — the car passing and the time.
        But perhaps it was not so.
     Perhaps the happy voices were
echoes in the walls, and the faces figments
       of my contemplation, a twist
  of the eyes in the blank room of summer.

JOHN PULLEN BOURNE
1900-1978

     At the end I was very ill.
I had been ill for years, but I told
no one, not even Bertha, my wife.
     At last the evil thing in my blood
asserted itself, grew visibly

     upon my heel. How then to put off
knowing one day more? How to motor
to the beach with my wife, my daughter
     and son-in-law, lay out the food,
ignore the crab scuttling in my veins? We watched the

     shadow of the beach umbrella
round upon itself, then sidle
east to touch the verge of Ocean.
     How to wait through to summer's end,
the brown and colored hills, the waning days,

     the hours of early snow against the bark?
Yet these, too, came to pass. I became
another voice in beams and ceilings...,
     but fresher, traces of blood upon the echo still,
my presence as strong in absence

Fearful Pleasures   *The Complete Poems*

      as in the flesh. I mourn their grief
for me, and I regret bitterly
my willed ignorance, my cowardice —
      for such it was. I called my stance
stoicism then, when still I might have been cured.

      It is much too late. I will fade
inexorably, despite their wish
to keep me green in memory. I shall turn
      gray as the lichen on the stone
that weights my body beneath the winter day.

BERTHA BOURNE
1901-1996

    I sang in my dreams, my voice
a point of stillness in the night.
        It was cold. There was snow
in the yard. These were the realities
        that forced themselves on us,

    yet they were to be made but
little of, the room light glinting
        in the blue glass along
the mantel. We made catalogs of things
        to be done while waiting

    for the spring to manifest
itself in the change of the brook's
        voice across the road
and in the appearance of jonquils. I heard,
        now and again, rumors

    of resurrection, but I was
little impressed, or perhaps
        I dreamt it, for it was
a season of spiders and of iron.
        The stove was our only

    consolation. He had gone,
my husband, the man with whom I
        spent my years faithfully.
Now his body is divorced from mine, his voice
        an echo from frozen springs.

MELINDA BOURNE
1901-1975

At the wake I spoke to the mourners, family
    and friends — of broken vessels, a clockwork
        kitchen running down. They did not know
            how to answer. There were dust
        and the piecemeal division of moments

on the mantelpiece. A loveseat and a coffin
    struggled for balance on the paisley carpet.
        They listened to our common sorrow
            and could not answer. I move
        now like the ghost of a gown filled with winds

here where our fingers discuss things of no moment
    over the pages of magazines and
        an ocean of tea brewed of seasons
            and herbs. I move furtively
        among my spheres and cannot tell how to

populate them except with lees and sentiment,
    with the empty turning of hands pointing
        at numerals that hum and click
            like beetles coming together
        at random intervals. I know my weeks

will turn themselves into a bag of years rustling
   on the porch. The doors will shut and open,
      windows come down and shades, to slice night
         or daylight into edible
      portions. What we waste can be used to fill

the spaces that must be filled until the garment
   of movement and the sack of waking lie
      replete, silent, floating in a round
         depth of unremembered hours.

JESSIE BAKER
1905-1979

    I came in my blue Buick to say
goodbye. I forgot the ancient albums,
      the object of my good intentions,
which lay still at home behind the kitchen door
    spinning fine tintype fables between their
        plush covers. I would have asked him, "John,

    do you remember these straight eyes that
line out over handlebar mustaches
      and whalebone stays?" Someone in those days
had forgotten to ink in the names. There'd been
    other days when younger eyes ran through
        evenings of conjecture, conjuring

    few words to put to those images.
"Did they move once, John, in dawns and evenings
      of someone's heydays, clothed in something
other than stiff collars and boas?" It was
    unwitting kindness, perhaps, that caused me
        to forget. It was hard enough that

    day to speak, let alone recollect.
The motor lulled me to and from with small
      talk of tappets and valves. There's nothing
of flesh devouring itself in that, nothing
    of cells raging like wild worms through the host
        of themselves. You would not ask yourself,

        when I had left, which of my poses
    you preferred. When I got back home I put
          the albums back upon the shelf by
the television console where images
        might flicker their uneasy glass dreams. Such
            thoughts were not to my profit. Now I've

entered this dream of a house with you, brother John.

RAYMOND CARR
1908-1979

It was late. I remember turning
    the odd fact over while the bees
gorged themselves in the dooryard. The pods
and days were full. Maples breathed deeply
of the setting suns; oaks held the squirrels'
    footprints until it was too late,

or nearly so. The fall impended.
    We hearkened to the distances...
we considered the alternatives,
discarded them as they arose out
of indecision. There were, of course, things
    to be counted — we took up nails

and set them in place. We took our meals
    and our time, though it was perhaps
the catbird's, guarding the goldenrod
in uniform gray: now and then
he dropped over the bank toward the road,
    stopping here and there to call his

ownership. The two old women clipped
    flowers in the season's heat,
then disappeared among the stones that
stood under the woods, came back to life once
more, their hands empty of stalk and blossom,
    for they had left them with the one

    who had left them. The catbird became
        the sole proprietor at last,
    but what does he own of the season
    beyond the shape of the maple leaf,
the silences and sorrows of houses
          and the warmth of the waning sun?

JOSEPH CARR
1917-1995

Out of the old noon sun still lifting
      wraiths from morning's gully,
   the phoebe's call assails the barn —
   its shingles are nearer the heart

of gray in the shadows of those deep
      eaves. Summer, the huckster,
   wends over Blinn's Hill, having sold
   snippets of blue thread, a needle,

some ribbon, perhaps a pan or two
      for a child to bang on
   in time to the oaten reed of
   phoebe's throat. The falls still murmur

out of the tannery's foundations
      past the millstones that lie
   below the culvert — everything
   is the same. The same thread of ink

stitching samplers of the hours; the same
      summer stretching to that
   familiar autumn perched like a chipmunk
   on the cask by the chicken coop.

We feed song sparrows seed the chipmunks
         steal. Winter huddles under
     pelt or plume, heedless of our will,
     whether we forestall the first frost

with words or let fly with silence. Child
         and birds wax fat and sleek.
     For the moment I need not sing
     that sad song I had in mind. But

I reserve the right to return to
         that old tune one day when
     summer's luster dims to the tone
     of morning mist, takes to itself

the patina and hue of pewter
         and dew lies like crystal
     on the varicolored vials
     of honey water hung on wires

to halt the flight of the hummingbird.

RUTH CARR
1919-1972

    This was our conceit: the brilliant
    gavel of the sun arched and fell
        just once on the treetops
beyond the river — going, going,

    gone. Summer had been sold item
    by item to the gathered
        bidders. That auctioneer
of hours reckoned up the proceeds

    as the crowd drove down the gravel
    drive, bits and snatches of odds and
        ends tied down on car tops,
tucked in trunks — goods bought in good barter

    with what rare currency. Our money
    grew on trees whose leaves measured, from
        green bud to russet leaf,
corrosions of the heart. From the spring

    founting in the valley there followed
    a hurliburl of foliage
        in thunder and in sunlight.
Summer spent itself at last. It broke

    into bankruptcy with a fine
       splurge — too late. We fair-weather folk
          fared well away. We'd know
nothing of that bleak grace with which the

    weather-beaten would sustain their
       penury. But we knew that when
          the gold was gone there would
be silver to spend. There was one last

    night by the river, then we locked
       the barn in the morning, turned off
          the tap, drained the kitchen
pipes, saw the lawn chairs, the croquet

    and badminton stowed in the shed.
       Then, the windows of the old house
          reflective of nothing
but sunlight, we drove ourselves away.

HERBERT TORREY
1919-1985

      That fourth of July a sly laugh
           dogged our fancy. Uncle John,
the old wag, taled off again. The children
    clamored in bushy shadow, and green
        grass grew all around all around

      under the vintage windows, rosy
          with the last of the sun. Like
time shrunken and drawn taut across the evening,
    the lawn tapped out its cricket sounds and
        Melora rapped her doldrums on

      the tabletop. Muzzy Aunt Nat
          turned over turning forty-
one, gave the women the once-over, thumbed
    down the thought. How to describe it? The park
        that day was ducks like sparks about

      the pair of snowflame swans burning
          out of blue sconces. The kids
had crackers and quacks — as many as they
    could swallow or toss; the trees had leaves
        thick as Moorish rugs. Their silhouettes

blotted sunlight, drank it off thick
banks and gravel walks. And flowers!
Bows of them, beds massed beneath Old Glory
poling it over the band shell, green
benches applauding its rustic

orchestration: flagstone, sandstone,
half-timber. All told, it was
a period piece, a dash of Edward —
a pause. But not ours, and surely not
the children's. Perhaps we elders

could remember when it was like
this all day long, nearly, day
in, well-nigh, and out. And what were we to
say when the night came mooning? When light
lay draped lightly about the hill,

and on the hill the old stone tower,
in it the four flights of iron
stair that we climbed counting that afternoon
to see the world unroll there beneath
the parapet? Not even the world,

merely our town: a tall tale told tongue-
in-cheek — to a child holding
buttercups and clover — by a sly old
mountebank, it well may be.

JASON PULLEN
1920-1943

There was an end of things when Hitler took
the violet from violets. I wound
a ribbon of desire around a flame
and set it under tinseled evergreens.
No siren admonitions could efface
the visions drifting up the chimney pile.

Beyond that short-lived spring gray willows wept,
and passionate midsummer suns espoused
the darker shadows of the dawn. Axe blades
bit deep while life-sap mercuries of pine
and fir recorded ebbing flames. Bring on
my Yule! — the hoarfrost-bitten log of pruned

and felled desires! Undo the wrappings!
It was not sleet that soughed and seeped upon
that German wind, merely the gift of twigs
and bark lining my box, only the soot
and cinders of a blaze. Burn autumn leaves
and grass grown in the spring upon bonfires

of the past! Strike sparks to tinder wood! Here
is mistletoe, holly and spruce — here where
I lie among the ashes of desire,
among the detritus of love and war
listening to the flames in the woodstove sing
lullays and carols to the chimney pile.

PHILIP BOURNE
1921 -1998

Like a friar asking alms, the chickadee
    proffered its black cap at the windowpane
        where the bankrupt feeder wove
    in the wind. Was I surrogate Father
Superior, head of a house of monks sworn

to poverty? The winter would not loosen
    my starved wallet — all my riches had gone
        to the cardinal. I heard
    the suppliant protest my cant with one
note chanted from a hollow throat, its surplice

ruffled. Yet my seed was gone truly, spilt on
    the white belly of the snow. I had been
        host to the chill chastity
    of ice, my novice mistress twisted in
her winding sheets in this winter cell. Twining

abstinence preyed in the cold air. Here there is
    no seed, my brother, but there is bread which
        I will break with you the while
    the lost seed siles down through the drifts until
it touches the sun's earth, blooms at last into

the flower we seek and shall forever seek.

NATHALIE MASON
1923-2002

    I would often visit that smaller village
        of stones set in the heart
of our village. I own a photograph still,
        not as the record of shadows cast
    among the stones, the sunlight

    in sheets of green studded with flowers; rather,
        as a still life of the boy's face
smiling the wraith of a smile we recall
        of older lips. He is partly
    in stipple, dandelions

    and stalks within his grasp. I recall as well
        the picnics on the hill
peopled now with those who are strange familiars —
        cousins once removed, nephews and nieces —
    smoke rising from the grill into the leaves

    of a horse chestnut, its husks transforming themselves
        into the green maces of autumn.
Those folk were visitors then among the stones,
    occasional and wandering, not yet
        themselves dwellers there.

> The dates are sometimes hard of recollection,
>   eroded by rains, etched in lichen,
> in time obscured by herbs and seasons.
>   The boy's face rises out of the long grass,
>   comes into focus before
>
>   our lenses, imprints itself on retina
>   and film. The road among
> the fields snakes over the hill out of range. What is
>   left behind is monumental, transient.
>   I keep this image in mind
>
> so that it will not fade in the vapor of
>   the river winding through
> our valley where these houses ruminate, telling
>   yet another story in the voices
>   of silences and shadows.

WILLIAM PULLEN
1925-1985

We were in our room, I at my desk
and she at the window looking out.
    She called me over, crying, "Look!"

A balloon floated above the pines.
In the gondola a bride and groom
    waved to the villagers at

the store where a boy spilled gasoline
down a fender in his wonderment.
    We watched them sail on the currents

over the Eastern river till they were out
of sight. To our minds now we recall
    the image of that day of stripes

riding the wind — recall it to play
among these eddies of air where we
    pretend still to be love's sailors.

BETTY BOURNE
1927-20__

      Those were bear shambles, night falling
over the cascades of cans, broken jugs,
retired tires gone bald, inner springs
   come out into the fall. We sat still
   in the auto, waiting, our lights out,

      everyone's lights flooding the sky,
not a cloud to worship, the gravid moon
giving birth to bone: starlight and moonlight
   over the land-fill. It was chilly
   waiting, the radio crooning to

      itself, muttering chanteys and
kyrielles under the dash. The watchman's
shanty blew in the wind, its shades flickering,
   watching for bears in darkness. And then,
   there they were in the naked headlamp-

      light catching them unawares where
they lumbered in cottage cheese and horsehair
loveseats gone to seed: nothing to cushion
   the bare beam transfixing them where they
   searched in the junk and offal. Only

    for a moment did they stand still,
limned against starlight. Then, when they turned from
the limelight back to lime rind and orange
    peel, we got out of the car to stand
    among the bears standing amid our

    castoffs. We felt like castaways
in the dark of the moon, in the thick black
fur of the umber woods, a hunger in
    our hides — the craving of outcasts that
    the ravened land can no longer fill.

ANN PULLEN
1929-20__

That day the kite, windcaught, rose along its line;
    the swallows went sweeping aloft
to tie sunlight in curious bows and loops
about the paper hawk. Ragtail and bobbin,

a skein of urchins tangled upon the beach
    below. Grandfather Pullen, in
the wind unwinding string, walked tugging at air,
his feet at blade tip but caught in the scrimmage

of children. There were the sun in the blue and
    the kite, the breezy surf rafting
it, the women laughing, all the men huffing,
the children at play in sand, the dog champing

at towels. It was the kite, though, that most loved
    the sun, that went to mate with flame
and was lost in fire. The rays flared and grasped.
Melora asked, "Will it burn, will it burn?" and

the answer was "No" — (but *yes, yes it will burn,*
    for the hawk will fly down afire
after its adoration, come down with its
tail of rag spread out in a huge hot shadow

to take the day into its talons and flap
    off to a place where the stars hatch
cold light and the kite will huddle till it has
turned to shell, bone-white and cratered).

LAWRENCE MASON
1930-2001

   Beyond the shadow of the blue spruce
Melora lay on the lawn. The morning
        sunshine laved her; shade shied away

   from her early flesh. The point is this:
she lay nonetheless within the compass
        of darkness, well within that cone

   of darker green which would spin out her
whirling hours and spill them upon her
        at last as a river of moons

   reeled out overhead, breached dawn, noon,
dusk, and fell finally into an old crone's
        eyes to drown. Meanwhile, goldenrod

   ran like the chain of a fob around
the yard. Summer dissembled by seeming static.
        In the orchard the greengages

   would never ripen, the grass never
turn to hay; the fever of movement that
        infested those small lives that crawled

and flew about the blue spruce would go
on endlessly — without end, it is true:
there will always be a girl on

the lawn under an old spruce, a tree
tipped with time's needles for knitting umber
to ravel up the morning flesh.

JEAN COURT
1934-20__

We lived that winter in separate houses,
    both of them white, set in fields apart,
    conjoining only at the gravesite,
        hearing on the verges the ghost
            of grandmother Carr's song.

In our house a mood of blue settled itself
    out of glass upon Christopher's tracks
    laid out on the floor where the cats, all
        three, watched carefully, groomed themselves
            as the sparking toy cars

ran their ovals under our gaze. It was cold.
    We took our meals with Mother Bourne and
    my eldest sister, Nathalie, in
        the old house. We were without our father
            for the first time,

but he was present whenever we closed our
    eyes. At last spring came slowly over
    the hill into the valley — we knew
        it would not know itself, but the brook
            spoke clearly among

the alders and then the smelt began their run,
flickering in the indigo currents.
We walked into the yard. Grandmother
noticed the grass coming alive,
but it was not part

of her nightsong. Summer, if it should
come, would be an age of brass and trumpets,
swallows, and the flight of swallows.

WESLEY COURT
1934-20__

Here among the dust is anywhere,
motes dancing among the coleus
    and pepper plants, lamps vamping
        the half-drawn shades — and we talk.

Clocks cluck, the rug lies low and listens
as the springtide slides under the door.
    The phone rings once, its bell hung
        among dim weather. The wood

of the room rubs a maple table
the wrong way. Gray slides from its mousehole
    to lie where we walk. Still we
        talk, ears weary of winter,

our words tucked in a hamper. And what
shall we say if all bells fail? Clockworks
    rattle. Sashcords in loveknots
        hang in the windows. Voices

fill the silence of our living room.

GARY CARR
1935-20__

      The angel hair of winter — come down to
      Spring from the Feast of the Nativity —
lies among crocus under the lilac:
a moss of spun glass among spears of green
and cream. Pendulous upon a limb, seed

      and suet dangle in the wind straining
      through the straining bush: a roof of birds.
Nut-hatch and chickadee, grackle
and cowbird — white with gray, black upon brown —
move among the branches and the sunlight,

      like a bright ladder for wings, which coaxes
      life out of the bark in furious buds.
The snow has melted, all but the false snow,
filaments spun from silica, mica
ice made for a metal tree topped by a

      star of tinsel whose light was wired to our
      wall. Carpets and curtains between us and
the wind, winter's emblem glistened above
gifts no Magi could have dreamt in their sands
or tamarinds — glistened for a space. Now

      the birds come tearing the angel hair, their
      eyes bright with birth. Our useless artifice
shall make a glass nest in a real tree. Its
dangle will be rare among sunlight and
showers, leaves, limbs, explosions of true wings.

JOHN PULLEN
1946-20__

    We waited in the next bright morning
  for whatever was to happen next.
      The sun flared in the hardwoods on the hill,
put a cold torch to the tips of the pines,
of the cedars pitching down the riverbank.

    The tide arose in the river's throat,
  pushing the current back to its source.
      The rushes of the middlegrounds all leaned
the other way around, their roots sucking
in silt where carp fed in the cloudy water.

    A snapper climbed like a rock onto
a rock. A muskrat swam ashore and
      disappeared. Downstream a heron waded
searching. The farmhouse waited in its fields
as it has always waited, the sun shining

    in its windows; cords peeled in the lean-
to. The barn, color of mist, breathed cool air
      out of its stores of night, and dew began
to rise as it had fallen, glittering
on the green blades of late summer. There was a sharp

    and sometime breeze following the stream
  past the ruined mill where willows grew
      among the fallen walls and alders rose
in the centerholes of the great round stones.
Where the stream met the river there were eddies

         and pebbles, waterstriders skating
    surfaces. I looked upward into
              the morning at flood now among the woods
and saw the great bird at last, its earthen
body, head and tail of snow, riding the drafts

         rising above the Eastern, wings spread
         like sails on the summer. In a stroke
the eagle was gone upstream and easterly
         where the river wells out of the spring.

WILLIAM MASON
1952-20__

    We gathered in the spring to make
the old women a winter place to live
      out of the shed of the old house.
We tossed the mathoms, the forgotten treasures,
out of the breathing window. We built with them,

    to start, a tell of years that rose,
oddment and shard, to the flower of debris.
      The women moaned, picking through their
lives, but we were ruthless. There was no place now
for the past in the ell, for the winter lay

    couching beyond the river and
its currents. When we were done we gathered
      in the loft to raise the floor, board
by board, the dust raining through cracks and gaps, guano
and beans falling like hail in a choking fog.

    Our lungs were sacks of wheezes, eyes
slick as onions. Outdoors the rain fell. Sere
      bridles soaked themselves to mud, and
lanterns leached a liquid rust — whatever was
left over from former light. None of us had

    ever seen a loft like that, its
eastern end suspended in the air by
      great chains slung over the rafters,
not a beam or a pillar to lend support.
We read a board inscribed last century by

>   the country inventor of this
>   system of instability; then we
>   salvaged his chains. We stared down through
> his joists, and took them up as well. When we were
> finished, we saw that we had created space.
>
>   In the air there hung a billion
>   motes, a slow universe of particles
>   silently descending, swirling
> in nebulae, great spirals of the past
> falling, moments coming to rest.

AT HOME

None have come with silver, none have come
with loud huzzahs to plight my flame or paint
my eyes with fame's delight. Nor are there many
who would condescend to nod my being
or to wave my fact along a voiceless street,
much less descend this slope and meet me here
where bottoms end. For who are you, my faceless,
who are you that they should come?

In the mirror there is glass; behind the glass
lies a river of mercury, frozen
perpendicularly against the bathroom wall.
Between the glass and the quicksilver
no longer quick, there is nothing: no flesh,
no frame, no bone hung with lip, eye, hair.
There is no beard, not even a bristle.
Outside the bathroom window there is morning,
and a bristling tree scraping the wind.

In this house are a thousand things singing
with use, swearing a thousand vows silently
that someone lives here, someone wears that sock,
warps that chair, twists that knob — but the phone rings,
the phone is ringing, shrilling the house apart,
halting the walls that press forward while
no one answers, no one answers, no one
goes to the telephone cursing to answer.

I live here. My face is not in the mirror,
my foot is not in the sock, my hand does
not haul the phone to my ear, and my voice
carries no weight from my lips to the phone,
to the wires that hum along the roadways
out into the world that does not wait for
any sound that I might make. I am not
to be found, although I live here.

Among the wool, among the hung frames, the dusty
shoes, the desks lumpy with papers, and the lamps
gone black with burning, let them come to find me,
let them come, if they will, to unbury me,
with or without silver, plus or minus praise,
happy with folly or squinting with blame.
Only let them come: the mirror is in need
of a beard, the phone wants a voice.
And a sock is not a sock without a foot
to belly it, and a shoe to harry it to holes.

INDEX TO TITLES OF POEMS

"A Squis'd Cat"	384
A New Year	445
A -Bao-A-Qu	187
A Dainty Sum	423
A Daughter Moves Out	399
A Dedication	39
A Dream of Roses	457
A Farewell to Melancholy	388
A Fin for the Melancholick's Thoughts	366
A Medicine for Melancholy	373
A Memoir of Evening	419
A Morning Picture	442
A Pearl Jail	437
A Rural Jetty	173
Adventure	462
Al	28
Albums	543
Amanda Pullen	571
Amherst Neighbors	470
Among the Stones	449
An Amherst Calendar	480
An Amherst Christmas	476
An Amherst Haiku	439
An Amherst Pastoral	453
An Old Acquaintance	60
An Old Tale	425
An Orator of Feather	460
An Ordinary Evening in Cleveland	66

ANN PULLEN	596
AS I READ MY GOOD FRIEND'S BOOK	162
ASEA	455
AT HOME	607
ATTIC POEM	398
AWAKEN, BELLS FALLING	96
BASILISK AND COCKATRICE	189
BALSAMUM APOPLECTICUM	351
BANJO	233
BEAVER MOON	281
BERTHA BOURNE	576
BETTY BOURNE	594
BLOOD DEEPER THAN NIGHT	344
BOB	20
BONE	235
BROWN STUDY	434
BUCK MOON	277
BURNING THE NEWS	85
CHIMERA	190
CALEB PULLEN	556
CANCER	401
CASS	12
CIRCLES	252
CLAMBAKE	88
COLD MOON	271
COMPANY	452
CONCEIT	406
CORRAL	405

CORRESPONDENCE	260
CRIMSON CHILDREN	415
CUPS	242
DYBBUK	191
DEACON SMITH	19
DEATH	255
DEATH	454
DELAY	451
DIALOGUE	246
DOROTHY	11
ENT	193
EMERALDA	353
EPHRAIM BOURNE	560
EPISTLE	475
EPISTLES	244
EPITHALAMION	417
ERCOLE THE BUTCHER	4
FETCH	194
FACETS	250
FADING THINGS	459
FAILED FATHERS	363
FATHER FIGURE	172
FIRST SNOW	450
FLOWER MOON	275
FLOWERS IN SEASON	466
FOLIAGE	234
FOUR SMALL SONGS	432

FOXFIRE	240
FRANCIS PULLEN	552
FRANK	22
GOLEM	196
GARY CARR	602
GENE	1
GINGER	14
GRANDDADDY DAGGER	27
GRANNY	25
GUIDO THE ICE-HOUSE MAN	6
HOMUNCULUS	198
HARRIET BOURNE	572
HE WHO FEEDS PIGEONS	50
HE — ACROPHOBIA	534
HE — AGORAPHOBIA	536
HE — ALEKTROPHOBIA	530
HE — AMBIVOPHOBIA	538
HE — AMNESIOPHOBIA	532
HE — APEIROPHOBIA	512
HE — ARACHIBUTYROPHOBIA	526
HE — ARACHNOPHOBIA	508
HE — CHOROPHOBIA	498
HE — CHRONOPHOBIA	522
HE — ENNUIOPHOBIA	516
HE — GAMOPHOBIA	502
HE — HOMILOPHOBIA	510
HE — HOMOPHOBIA	500
HE — IDEOPHOBIA	528

HE — MELANCHOPHOBIA	518
HE — MNEMOPHOBIA	520
HE — MUNDANOPHOBIA	524
HE — PAPYROPHOBIA	494
HE — PEDOPHOBIA	504
HE — PHALACROPHOBIA	506
HE — QUIESCOPHOBIA	514
HE — SENILOPHOBIA	540
HE — ZELOPHOBIA	496
HENRY BOURNE	550
HERBERT TORREY	587
HESTER PULLEN	547
HOME	429
HOME THOUGHTS	157
HOT MOON	276
HOUSE AND SHUTTER	98
HOUSEKEEPING	448
HUNTING MOON	282
*I*MAGO	200
I AM PETER	184
I PRAY TO A GENITAL GOD	375
IN A WHITE DIRECTION	41
*J*UGGERNAUT	202
JASON PULLEN	589
JEAN	23
JEAN COURT	599
JEREMY CARR	564
JESSIE BAKER	579

JOHN	9
JOHN BOURNE	544
JOHN BOURNE, JR.	549
JOHN PULLEN	603
JOHN PULLEN BOURNE	574
JONES	17
JOSEPH CARR	583
JUDGMENT	259
JULIA PULLEN	570
JUST GOD	456
KAMELOPARD	203
LEVIATHAN	205
LAMPS	458
LANDSCAPE	285
LATE FALL	469
LATE SUMMER	468
LAWRENCE MASON	597
LENA	31
LETTER TO W. D. S.	45
LEWIS	36
LINES FOR MR. STEVENSON	48
LORRIE	29
LOST GIRL WITH DOG	43
LOUIE THE BARBER	5
LOVERS	160
LUIGI	10

MINOTAUR	207
MAIZE MOON	279
MANSIONS OF MIRAGE	421
MARBLE ROOMS	424
MARGARET PULLEN	559
MARY MOODY EMERSON, R. I. P.	176
MAUREEN	13
MAY	8
MAY, MERELY	438
MELANCHOLY LOVE	381
MELANCHOLY'S HERBAL	355
MELINDA BOURNE	577
MELORA	24
MICE IN THE SUNDAY WALLS	46
MICHAEL PULLEN	565
MILLPOND	62
MISS AGATHA	15
MISS BURNSIDE	18
MISS MARY BELLE	34
MORGAN	7
MORNING MUSIC	426
MORTON	32
MR. MELL	16
MRS. MARTINO THE CANDY STORE LADY	3
MY COUNTRY WIFE	55
MY WIFE OF THE TOWN	56
MY LORD LIFE	170
NASNAS	209
NARCISSUS TO HIS FLESHLY SHADE	59

Nathalie Mason	591
No Reflection on You, but…,	57
Nocturne	435
*O*dradek	210
Old News	73
*P*hoenix and Salamander	212
Paradigm	247
Passages	472
Passing	443
Patience Cobb Pullen	554
Patience Pullen	567
Paul Pullen	546
Pentacles	236
Philip Bourne	590
Playhouse	61
Poetry	477
Priscilla Bourne	545
Proem: Cloth of Dreams	413
Prothalamion	319
Pumpinode	94
*Q*uerule	213
*R*oc	214
Raceway	92
Randall Bourne	568
Ray	21
Raymond Carr	581

Reflections at Forty-Nine	393
Roots	337
Ruth Carr	585
Sasquatch	215
Sampler	430
Scarecrow	91
Scarlet Expectations	420
School Drawing	65
Season	100
Seasons of the Blood	245
Seed Moon	274
SHE — Abandophobia	497
SHE — Acousticophobia	513
SHE — Aelurophobia	507
SHE — Alliumphobia	525
SHE — Amathophobia	505
SHE — Ambiguphobia	529
SHE — Apocalyptophobia	511
SHE — Arithmophobia	527
SHE — Bibliophobia	539
SHE — Brontophobia	509
SHE — Catoptrophobia	515
SHE — Claustrophobia	501
SHE — Dementophobia	537
SHE — Gerascophobia	521
SHE — Meteorophobia	531
SHE — Monophobia	495
SHE — Mortophobia	535
SHE — Nebulaphobia	519

SHE — NOMATOPHOBIA	503
SHE — ONEIROPHOBIA	523
SHE — PARTURIPHOBIA	499
SHE — *PROEM*: ERATOPHOBIA	493
SHE — SABBATIPHOBIA	517
SHE — SOMNOPHOBIA	533
SMALL VICTORY	447
SNOW MOON	272
SOME FOOD FOR MELANCHOLY	374
SOME PINFEATHER BLUES	90
STONE AND SHADOW	362
STURGEON MOON	278
SUMMER'S CHARIOT	446
SWORDS	243
*T*ROGLODYTE	217
TAURUS SIRES AQUARIUS	379
THAT PARTICULAR AIR	359
THE AGE OF AQUARIUS	377
THE AMHERST FIRE	436
THE ATTIC	113
THE AUTHOR OF MELANCHOLY	342
THE AUTOMOBILES	326
THE BARN	318
THE BASEMENT	137
THE BATHROOM	135
THE BEDROOM	131
THE BURNING BUSH	76
THE CAGE	431
THE CAT	129

THE CELL	164
THE CHARIOT	258
THE CHURCH	317
THE CLOCK	484
THE COLLEGE	297
THE COLONY	286
THE COMPLEAT MELANCHOLICK	335
THE COUCH	119
THE COURTHOUSE	298
THE COVERED BRIDGE	309
THE DEAD SAILOR	166
THE DEEP STRANGER	433
THE DEPOT	312
THE DESERT OF MELANCHOLY	357
THE DEVIL	237
THE DINING ROOM	120
THE DOOR	107
THE DREAM	181
THE DWELLING-HOUSE	151
THE EAR OF SILENCE	416
THE FACE IN THE STONE	178
THE FACE ON THE CHEQUERED FIELD	79
THE FENCES	329
THE FERRY	299
THE FOOL	262
THE FOREST BEYOND THE GLASS	74
THE FOREST OF MY SEASONS	86
THE FORT	294
THE FOUNTAIN	167
THE GARDEN	150
THE GARDEN OF MELANCHOLY	368

THE GIFT	428
THE GIRL FROM THE GOLDEN WEST	82
THE GIRL YOU THOUGHT YOU LOVED	397
THE GLIDER	144
THE GOD OF MELANCHOLY	386
THE GUESTROOM	145
THE HABITATION	394
THE HALLSEAT	110
THE HALLWAY	109
THE HANGED MAN	257
THE HARPER OF STILLNESS	414
THE HERMIT	254
THE HOMESTEAD	314
THE HOUSE	307
THE ICE HOUSE	304
THE KITCHEN	122
THE LATE, LATE SHOW	80
THE LINEN CALENDAR	123
THE LIVINGROOM	117
THE LOOKING-GLASS	147
THE LOVERS	238
THE MANDARIN OF MELANCHOLY	365
THE MAPLE WORKS	288
THE MEETINGHOUSE	290
THE MELANCHOLICK ART	371
THE MENU OF MELANCHOLY	339
THE MILL	302
THE MILLER'S TALE	440
THE MIRROR	136
THE MISTRESS OF MELANCHOLY	383
THE MOON	241

THE MOON OF MELANCHOLY	345
THE MOWER	418
THE NAKED EYE	441
THE NEIGHBORHOOD	323
THE OBSERVATION TOWER	316
THE OLD PROFESSOR AND THE SPHINX	70
THE ORCHESTRA	158
THE PHARMACY	296
THE PHOTOGRAPH	115
THE PILLOW	134
THE PILOT	179
THE PLAYROOM	124
THE POND	328
THE PORCH	141
THE PORTRAIT OF A CLOWN	126
THE RECURRING DREAM	403
THE RIVER	251
THE ROPE WALK	305
THE SCHOONER	306
THE SCYTHE	139
THE SHIFTING WEB	408
THE SIDEBOARD	121
THE SILO	308
THE SNOW DEVIL	101
THE STABLE	311
THE STOCKYARD	315
THE STREET	327
THE STROLLER	103
THE STUDY	127
THE SUMMERHOUSE	148
THE SYMPTOMS OF MELANCHOLY	347

THE TAVERN	291
THE TEST	248
THE TOBACCO SHED	310
THE TOLLHOUSE	301
THE TOWER	261
THE TOWNSFOLK	40
THE TRADING POST	292
THE TREES	325
THE TRESTLE	313
THE VALLEY	330
THE VISTA	331
THE VOYAGERS	168
THE WEED GARDEN	169
THE WELL	64
THE WELL OF HOLY HEAVEN	72
THE WINTER GARDEN	461
THE YARD	324
THEME AND VARIATION	444
THOMAS BOURNE	551
THOMAS BOURNE, JR.	555
THOMAS CARR	566
TICK	183
TIMOTHY BOURNE	557
TOAD	256
TOMASO THE BAKER	2
TRAVELERS' MOON	280
TRILOGY FOR J. F. K.	51
TURN	239
TWILIGHT TOUCHES AMHERST	427

*U*ROBOROS	218
UNCLE LARRY	26
*V*IELFRAS	219
VERN	33
VIGILANCE	395
*W*EREWIND	221
WAKE DISTURBING SURFACES	175
WENDELL PULLEN	562
WESLEY COURT	601
WHEEL OF FORTUNE	231
WILLIAM MASON	605
WILLIAM PULLEN	593
WINTER BOUQUET	463
WINTER IN MUSCOVY	360
WORM MOON	273
*X*OANON	223
*Y*ETI	225
*Z*OMBIE	227

Index to First Lines of Poems

"…ill-favored, wrinkled, pimpled, pale,	381
"How many you want?" asks Ercole slowly,	4
"I am drowning in the wind,"	172
"Of seasons of the year,	335
"Ragtail Gene, don't tag along here;	1
"Six weeks gone," the doctor said,	73
"Some signs are secret, some manifest, some	347
"Take the distill'd Oil of Cinnamon,	351
"Thank you," it said when she uncovered it,	198
"Why?" it asks, and snivels.	213
A circus passed the house this morning —	462
A continuous curtain, the	61
A gust of smiles behind his beard,	32
A one-armed man conveyed the flowers.	428
A shadow falls upon my	442
A stick strolling with an old man. Trees	103
A thousand little winds wafted	450
A true October —	252
After the wind-tempest, when	215
Al's eyes paced the cell of his head;	28
Am I in love? Birds are flying.	235
Among the lianas there lies a pool	200
And I was the last of the old man's sons,	551
And in the morning it is a wedding	319
And so it was with Morgan,	7
As he drowned he saw	166
As the boat rounds the river bend	278
As the storm comes now like a cage of dark air,	331
As the summer was gathering to its end	572
As we stand talking, his eye	60

As you stand there, Melora, winking at	90
At first one might take it	210
At first she jerks awake time after time,	533
At noon I heard a well-known rap.	447
At the age of thirty-one I left Gardiner	552
At the end I was very ill.	574
At the first blare of the Federal trumpet	564
At the wake I spoke to the mourners, family	577
Atmospherically, it was the most	476
Autumn is coming on	443
Behind the locked doors	318
Beyond a doubt, there was no other dusk	33
Beyond the shadow of the blue spruce	597
Black sphinx, white sphinx, pull.	258
Bob came down with a *rumblededum*	20
Cass looked the lecher I was not	12
Christ, you made me sad	45
Deacon Smith was older than the pews,	19
Dear Cousin, she wrote, *Thanks*	493
Dear Granddaddy Dagger slyly grew berries	27
Denuded by the	366
Desire today is a cavern of snow;	86
Destitute of sound, I rely upon the room	571
Do you hear the voice	250
Do you recall old Mrs. Ay,	470
Does mallow whistle	240
Does this dark blade strike	243
Even as she slides down the ways	306
Evening called with a twilight of you.	475
For a moment he forgot to be afraid.	532
Frank was the Maelstrom in the stream	22
Ginger loved things small and furry:	14

Glistering on the horizon,	190
God is kept in this box of pine	290
Grandfather of mammoths,	202
Having dumbled through	196
He and his go to the spring, have gone	64
He awakens in the darkness hearing	514
He couldn't eat them, the dopey birds, not even	530
He feels it first in his belly: a dying fall,	518
He hears his timepiece ticking in the night	522
He inhabits a precious pelt,	219
He is the Mandarin of silence:	365
He lies awake in his bed	512
He looks at the bottles on his shelf —	540
He opened the door of the fridge, and there it was:	526
He sees that the night is a dark web	508
He sees them on the sidewalk before his doorway	504
He starts to worry. The job is almost done.	516
He thought she was a vampire, she felt sure —	525
He touched the switch	76
He wanted him to shake his hand? No way!	500
He was on a pale horse when he came	82
He washes his hair carefully in the shower,	506
He watches the dancers skimming across the floor	498
He will go to the valleys of Andorra; *He will stay*	538
He will have his will,	237
He will wash away the dross of sleep	135
He's not for her, no matter who he is.	499
He's walked these halls for nearly thirty years:	520
Her eyelids will not close. She stares awake	523
Here, music	48
Here among the dust is anywhere,	601
His feet point inward at	386

His son's dinosaurs surround me.	434
his words make choochoo trains that	162
Hours accumulate.	565
How I love to see them, a beautiful company	452
Hundreds of yards of woodland	74
I am a cat with a tick	183
I am Peter,	184
I am pleasantly located	455
I am saving a miller moth.	440
I am the ghost of the weed garden.	169
I am wearing blue	246
I am writing you	244
I call you Death, you mouse.	170
I came in my blue Buick to say	579
I grant you your grain of sand,	31
I have always wanted to write	94
I have come, cousin,	41
I have had little	262
I have not been here long.	50
I have put on my badge, and I repose me	342
I have tried to delay the frosts,	451
I have waited so long for all the mails to come —	383
I hear the wind blow the wide way	425
I live in mansions of mirage	421
I love to have the lamps shine	458
I met Ray just as we first thumbed	21
I remember, briefly,	550
I sang in my dreams, my voice	576
I seek my father — that minister	403
I sprang to the window and each	436
I thought I would write again.	457
I want her to be what I need	59

I was the aunt who made the collection	570
I was the eldest, the oldest daughter.	547
I was the odd one, the merchant.	556
I would often visit that smaller village	591
If he goes out they'll see his fly is open,	536
If I were you, I wouldn't listen	406
If it is true that	39
If night is staining the window,	388
If roses had not faded,	459
If she closes her eyes, before she can drop	505
If she looks into the mirror she will see	515
If we come by water,	175
If you should waken	239
If you walk these acres today,	549
Improbably fair, picture girl, your hair	43
In a drawer he found	79
In her New England house as old as moss	539
In my dream there is light	207
In the basement it is cool	317
In the dooryard a stand of milkweed	468
In the garden of odd seed, no	368
In the kitchen the dishwasher is eating the dishes.	122
In the lowlands lie his reaches,	217
In the maple grove wind moves	288
In the mirror this	136
In the morning there is the east wind	314
In the night there was a crescent	274
In the pastures the wind walks	329
In the street the wind gutters, moving papers	327
In this season light	100
In what shall I be clothed today?	413
Is it winter? Blood is warm.	245

It has a black throat,	316
It has been	179
It is a dawn quick as swallows	96
It is a dry word in a dry book	70
It is anomaly and paradox: Somehow,	379
It is as still as falling	362
It is dark in the dining room.	120
It is in her eyes — the odd light,	191
It is not far from here to	357
It is November. The noons are more	461
It is now ten minutes after midnight,	80
It is stuffed with	134
It is the age of Aquarius;	377
It is the morning,	233
It is time to write a poem.	408
It is unwise	115
It must hop, having but one leg,	209
It ought to be a large old knot hole,	373
It stares back at him, a blank white sheet	494
It storms in Amherst five days —	463
It waits against	119
It was a blue day	248
It was a grain of sand, grand	25
It was a quiet June evening;	141
It was difficult. I was starved,	353
It was late. I remember turning	581
It was late when they came in	345
It was only six weeks away, and then it would be	511
It was such a day. The gulls in the park	537
It was there, lying in the grain,	178
It was tidal.	251
Its body is like that	223

Jealous beyond love or hate, he walks	496
Jean's flesh proved sheerest silk:	23
John had a holy eye or two	9
Just so it goes: the day, the night —	66
Like a fleet thief, this sparrow has	98
Like a friar asking alms, the chickadee	590
Like a great eye it lies	187
Listen to the hum	3
Loaf here on a cool day	2
Long-haired and black as shadow	129
Lorrie looked good — man,	29
Many an angel, with its needle,	430
Mary of the Charms, Mary Belle,	34
Melancholy kitty, nice pussy,	384
Memory's fog is rising: I had a terror	477
Miss Agatha was a spinster	15
Miss Burnside knew a ruler's job	18
Moon takes the tide where	242
Morning. The sun is a fried egg in a pastel	374
Morning touches the waves and breaks	205
Mother named me Lewis,	8
My country wife bends to rinse. Her skirt is	55
My cousin James showed me how to skate	562
My mother called me Lewis,	10
My raceway of sheets last night became	92
Neither hear nor dare to utter them:	529
None have come with silver, none have come	607
None knows how long the Phoenix lives,	212
Nor was it the moon,	88
Not what the stars have done,	416
Nothing is to be seen	393
Now the grass is glass	427

Old man Jones unwound twine	17
Old Uncle Larry, leery of losing,	26
On the morning of the first day	151
Once in a while	147
One is a dainty sum!	423
Once upon a blue moon, legend has it,	568
Onetwothreefourfivesixseveneightnineten	527
Open any grate, any glass gate	360
Open the trunk: She is there,	397
Out of a single shell these twins emerged:	189
Out of the old noon sun still lifting	583
Out of the weather, in the first room,	292
Outside the door, the noises of the sleugh.	227
Past the worm reef and the coral,	168
Ralph Waldo's Aunt Mary,	176
Rising out of the summer woods	286
Say that the night was starred, the year not far	203
Second of March and the crow	420
Seen from the side of this hill	330
September comes smoking over the hills	310
She cannot hear me now, but once she could.	546
She cannot stand their eyes, the way they stare	507
She has left	399
She heard her mother say the word that struck	497
She looks at the calendar. It's February now,	531
She loved her son, but oh! the blare they made —	513
She sees that he rides a dark stallion.	535
She sits by herself at a table, not the bar,	495
She wakens gasping, feeling as though her throat	501
Smoke Hole, Coeur d'Alene —	566
Snow nearly hard as hail	282
So what if it's hot in the sunny streets	6

Some call him Uroboros:	218
Sometimes as I am drifting	433
Somewhere within these houses a woman looks	521
Stones are falling from the sky	214
Stories are done for the evening.	124
Such a purple morning, even to	466
Summer? Was there a summer?	460
Summer is past and gone;	446
Take two	150
TAROT in the Wheel;	231
That day the kite, windcaught, rose along its line;	596
That fourth of July a sly laugh	587
The ancient albums lie	543
The angel hair of winter — come down to	602
The ashen birds light	167
The background hours are	123
The bed frames them.	160
The bell rings once and then the woods are still.	301
The book is fair and lonely,	419
The buck on the hill	277
The building is a telescope of wood,	305
The cable bows downward,	299
The calendar is her nemesis. The days drip off	517
The carved elephant	234
The chairs of his livingroom lounge thinking in groups.	117
The chickens grow very fast —	441
The Conceit of Melancholy	371
The crescent blade with its snake	139
The crocuses are with us	472
The fire is eating	85
The first time she could remember hearing thunder	509
The floating dead will	259

The fog is rising...but not like Lazarus,	519
The forests are at home —	429
The gazebo looks at summer	148
The geese make a sound like vee in the air	484
The gray rain, like mice scurrying about the house,	46
The heart is a coin	236
The hook has let go,	359
The houses are settling into their foundations.	323
The Inhabitant descends to find	137
The Inhabitant must go around thinking of Death.	145
The Inhabitant stands in his hallway.	109
The lake drifts in the starfall,	271
The lake that looks like a sea	315
The lamp is standing in the corner of the study	127
The lawn is full of south	414
The legal arm has reached up from the sea	298
The maize is shin high	276
The man's breath	280
The maple across the street says something deeply	524
The mill grinds the night	302
The mirror on the morning wall listens	131
The monster in	121
The moon rides like a girl	417
The morning in the windows smells blue.	311
The mountain of snows,	254
The mower is tuning his scythe	418
The odor is of sulfur and autumn.	296
The orchestra of winds performs	444
The path that passes is of mud.	291
The pond at the edge of town	328
The rails pause barely to tie the horizons	312
The rails shine like new wire	313

The rooms were marble	424
The sky is a curtain of slate	273
The snow is thin and wet	309
The stairs are teeth that chew her heels.	56
The stars rattle the window	337
The storm seems to gather	326
The stove is singing the merry song	469
The sun blossoms in the sky,	275
The sun came out when you were gone.	432
The sun has barely	448
The sun through the clouds,	281
The ugly table is	158
The vane defies the wind.	480
The wall is of brick. The buildings	297
The walls are of rough plank.	304
The weeds pant	438
The well of holy heaven has gone sec;	72
The wind is telling rumors	101
The wind moves in the maize	279
There are others: Black Hellebore, being an herb	355
There is, first, the road,	40
There is a black hole	260
There is a door	107
There is a road: no	65
There is a subject on which	454
There is no way out.	394
There is the room	164
There was an animal in the sun	557
There was an end of things when Hitler took	589
There was no house here when I came	544
There was time until there was no time.	545
These do generally ingender gross humours	339

They are falling out	261
They converge here,	173
They stand there	325
Things, the work of dust and summer flies,	113
This is a stern Winter,	437
This is already old. When you find these pages	398
This is the place where	110
This is the place where peace grows	62
This is the story of a dream:	181
This is the way I played with my dolls,	567
This is the world that opens and shuts	435
This is your house as well,	36
This was our conceit: the brilliant	585
This morning sang at the windowpane	431
This year's garden is a series of ridges	324
Those were bear shambles, night falling	594
Time buzzes in the ear.	157
To step out of a bedroom	194
Today is very beautiful —	453
Tonight it is cool and quiet,	449
Tonight the crimson children	415
Two great elms. Hills beyond them;	308
Under Orion nothing	144
Up the block, all you kids,	5
Upstairs there is a bed	307
Waken one clear morning and look to where,	193
Was hers the blame? Blossoms flare.	238
Was it the sound a blue spruce makes	294
Was there sense in that	256
We did not know, then, what the wen	401
We do not know whether the tales are true	225
We gathered in the spring to make	605

We pumpkins worship you. We orange globes,	91
We lived that winter in separate houses,	599
We shall find Death	51
We waited in the next bright morning	603
We wandered gently, Dorothy, and long	11
We were in our room, I at my desk	593
Weep, Melora, weep and stay;	24
What could he have been thinking? He'd thought	502
What good were they? The only thing they did	528
What has become of	241
What shall she name it? She cannot bear to think —	503
When he was young he thought nothing of climbing	534
When he was young they'd called him "preacher's kid,"	510
When I pointed out the pun	375
When she died she became a wind.	221
When the angels came to fetch me	560
When the call came, I was ready.	555
When you were small I lay awake at night	405
Where do all the failed fathers	363
Where have these strangers come from,	344
Where is the morning music,	426
Which way will he go	126
White and yellow, its flight	559
who are you? he asked me	57
Who is approaching?	445
Who is the Hanged Man? Golem.	257
Who may withstand them,	255
Who writes these funny accidents	456
Why do I recollect Maureen? —	13
Why does the brook run?	247
Will you bring me a	439
Wind calls over the lake;	272

Winter is hanging fire behind the sun.	285
You mustn't listen to him.	554
You stand waiting. You listen.	395

LEWIS TURCO began teaching in 1960 at what is now Cleveland State University, where he founded the Cleveland Poetry Center in 1962. In 1965 he began teaching at the State University of New York College at Oswego where he founded the Program in Writing Arts in 1968 and from which he retired in 1996. His *First Poems* appeared in 1960 as a selection of the Book Club for Poetry, and in 1968 he published *The Book of Forms: A Handbook of Poetics*, which has since become known in the field as The Poet's Bible. His book of literary criticism, *Visions and Revisions of American Poetry*, won the Poetry Society of America's Melville Cane Award in 1986, and his *A Book of Fears, Poems, with Italian Translations* by Joseph Alessia, won the Bordighera Bi-Lingual Poetry Prize in 1998. Two selections of poems from his 2002 collection of poems titled *The Green Maces of Autumn, Voices in an Old Maine House*, won the earlier Silverfish Review Chapbook Competition in 1989 and the Cooper House Chapbook Competition in 1990. A compendium of his rhymed and metered poems, *The Collected Lyrics of Lewis Turco / Wesli Court 1953-2004* appeared in 2004 and should be considered the companion volume to this collection of his non-traditional poetry. He lives in Dresden, Maine — with his wife, Jean, and cat, Sweetie-Pie — where he is currently working on a series of poems provisionally titled *Attic, Shed and Barn*.

The Companion Volume to
Fearful Pleasures: The Complete Poems, 1959-2007

The Collected Lyrics of Lewis Turco / Wesli Court, 1953-2004

ISBN: 1-932842-01-4 (cloth edition), $ 49.95
ISBN: 1-932842-01-2 (paperback), $ 26.95
Publisher: Star Cloud Press

PAGE COUNT: 450, 6 x 9

StarCloudPress.com

A Sheaf of Leaves: Literary Memoirs
LEWISTURCO

ISBN: 0-9651835-6-4 (cloth edition), $ 36.95
ISBN: 0-9651835-4-8 (soft cover), $ 24.95
Publisher: Star Cloud Press

page count: 254, 6 x 9

StarCloudPress.com

Lewis Turco and His Work: A Celebration
Edited by Steven E. Swerdfeger

A festschrift published in honor of the poet's 70th birthday (May 2, 2004), this book is a collection of essays, interviews, and tributes from major poets and scholars, including R. S. Gwynn, Donald Justice, Mary Doll, Donald Masterson, Hyatt H. Waggoner, William Heyen, Herbert R. Coursen, Jr., Gene van Troyer, Gerhard Zeller, De Villo Sloan, Felix Stefanile, and Kathrine Varnes, as well as from friends and former students.

ISBN: 0-9651835-9-9
page count: 243, 6 x 9   Cloth, $ 36.95

StarCloudPress.com

www.ingramcontent.com/pod-product-compliance
Lightning Source LLC
Chambersburg PA
CBHW021303240426
43669CB00041B/47